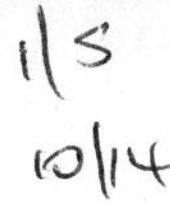

THE PROFESSIONAL SERVER

NEWCASTLE COLLEGE
WITHDRAWN
LIBRARY

THE PROFESSIONAL SERVER

SECOND EDITION

Edward E. Sanders
New York City College of Technology

Marcella Giannasio
Johnson & Wales University

Paul C. Paz
WaitersWorld

Ron Wilkinson
Profit Power Systems

Boston Columbus Indianapolis New York San Francisco Upper Saddle River
Amsterdam Cape Town Dubai London Madrid Milan Munich Paris Montreal Toronto
Delhi Mexico City Sao Paulo Sydney Hong Kong Seoul Singapore Taipei Tokyo

Editorial Director: Vernon Anthony
Senior Acquisitions Editor: William Lawrensen
Editorial Assistant: Lara Dimmick
Assistant Editor: Alexis Biasell
Director of Marketing: David Gesell
Campaign Marketing Manager: Leigh Ann Sims
Curriculum Marketing Manager: Thomas Hayward
Senior Marketing Coordinator: Alicia Wozniak
Marketing Assistant: Les Roberts
Associate Managing Editor: Alex Wolf
Project Manager: Kris Roach
Production Project Manager: Debbie Ryan
Art Director: Jayne Conte
Cover Art: © iofoto/Shutterstock
Lead Media Project Manager: Karen Bretz
Full-Service Project Management: Integra
Composition: Central Publishing – Integra
Printer/Binder: Edwards Brothers Malloy
Text Font: 11/13, Adobe Garamond Pro

Minion Credits and acknowledgments borrowed from other sources and reproduced, with permission, in this textbook appear on appropriate page within text.

Library of Congress Cataloging-in-Publication Data
The professional server / Edward E. Sanders ... [et al].—2nd ed.
p. cm.
Rev. ed. of: Service at its best / Ed Sanders, Paul Paz, Ron Wilkinson. 2002.
Includes index.
ISBN-13: 978-0-13-170992-8 (alk. paper)
ISBN-10: 0-13-170992-5 (alk. paper)
1. Table service. 2. Waiters. 3. Waitresses. I. Sanders, Edward E. II. Sanders, Edward E. Service at its best.
TX925.S26 2013
642'.6—dc23

2011019813

10 9 8 7 6 5 4

PEARSON

ISBN 10: 0-13-170992-5
ISBN 13: 978-0-13-170992-8

brief contents

contents

2

3

4

Foreword

This updated second edition further defines the level of professional training for people working as servers in the hospitality industry. The foreword from the first edition by industry legend Herman Cain has been proudly honored with technology updates and the addition of new material and timely information.

Edward E. Sanders
Lead Coauthor

FOREWORD FROM THE FIRST EDITION, *SERVICE AT ITS BEST*, 2002

In today's competitive market, the need for restaurants to sell on tight margins while satisfying the customer is at an all-time high. Restaurant patrons have expectations that they want to have satisfied. At the top of their lists are quality, value, and service. In the final analysis, only those restaurants that continually seek to improve their service will survive and flourish. Exceptional service doesn't simply happen. It is the result of careful initial training and constant attention to ongoing training.

Service At Its Best is a comprehensive and informative training and reference manual. The book has brought together all of the basic elements that can effectively inform and train the new waiter or waitress in all aspects of professional table service. It presents the material in an easy-to-read and understandable format. The book can further serve as a reference manual for the experienced server as new situations and circumstances arise.

This book has everything—from tips on professionally serving wines, cocktails, beers, and specialty coffee drinks to the latest in restaurant technology that will advance the lėvel of table service. Exceptional service starts with exceptional training.

Herman Cain
CEO, T.H.E., Inc. (The Hermanator Experience)
Former CEO and President of the National Restaurant Association
Former CEO and President of Godfather's Pizza

Perspective

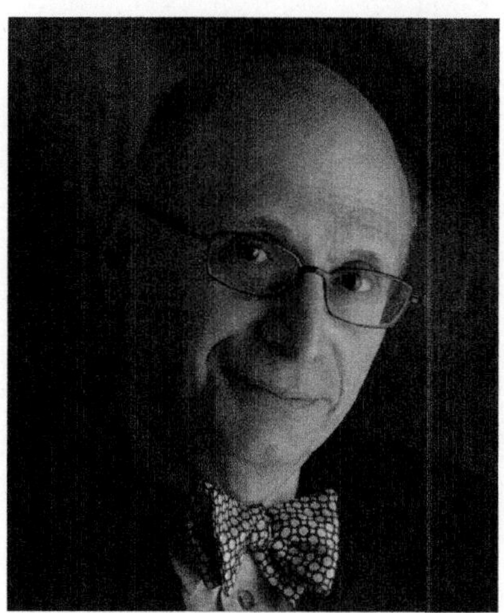

Edward E. Sanders
Lead Coauthor

Experienced restaurateurs recognize that customers will return to restaurants that consistently demonstrate exceptional service. The competitive nature of the restaurant business demands more than just great food and creative presentation. Customers return to the restaurants that cater to their dining-out needs.

Along with presenting the proper techniques of professional dining room service, this second edition discusses the importance of "reading the - needs" of the customer in providing exceptional service.

As a professional server, management professional, and culinary and hospitality educator, Marcella Giannasio of Johnson & Wales University has infused the added touches that go beyond the basics of good service. She explains how to develop the emotional connection that transforms a new customer into a familiar guest who returns to be served by friends.

Learning modules and projects will advance the students' understanding of dining room service and aid in developing the skills of "reading the - needs" when serving guests.

The casual professional atmosphere that prevails in most full-service restaurants across America can be further enhanced with well-trained professional servers.

The Professional Server: A Training Manual, 2e, provides the necessary information to adequately prepare servers for a rewarding career.

WE WELCOME YOUR COMMENTS

We would like to know your thoughts about professional table service and welcome your comments on this edition of *The Professional Server: A Training Manual.* Please address comments to Marcella Giannasio, Associate Professor, Johnson & Wales University, 801 West Trade Street, Charlotte, NC 28202, marcella.giannasio@JWU.edu

Acknowledgments

We would like to thank the following people:

Jerry Lanuzza, for the pictures that he took which appear in most of the chapters and for his never-ending support.

Kristen Depaul, for her input on Chapter 6, in the coffee and barista section. She was ready, willing, and able to help as soon as she was asked. Kristen is a 1999 graduate of Johnson & Wales University, Charleston campus, with ten years of food and beverage experience, currently working as a Specialty Coffee Bar manager.

John Abbott of Positech for his contribution and guidance with Chapter 8. His knowledge of restaurant technology and POS systems was so important and valuable.

Associate Professor Brad Beran of JWU, who contributed his expertise on craft beer in Chapter 6. He is not only knowledgeable but also passionate about beer and beer making.

Martin Lovelace, who was always available to help with any technical questions, as well as his cake and dessert photographs.

The family and friends who supported me before and during the writing of the second edition. My parents, Hilda and Joseph A. Giannasio, who always told me I could do whatever I put my mind to. They love good food and service and expose all four of their children to the pleasures of both.

Alva W. Alsbrooks, who is always ready to offer a kind and thoughtful word. His support is greatly appreciated.

A special thank-you to Alain Sailey, Franz Meyer, and Dean Karl Guggenmos, restaurateurs and mentors, who gave me an opportunity to work and learn from them for twenty-five years. Their generosity of spirit inspired me to become a teacher.

William Lawrensen, Senior Acquisitions Editor; Lara Dimmick, Editorial Assistant; Kris Roach, Project Manager; Alexis Biasell, Assistant Editor; and Debbie Ryan, Production Manager.

Shiny Rajesh, Senior Project Manager, Integra Software Services, for the exceptional attention to detail during copy editing and production.

The following professors from the *Hospitality Management Program, New York City College of Technology*: Jean F. Claude, John Akana, and Karen Goodlad for comments and suggestions, James Reid for many discussions on the subject of exceptional service and for his observation comments on the bartender/server in Chapter 4.

Dr. John Avella for reviews and suggestions, along with contributing to Chapter 7, "Guest Communication."

The spring 2010 Hospitality Marketing Class taught by Ed Sanders for having contributed ideas for the development of the second edition title: *The Professional Server: A Training Manual*

Kanda Rodpothong, photographer for the New York City College of Technology photo used in Chapter 10.

Miles Small, Editor-in-Chief, *CoffeeTalk,* for his expert review of the coffee and tea material presented in Chapter 6, "Wine and Beverage Service."

Alan Kimmel, Catering Manager, Lake Isle Country Club Caterers, for discussing catering applications with photos.

Dick Cattani, CEO, Restaurant Associates, for providing photos used in Chapter 10, "Banquet, Catering, and Buffet Service."

Wilfred Beriau, Southern Maine Community College; Alan Gross, the Art Institute of Philadelphia; and Michael Wray, Metropolitan State College of Denver Campus, for their time spent reading and reviewing.

The authors would like to acknowledge the following people for their help and guidance as the first edition was being developed:

Vernon R. Anthony, editor-in-chief, Pearson-Prentice Hall Education, for enthusiastically supporting the authors' vision for the book from the time of inception through its completion.

The professionals who reviewed the manuscript during its development and offered critical input that allowed the authors to bring additional focus to important topics, and further add to the book's detailed descriptions and accuracy.

Nick Fluge, CCE, Le Cordon Bleu Schools North America, for developing Chapter 6, "Wine and Beverage Service"; Eric Stromquist, Western Culinary Institute—Le Cordon Bleu Program; Tim Hill, Ph.D., FMP, Central Oregon Community College; Vivienne Wildes, Ph.D., The Pennsylvania State University; Chef Gene Fritz, Ed.M., CCE, Washington State University; Ray Colvin, Le Cordon Bleu Restaurant Management Program; Jim Sullivan, CEO, Sullivision.com; John Antun, Ph.D., CEC, CCE, FMP, CHE, University of South Carolina; and Richard D. Boyd, *Boyd Coffee Company,* for his review and suggestions for the coffee and tea section of Chapter 6.

Mark Sanders, who encouraged his father to do another textbook, and Jay Sanders, who worked as a busboy and server during his senior year in college, and who shared personal experiences that brought focus to several topics. Katherine Sanders, who always takes the opportunity to recognize, appreciate, and compliment "good service" whenever and wherever she finds it. Dad needed and appreciated the critical input. Linda Sanders for her suggestions, ideas, and constructive comments, who again brought great value to another of her husband's writing projects. In memory of Nick and Dorothy Drossos, lifetime restaurateurs, who introduced Ed Sanders to formal dining room service in 1971, and were still able to show him a few more tips in 2001 for the first edition.

Robert E. Farrell, whose philosophy and book *Give'Em the Pickle* inspired Paul Paz never to lose touch with the only reason any of us have hospitality careers: to serve the customer. Besides once being Paul's employer, his professional and personal friendship is profoundly appreciated.

Paul J., Jacqueline, and Dominic Paz for providing respect, love, and pride to their father, the waiter.

Darla Wilkinson for her insight and expertise on the subject of server training. Her suggestions and constructive comments contributed additional value to the book—from a most appreciative and loving husband.

Organization of the Text

This book is written in such a way that the chapters flow in a logical sequence, establishing a step-by-step procedure for understanding and learning appropriate server skills. The chapters are also self-contained, so that the reader can go directly to any chapter for specific information. Therefore, the book can be used as a training guide or a reference manual for specific service questions.

Chapter 1, "The Professional Server," introduces the reader to restaurant industry statistics and income opportunities, and explains how tip credit is calculated. "The Saturday Market Theory of Waiting Tables" reflects how a server takes ownership in his or her job. The nature of tipping and tip income reporting responsibility to the Internal Revenue Service are explained. Occupational advantages and disadvantages are identified, along with the job qualifications and descriptions of advancement opportunities for servers.

Chapter 2, "Professional Appearance," discusses the many aspects of grooming standards, the importance of body language, poise, and posture, the types of uniforms and aprons that may be used, the value of safe shoes, and the importance of server health.

Chapter 3, "Table Settings, Napkin Presentations, and Table Service," identifies the basic table settings for breakfast, lunch, and dinner as the table is preset and as the meal is served, along with the appropriate wine and beverage settings. The use of place mats and the correct placement of salt and pepper shakers, sugar and creamers, and rolls and butter are explained. Napkin presentations are discussed along with the correct procedure for placing tablecloths. The specific types of table service are explained in detail, including the following: American service (individual plate service), butler service, English service, Russian service, French service, as well as counter service, banquet service, and room service. The use of salad bars and dessert tables and carts is highlighted.

Chapter 4, "Serving Food and Beverages," sets forth twenty-five tips for proper table service that include the technique of carrying multiple plates, and also the correct procedures for loading and carrying trays. Service priorities and timing, along with effectively handling difficult situations, are identified and supported with positive responses. Table bussing is detailed with procedures for using a cart or tray, as well as the procedure for setting up with the use of a tray, along with identifying additional server's assistant/busser responsibilities. The role of the bartender/server is also discussed.

Chapter 5, "Service Readiness," presents the responsibilities of a server that support good service, which include completing side-work as well as following opening and closing procedures. The chapter further illustrates breakfast, lunch, and dinner menus, along with a wine list. The importance of menu knowledge by the server is emphasized along with the role of the server in helping the guest understand the menu and menu terms.

Chapter 6, "Wine and Beverage Service," begins with identifying the proper temperatures for serving wines along with the correct procedures for using an ice bucket. The presentation and service of wine is illustrated step by step, beginning with presenting a bottle of wine to a guest, properly opening it, and the appropriate method of pouring the wine. The reasons and the procedure for decanting wine are also discussed. The various shapes of wine glasses are shown, identifying their appropriate use for the type of wine being served. Wine varietals are introduced and explained so that the reader gains a basic understanding of wine. Spirits and cocktails are discussed, along with popular spirit brands, cocktail choices, and related terms the server should know. Beers, lagers, and ales are defined, and the correct procedure for serving beer is explained. Responsible alcohol service is reviewed and emphasized. The correct procedure for serving bottled waters is discussed. Coffee drinks that include espresso, café lattes, cappuccino, mochas, and the application of coffee with a spirit beverage are explained, along with the use of the French Press for coffee service. Tea varieties and service are also presented.

Chapter 7, "Guest Communications," begins with the server personally connecting with the guest through an individual sense of enthusiasm. Varieties of possible guest types are discussed, along with tips for anticipating the guest's needs and how to look for nonverbal cues and prompts. Suggestive selling is detailed, with techniques for upselling to the guest, suggesting related menu items, new menu items or the chef's specialties, items for special occasions, and take-home items. The guidelines for suggestive selling are presented and illustrated. The correct procedure for taking the guest's order is discussed, as is the guest check and the importance of service timing. Correct reaction in a professional manner to emergency situations is also addressed.

Chapter 8, "The Technology of Service," identifies the basic POS (point-of-sale) terminology and presents technology applications. Table service management, guest paging system, product management software, handheld touch-screen terminal, server paging system, staff-to-staff/customer-to-staff paging, and various software applications are discussed, along with the benefits of technology. The uses of restaurant websites are reviewed, as is employee training with technology.

Chapter 9, "The Host," begins with effectively greeting guests and table selection. Professional courtesies, handling complaints, taking telephone reservations and "to go" orders, server supervision, and menu meetings are all detailed in the discussion of the responsibilities of this important position.

Chapter 10, "Banquet, Catering, and Buffet Service," defines the three distinct types of service. The importance and value of an Event Plan Details work sheet is clearly explained in a manner that covers all of the essential details for any planned banquet, catered, or buffet service event. Such details as knowing the difference between "approximate, guaranteed, and confirmed" number of guests; the differences between an open bar, cash bar, and open–cash combination bar; understanding how to calculate a room's capacity for comfortable seating; and a knowledge of the various accessory details that can be added to an event are discussed.

Appendixes A, B, C, and D have been designed to provide the reader/user with a quick reference source for common menu terms; wine terminology; spirit brands and related cocktails; and ales, lagers, and nonalcohol beers.

An Effective Server

An effective server is a person who:

- Has a pleasant manner and truly enjoys people. The server is able to sustain a friendly demeanor with poise and self-confidence while under pressure.
- Is organized and systematically follows up. The server is always on time for work, provides prompt service to guests, completes all tasks including opening, shift change, closing cleanup, and restocking service areas.
- Has a positive professional attitude that generates positive results. The server enjoys pleasing people and contributes to an atmosphere of trust and unity with coworkers and guests.
- Takes charge of his/her station, recognizes when and what kind of service guests need, and responds with a sense of urgency. The server enjoys working at a fast pace.
- Has a good cultural awareness of the lifestyle, ethnic, and nationality mixes of coworkers and guests. The server enjoys and desires to work with many people of diverse backgrounds.
- Has the ability to be flexible, diplomatic, patient, understanding, and cooperative. The server cooperatively works with coworkers in the fast-paced work environment that supports a common goal of providing the highest quality of guest service.
- Is sensitive and is able to anticipate guest needs. The server has the ability to be a good and active listener, enabling guests to feel at ease. The server is able to quickly discern and understand guests' needs, and is concerned with accuracy and quality.
- Demonstrates loyalty and commitment to the restaurant operation and coworkers. The server has a strong sense of honesty when handling guest payment transactions, when sharing tips, and when sharing work responsibilities equally.
- Has the ability to adjust timing and service according to the expectations and needs of multiple guest situations. The server continually develops and refines his or her service skills based upon personal experience.
- Understands food and beverage menu descriptions and is able to comfortably guide guests through meal selections. The server constantly takes the initiative to keep informed about new food and beverage items.
- Demonstrates politeness, courtesy, and respect at all times, enabling coworkers and guests to feel comfortable. The server works to support an environment that is relaxed and free from discord.
- Has endurance and a high energy level and enjoys working at a quick, steady, and methodical pace. The server is enthusiastic and has the ability to step back and find a sense of humor in order to minimize the stress and tension of the job.
- Can effectively create an emotional connection with guests that results in creating guests' loyalty.

From the Authors

A professional server has the opportunity to earn an unlimited income, work flexible hours, be involved in a life's work that can result in great personal satisfaction, and pursue career advancements within the hospitality industry.

The Professional Server: A Training Manual introduces the student to the many aspects of being a professional server. The experienced server will also find the book to be an excellent reference to consult for various techniques and service situations.

The key topics include the rules of good service, typical experiences for which a server needs to be prepared, how to deal with and solve problems, the value of good communication skills, and some of the best techniques used for professional servers.

As a working server involved in practicing the correct principles and procedures of good service, coauthor and professional server Paul Paz brought reality to every chapter. Coauthor Ron Wilkinson recognized the need for a thorough guide to successful server training and initially developed training methods and guidelines as a restaurateur and consultant. That material became the foundation to which lead coauthor Ed Sanders added his foodservice and academic experience to bring forth the first edition.

The basics for becoming a successful server have not changed, but the methods and procedures continue to be refined in many areas, including technology. Coauthor Marcella Giannasio, with hands-on restaurant experience and the knowledge of a respected educator, has brought those advancements to the second edition.

INSTRUCTOR RESOURCES

To access supplementary materials online, instructors need to request an instructor access code. Go to www.pearsonhighered.com/irc, where you can register for an instructor access code. Within 48 hours after registering, you will receive a confirming e-mail, including an instructor access code. Once you have received your code, go to the site and log on for full instructions on downloading the materials you wish to use.

Welcome to the second edition of *The Professional Server: A Training Manual,* an indispensable guide to becoming a successful server.

About the Authors

Edward E. Sanders ***New York City College of Technology*** Ed is an Adjunct Professor of hospitality management at New York City College of Technology. He has enjoyed a career in business management, foodservice, journalism, and academics—owned a restaurant, operated a chain of restaurants, founded and operated *Hospitality News,* a mega-regional trade journal, been an associate professor of business and cofounded and directed a hotel, restaurant, and resort management university program. He is also the lead coauthor for *Understanding Foodservice Cost Control, 4E,* and *Catering Solutions: For The Culinary Student, Foodservice Operator, and Caterer,* published by Pearson Education. Ed is a Certified Food Executive and Certified Purchasing Manager and has a master's degree in international management from Thunderbird School of Global Management and a doctor of business administration degree in management and organization. Through his career in business and education he has been associated with Xerox Corporation, Sky Chefs-American Airlines, Marriott, Delaware North, North's Restaurants, Brigham Young University, Oregon State University, and Southern Oregon University.

Marcella Giannasio ***Johnson & Wales University*** Marcella is an Associate Professor at Johnson & Wales University, Charlotte, North Carolina, and teaches in the culinary and hospitality departments. She has also taught and supervised students in Koblenz, Germany, at the Deutsche Wein und Sommelierschule, and at Sun rice global academy in Singapore, and participated in the Banfi scholastic tour in Italy. Marcella is a graduate of the College of Charleston and earned a master's degree in management from Southern Wesleyan University. Her certifications include: Certified Hospitality Educator (CHE) through the American Hotel & Lodging Educational Institute, Foodservice Management Professional (FMP) through the National Restaurant Association, and a Court of Master Sommelier Level1. She is a Bordeaux wine ambassador and holds an advanced wine & spirits certification from WSET, a division of the Wine & Spirit Education Trust Limited based in London, and is a Hospitality Grand Master (HGM) through the Federation of Dining Room Professionals. She joined the Johnson & Wales University faculty in 1997 with having several years of management experience within the hospitality industry.

Paul C. Paz ***WaitersWorld*** Paul has been a career professional server for over thirty years. He began working as a server knowing very little about it to being featured in his profession by *The National Restaurant Association, Nation's Restaurant News, Restaurants and Institutions, The Washington Post, The Wall Street Journal,* and many other publications. He has also appeared on ABC's 20/20 news show. He has written numerous articles on tableside service-sales and is an active contributor to the restaurant social media group, www.FohBoh.com. He posts regularly on his Facebook page, "WaitersWorld—Paul C Paz." He is a hospitality consultant and has presented a variety of seminars throughout the Pacific Northwest and nationally. Furthermore, he has delivered *WaitersWorld* service-sales workshops for such organizations as SYSCO, Food Services of America, Ben E. Keith Distributors, National Association of Catering Executives, and IHOP International. He also serves on the policy advisory committee for the Oregon Restaurant Association.

Ron Wilkinson *Profit Power Systems* Ron is the founder and CEO of Profit Power Systems, developers of Foodco—Cost Control Systems—RestaurantMarketingGroup.org, and AIMHIRE—Employee Selection Systems. He is also the founder and director of the International Food Service Foundation. His career has spanned over fifty years and has included owning and operating quick-serve, family, and formal dining restaurants, and he has been a training director and vice president of operations for several large restaurant chains. He has developed and written operational and service training manuals and has taught college foodservice and restaurant management courses. Ron has also served on academic advisory boards for restaurant and hospitality programs. He has presented numerous workshops at food shows, hospitality association conferences, and restaurant chain management meetings. Ron is a recognized expert at maximizing profit for foodservice operations of all types.

THE PROFESSIONAL SERVER

1

The Professional Server

The culinary and service aspects of the food and beverage industry have significantly advanced in recent years. Today the food and beverage industry offers diverse careers with great opportunities for earnings and advancement. The stereotype of a server being a transient job filled by college students and part-time employees has changed. There are many professional servers who raise families while enjoying the flexibility of a server's schedule, a fun and exciting career, as well as a good income. The restaurant industry, in general, offers boundless opportunities in all segments of hospitality service (Table 1–1).

Service has become so important to the dining-out public that it is not unusual for neighbors, friends, and colleagues to discuss and critique the food along with the service that they enjoyed at a particular restaurant. In addition, there is a new focus on healthy and organic restaurant food. There is an increased interest in where food comes from and how it is prepared. The use of fresh, local ingredients is a popular movement in the restaurant industry. There is an interest in local farming and how to bring these ingredients to the rising numbers of guests who are asking for this.

The following list represents some impressive facts and figures taken from the 2000 and 2010 *National Restaurant Association Restaurant Industry Pocket Factbook* (Table 1–1)

Additional information can be obtained from the National Restaurant Association at www.restaurant.org or from The Education Foundation at www.edfound.org.

The restaurant industry continues to sustain record growth with increasing employment opportunities in all segments of the industry. This is a positive outlook for many people who are interested in a career in the hospitality industry.

learning objectives

After reading this chapter and completing the discussion questions and exercises, you should be able to:

1. Understand the size and economic importance of the restaurant industry.
2. Analyze and project potential income opportunities derived from wages and tips.
3. Identify factors that can influence annual income.
4. Understand the entrepreneurial side of being a professional server.
5. Relate the standards and rules for table-service tipping.
6. Understand why a tip may be small or not given at all.
7. Understand that tips are taxable income and that accurate record keeping must be maintained.
8. Recognize occupational advantages and disadvantages.
9. Identify professional server job qualifications.
10. Recognize career advancement opportunities.

INCOME OPPORTUNITIES

Professional servers are often stereotyped as having low incomes and poor prospects of ever achieving a successful career. However, server income averages and industry advancement opportunities do not support these assumptions. Serving tables of customers should be viewed as an entrepreneurial business opportunity.

A server's income is usually derived from two sources: wages and tips. There are few other businesses that the employee has so much control over their own income. A server's income is typically based on tips which are directly linked to sales. There are many types of servers in many different areas of a hotel or restaurant. We must mention room service attendants, banquet servers, and any tipped associate of a large hotel such as a bell person or a parking attendant for valet parking. Some of these positions, such as banquet servers and room service attendants, receive their tips on a paycheck. Banquet servers pool their tips, which

TABLE 1–1
U.S. RESTAURANT INDUSTRY STATISTICS, 2000 AND 2010

Facts 2000	Facts 2010
$376 billion in annual sales	$558 billion in annual sales
831,000 locations	945,000 locations
11 million people employed in the industry	12.7 million people employed in the industry
45.3 percent restaurant industry share of the total food dollar	49 percent restaurant industry share of the total food dollar
One-third of all adults in the United States have worked in the restaurant industry at some time during their lives	Half of all adults in the United States have worked in the restaurant industry at some time during their lives—32 percent of all American adults got their first job in the restaurant industry
	73 percent of adults say they try to eat healthier now at restaurants than they did 2 years ago

means their tips are divided among the number of servers scheduled for a particular banquet function. A professional server is more than an order taker; they are instead a salesperson who can increase their income as well as the income of the restaurant by increasing the food and beverage sales at each of their tables. Listed below are several sales techniques that are commonly used in the restaurant industry to increase guest checks, thereby increasing the potential income for the restaurant owner and the servers themselves:

1. Suggestive selling—suggesting additional items to a guest's order.
2. Upselling—increasing the value of the items a guest orders.
3. Highlighting—pointing out the specials to a guest; favorite or popular items on the menu to encourage the guest to order them.
4. Open-ended questions—a question the guest cannot answer with a yes or no. A question that allows the guest to think about ordering an item that they were not considering until they were asked.

These sales techniques, which are further discussed in Chapter 7, are used to encourage guests to have the most enjoyable meal possible and to increase the guest check total, as well as the server's potential tip. Table 1–2 is an example of the results when sales techniques are effectively applied.

There are additional factors that can influence a server's income, such as the following:

1. Working more or fewer hours
2. Working at two or more eating/drinking establishments
3. Shifts worked: breakfast, lunch, or dinner
4. Weekday or weekend
5. Banquet or special functions
6. Equipment failures
7. Weather
8. Holidays
9. Seasonal fluctuations in customer counts
10. Product availability
11. Staffing shortages

TABLE 1–2
COMPARISON OF TWO GUEST CHECKS REPRESENTING FOUR GUESTS

Guest Check #1 Low Salesmanship		Guest Check #2 High Salesmanship	
1 Crabcake Appetizer	$7.95	2 Crabcake Appetizer	$15.90
1 Cream Soup	$4.95	1 Cream soup	$4.95
		1 Caesar Salad	$6.95
2 Trout	$33.90	1 Trout	$16.95
2 Chicken	$25.90	2 Chicken	$25.90
		1 Lobster Special	$19.95
1 Dessert	$5.95	2 Desserts	$11.90
2 Coffee	$3.90	1 Coffee	$1.95
		1 Cappuccino	$3.95
TOTAL	$82.55	TOTAL	$136.20
15% TIP	$12.38	15% TIP	$20.43

12. Tip pooling. This (where legally allowed) occurs when all tips go into one pot and are divided equally among selected staff. Usually the employer determines who will share the tips and the percentage formula.
13. Tipping out other positions. Under this system, a percentage or specific amount goes to any one or a mix of the following positions: host, bartender, cocktail servers, or bus attendants. Again, the employer usually sets the house policy on distribution.
14. Menu prices.

So how does a career professional server get a raise? The answer is in one word: *tips.* The customers provide the raises. Furthermore, the level of the server's competence determines the size of the raise. But can one really make a living at this profession? The average dollar amount in guest check sales vary and are correlated to the style of restaurant. Typically, a fast-paced diner or deli may average $7–$10 per person, a chain or family restaurant may average $9–$15 per person, and a fine-dining restaurant may average $25–$50 per person, not including wine or other alcohol beverages. Guest check sales also vary at breakfast, lunch, and dinner, as the dollar amounts are smaller for breakfast, increase with lunch, and are greater for dinner.

There are technical skills needed to be a successful server, such as serving with the correct hand from the correct side, carrying a beverage tray, and working in a timely and efficient manner. Guests do not like to wait for long periods of time to eat. A server must understand the sequence of service which should have a steady flow that seems natural and unrushed.

Service skills are trainable; a server can learn the technical skills and can become proficient in them. But in addition to the technical skills, a server's success is greatly linked to the innate desire to serve. This desire to serve is difficult to teach and is something that the server must naturally possess, which can be further enhanced with good training. Below are examples of variables that directly impact a server's success. The combinations of the three variables are the foundation for excellent guest service and satisfaction.

The three critical variables within the server's control that directly impacts his or her earnings are as follows:

The Desire to Serve: Genuinely and sincerely wanting to create a pleasant dining experience for all your guests. Reading what your guest needs from you, through observation.

Personalized Service: Consistently creating and delivering a distinctively personalized service that increases tip percentages. This is accomplished by rendering the highest possible quality of service. A server can achieve this by using basic technical service skills.

Marketing Skills: Suggestively selling items such as appetizers, beverages, and desserts to increase the dollar amount of guest checks.

These variables will be further discussed in Chapter 7, Guest Communication.

CHALLENGES FOR THE INDUSTRY

Even though becoming a professional server has many advantages, the turnover rate in the restaurant industry remains quite high. This is one of the biggest challenges facing the industry today. Keeping talented employees has become increasingly difficult and has driven some employers to become more creative with incentives, including signing bonuses, health insurance with shorter waiting periods, paid vacations, and 401-K pension plans. For the most part, the wage standard for a server in the United States remains at minimum wage for the entire length of employment. It is not the industry standard for employers to offer merit increases based upon performance or length of employment. Weekly, monthly, or quarterly incentives help to keep servers interested in their job and create healthy competition among the staff. It is not uncommon for a restaurant to offer its servers a chance to win a night off of their choice, a gift certificate to another restaurant, or free merchandise for high sales, perfect attendance, or loyalty to the restaurant. These incentives are becoming more and more common and can be an excellent way of maintaining a positive work environment.

TIP CREDIT

Many states have mandated the legal authority to apply what is known as a "tip credit." The formula is simple: The more one makes in tips the less the employer is required to pay in wages. These formulas vary from state to state but, for the most part, duplicate federal guidelines. It should also be noted that there are some states whose minimum wage is higher than the 2011 current $7.25 federal minimum wage.

To answer the question, *What is the minimum wage for workers who receive tips?* The Fair Labor Standards Act requires payment of at least the federal minimum wage to covered, nonexempt employees. An employer of tipped employees is only required to pay $2.13 an hour in direct wages.

FEDERAL ($7.25) 2011 MINIMUM WAGE FOR TIPPED WORKERS

Basic combined cash & tip minimum wage per hour	Maximum tip credit against minimum wage per hour	Minimum cash wage per hour
$7.25	$5.12	$2.13

If that amount plus the tips received equals at least the federal minimum wage, the employee retains all the tips. If an employee's tips combined with the employer's direct wage of at least $2.13 an hour do not equal the federal minimum hourly wage, the employer must make up the difference. See U.S. Department of Labor website: www.dol.gov/whd/state/tipped.htm

Table 1–3 demonstrates the effect of the tip credit application.

TABLE 1–3
POTENTIAL SERVER EARNINGS

Annual sales of $125,000
(Amount taken from customer guest checks)
$500 per day in customer sales × 5 days a week = $2,500 × 50 weeks = $125,000
(A total of $500 per day in customer sales based upon serving 50 people with a $10 per person average guest check)
Working 30 hours per week × 50 weeks = 1,500 annual work hours

Annual Sales	Tip (%)	Annual tip income	Hourly + Fed.Min. = Hourly Wage
$125,000	× 10	= $12,500 ÷ 1,500 hours =	$8.33 + $2.13 = $10.46
$125,000	× 15	= $18,750 ÷ 1,500 hours =	$12.50 + $2.13 = $14.63
$125,000	× 20	= $25,000 ÷ 1,500 hours =	$16.66 + $$2.13 = $18.79

THE SATURDAY MARKET THEORY OF WAITING TABLES

The following story, in his own words, is from the experience of a professionally trained server:

> It's my morning opening shift for the restaurant and I have a new server trainee following me. We are going through the scheduled routine of opening and cleaning, including waxing tabletops and scraping gum off table bottoms. My trainee says, "For such a big company why don't they have a cleaning company do this? They're probably just trying to save a buck."
>
> I looked at him and said, "Have you ever been to a Saturday Market?" You know, the craft fairs and flea markets where entrepreneurs gather to sell their crafts and services.
>
> "Yep," he answers in a quizzical tone.
>
> Well, here in this restaurant, I'm in the same boat as the entrepreneurs at a Saturday Market. You see *my* "sales booth" is *my* five-table section and *my* success is completely determined by what I am willing to do with it. Okay, yes I am an employee. But, when I encounter my customers, they only see me. I am the owner. I facilitate what they expect to happen. In my customer's eyes, I am responsible for everything they experience during their visit at my Saturday Market sales booth.
>
> Now on a practical basis, that's a ridiculous concept. But, the reality of my professional and financial success is to understand and appreciate the entrepreneurial opportunity that has been given to me as a professional server. It's an opportunity to be rewarded based upon my personal performance.

The server continues his story.

> Well, I got hired as a server by a restaurateur who allowed me to take a theoretical ownership in a restaurant that cost over $1,000,000. The restaurant operation had a food and beverage inventory exceeding $70,000 that I could offer to my customers. It also provided an accounting department to calculate my business costs such as taxes, health insurance, vacation pay, and even retirement. There was a manager that planned the daily operations, staffing levels, and provided guidance and personal

support in helping me to better serve my customers. A professional support staff consisting of other servers, hosts, bartenders, cocktail servers, cooks, and dishwashers all worked as a team so I could focus on my customers' needs and requests. Then the restaurateur spent thousands of dollars for advertising to bring in customers for me. All of this for my own personal use!

You know what's crazy? The first day I showed up they paid me an hourly wage before I ever sold a thing. But you know what is really, I mean really nuts? I get all this opportunity handed to me for nothing. I didn't have to pay a dime for any of it. All I have to do is show up and invest an entrepreneurial effort using the resources given to me. I am responsible for my future. My challenge is how am I going to maximize all this opportunity given to me at no cost?

Who says I'm not an entrepreneur? All I have to do is think like a businessperson. I have my own business as a server.

A dignified profession, I must add!

TIPPING

The current national tipping standard for table service is 15–20 percent of the meal's cost, excluding taxes. Tipping over 15 percent is quite acceptable and in certain establishments can average 20–30 percent. Table 1–4 shows the tip amounts when the percentages are applied. Who made up this rule of thumb? It evolved as a "customary" standard via the hospitality industry and consumers. There are numerous stories of servers being "stiffed" (left with no tip) or of being given outrageous tips. Newsmaking stories include those of the Chicago cocktail server who got a $10,000 tip from an English doctor, or the Boston bartender who shared her restaurant concept with a customer who turned out to be an investment banker. He liked her idea and as a result, made her a partner and put up over $1,000,000 to launch her dream restaurant. A server can never know in advance whether the person that he or she may be serving could in some way reward personalized service with an extraordinary benefit.

Tips are not mandatory. Some servers think that they are, and they are routinely outraged when a customer leaves a tip that is less than they think appropriate. Some establishments set automatic gratuities or a service charge of 15–20 percent for certain circumstances, such as special events, banquets, and groups of diners

TABLE 1–4
TIP GUIDE 15% AND 20%

Check Amount	15%	20%
$10.00	$1.50	$2.00
20.00	3.00	4.00
30.00	4.50	6.00
40.00	6.00	8.00
50.00	7.50	10.00
60.00	9.00	12.00
70.00	10.50	14.00
80.00	12.00	16.00
90.00	13.50	18.00
100.00	15.00	20.00

over a certain size. In these cases the customer is notified either on the menu, during the process of making reservations, or by the server.

All too often, a server can look at a guest in a restaurant and make an incorrect judgment based upon the guest's appearance. This can be a big mistake and a valuable lesson can be learned from the following true story. A young college student, named Kristen, was working part-time as a server in a popular small French restaurant. The restaurant had a reputation for excellent food and wine at reasonable prices. The restaurant was always busy and the servers had a heavy workload, being responsible for seating and clearing their own tables.

restaurant reality: never judge a book by its cover or a guest by how they are dressed

On a busy weeknight, a gentleman walked in the front door. He had a disheveled appearance and was dressed very causally. Several servers walked by him. Kristen was extremely busy; she had several tables that needed to be bussed. The other servers had one available table each but did not seat the guest. Kristen asked her fellow servers why they allowed the guest to stand at the front door. They told her that she could serve the guest because they were not interested. Kristen was disappointed with the servers. She politely acknowledged the guest and bussed one of her two dirty tables, then seated the guest who explained that he would be joined by two more guests. He asked that she present him with the bill at the end of the meal, and proceeded to order the most expensive bottle of wine on the wine list and waited for his guests to arrive. The two gentlemen who joined him were neatly dressed in classic business suits. Kristen waited on the three gentlemen who ordered several meal courses along with two additional bottles of high-end wines. The guest check was quite substantial, and as the meal came to an end it was time to present the bill to the guest. It was one of the highest bills Kristen had ever experienced since her employment at the restaurant. She presented the bill and the guest looked at it and placed a credit card in the leather check presenter.

He expressed his appreciation for her excellent and professional service. When she returned with the credit card and authorization slip, the guest signed the credit card slip and wrote the word "CASH" in the space for the tip. He then reached for his wallet and gave her a 50 percent cash tip. She was shocked and told him that it was too much. He disagreed and further complimented her on her professionalism, and commented on the other servers passing him by as he patiently stood at the door. He felt that the other severs judged him by his appearance, but that she was respectful and professional in every way.

He told her that he was new in town and involved with a successful business, and enjoyed his meal immensely, therefore would be coming back to the restaurant often. He wanted her to be his server whenever he returned. He came in frequently and always gave Kristen a 50 percent tip.

GETTING STIFFED (LEFT WITH NO TIP)

Many servers have experienced the "penalty" of a short tip or no tip as the result of a customer's dissatisfaction. There are occasions where indeed the server did not deliver the service expected and should be tipped (or not tipped) accordingly. Some conditions are beyond the server's control, such as being short staffed, being out of certain food items, and a kitchen equipment failure. As a result, the tip is reduced or lost. For the most part, customers are forgiving of momentary glitches if they are informed of the circumstances and the restaurant makes a sincere attempt to reconcile the inconvenience. What customers will not excuse is a bad attitude on the part of the server or a projected sense of "entitlement" when it comes to tipping. Sometimes the best tip is no tip at all. Table 1–5 compares the best tippers and the worst tippers.

TABLE 1–5
BEST/WORST TIPPERS

Best Tippers	Worst Tippers
Businesspeople	Businesspeople
Regulars	Regulars
Hospitality industry workers	Hospitality industry workers
Restaurant managers & owners	Restaurant managers & owners
Alcohol drinkers	Alcohol drinkers
Seniors	Seniors
New Yorkers	New Yorkers
Church people	Church people

Get the picture? It's not who you serve but how you provide service.

Serving tables of customers is a craft. The level of income that one can earn is relative to professional customer service delivered. Servers certainly do not sustain their careers via minimum wage, although it is still an important part of their income. "Raises" are provided by the customers and not by the employers. If servers want to improve their income levels, they must enhance their craft and skills.

There are certain customers who do not believe in tipping. That is their choice; and it is one of the occupational hazards of the profession. Most people prefer having the option on tips and rebel at being told that they "owe" tips. A typical server can serve over 11,000 people each year; perhaps 1 percent are not satisfied with the service. That leaves 10,890 fabulous guests, who were a pleasure to serve and were willing to reward professional service. The tips of these fabulous guests allow the server to enjoy a good income.

The rule to remember when getting stiffed is: Get over it! Reset the table for the next party and work toward a 25 percent tip or more.

TIPPING AND THE INTERNAL REVENUE SERVICE

Workers in general have tax responsibilities and are required to pay their legally owed taxes on income. The Internal Revenue Service (IRS) estimates that $11 billion in tips are unreported by restaurant employees annually. Recent court rulings have reinforced the fact that employers are responsible for undeclared employee tips on payroll taxes. These were taxes that the employee should have paid if they had declared their tips properly.

The IRS is stepping up enforcement on undeclared tips with employers. This increased IRS activity is the result of court decisions ruling in favor of the IRS putting pressure on employers (not employees) to account for tip income. Potential penalties to tipped employees for underreporting tips are:

1. Prison sentence for failing to declare income
2. Additional tax
3. Federal Insurance Contributions Act (FICA) (7 percent of unreported income)
4. Fifty percent penalty on FICA
5. Twenty percent penalty on the total tax liability for the year
6. Interest charges
7. A big fat headache!

Benefits of reporting tips:

1. Higher social security benefits
2. Higher unemployment benefits
3. Higher credit rating for loans
4. Higher amounts paid into participating 401-K plans

IRS-allocated tip formulas are used to track the sales of restaurants against the percentage of declared tips by the employees. If the declared tip ratio falls below 12 percent of the gross sales, the employer may "allocate" tips on W-2's at the end of the year to those employees who under-declared tips throughout the year. The 12 percent figure is the minimum total tax due. If the IRS audits a server, they will be looking for all tips and will calculate the tax liability along with any penalties accordingly.

Because of increased payroll tracking technology, it is very difficult to not report tips, especially charged tips. It is recommended that servers keep a record of sales, tips, and other employees who shared in their tips. If the IRS audits a server, and no records are available, the IRS can assess a calculated amount.

Ultimately the law is clear and simple. Tips are taxable income and, by law, must be reported to all applicable tax agencies.

Additional information on tip-reporting requirements can be obtained from the Internal Revenue Service by calling 800 TAX-FORM or by visiting www.irs.com. The following tax-reporting forms are also available from the IRS upon request:

IRS Form 4070A, *Employee's Daily Record of Tips*

IRS Form 4070, *Employee's Report of Tips to Employer*

IRS Form 8027, *Employer's Annual Information Return of Tip Income and Allocated Tips*

IRS Publication 531, *Reporting Income from Tips*

OCCUPATIONAL ADVANTAGES

The following advantages are attractive and motivating to many people:

1. ***Time flexibility:*** The server's time can be flexible to accommodate other things in life, such as family activities, continuing education, a second job, leisure time, and other professional endeavors. The nature of the business allows for flexibility in scheduling work hours and days off.
2. ***Income flexibility:*** The server can control his or her income by working more or less hours.
3. ***Performance reviews:*** The server gets immediate feedback on the success or failure of his or her work in the form of tips and/or customer compliments or complaints.
4. ***High hourly wage:*** The potential to earn a high hourly wage (wage plus tips) is substantially greater than in many other occupations and can be achieved faster.
5. ***Job mobility:*** When the server has mastered the basic skills of the craft, those skills are then easily transferable to any restaurant in the world, along with other occupations. Everybody wants good service in one form or another.
6. ***Minimal clothing expense:*** The investment in work clothing can be minimal, as most employers provide uniforms.

7. ***Complimentary or discounted meals:*** The server is typically provided either a complimentary or discounted meal during his or her work shift. The average discounted meal is 50 percent off the menu price.
8. ***Minimal after-work stress:*** When the server clocks out at the end of a shift, the job does not go home with him or her. The server is done for the day until the next shift.
9. ***Physical fitness:*** The nature of the work provides a high level of physical activity.
10. ***Opportunity to meet interesting people:*** The server has the opportunity to meet a wide spectrum of people every shift. Friendships and lasting customer relationships often develop.
11. ***Interesting work:*** The work is never boring, as different things occur during every shift.
12. ***Entrepreneurial experience:*** The server learns how to be an entrepreneur by being exposed to selling and the rewards of providing personalized service.
13. ***Work unity:*** There can be a unique sense of family and camaraderie among restaurant employees that is not often found in other occupations.
14. ***Sales training:*** The server has the opportunity to learn the art of sales and merchandising. This training to increase sales will result in increased income and greater customer satisfaction.
15. ***Teamwork participation:*** The server can learn to appreciate the value and importance of teamwork.

OCCUPATIONAL DISADVANTAGES

The disadvantages can be discouraging for people who are not cut out for server work.

1. ***Working weekends, nights, and holidays:*** The nature of the restaurant industry often requires working weekends, nights, and holidays. These are typically the busiest times in most establishments.
2. ***Work stress:*** The work can be physically, mentally, and psychologically intense, and can be emotionally demanding. The burnout possibilities are high for those who do not take the time to relax physically and mentally after work.
3. ***Minimal employee benefits:*** The employee benefits are often minimal, although recent competition for labor has motivated the industry to offer better benefits than in the past. Examples include medical insurance, paid vacations, pension plans, access to free or discounted activities such as health clubs, and meal discounts as a customer.
4. ***No employer-provided disability insurance:*** Restaurant employers typically do not provide disability insurance or short-term income replacement benefits. This is not to be confused with Workers Compensation or Social Security Disability.
5. ***Minimum wage:*** Minimum wage is the industry standard and merit wage increases are the exception.
6. ***Reduced minimum wage:*** In states where tip credit is applicable, the hourly wage payable by the employer is reduced to below the federal minimum standard.
7. ***Lost income:*** Events beyond the server's control, such as shutdowns because of weather or equipment failure, mean the server will not be working.
8. ***Financial budgeting:*** Those who have difficulty managing a cash income may have budgeting problems.

JOB QUALIFICATIONS

To be successful as a server, an individual should review the following personal competencies:

Education

There are very few training schools for professional servers. Formal education is important but not necessary. The aspiring server should possess the ability to learn quickly on the job. Having the desire to serve and being willing to do your best is an asset to becoming a professional server.

Intelligence

A successful server should be alert and mentally sharp at all times. The job requires quick organized thinking under stress, with the ability to adjust timing and service according to the expectations and needs of multiple guest situations.

Product Knowledge

The server must understand the menu descriptions of the food and beverage items in order to guide the guests through meal selections. Given the wide selection of products available, and new ones continually being introduced, the individual must take the initiative to stay educated about the latest food and beverage items.

Service Knowledge

A number of service methods, techniques, and standards require training (usually on the job) and experience to gain practice at understanding and executing basic tasks. The seasoned server will develop a personal style by drawing from what he or she learns of the basics. With a little imagination and creativity, the server will become increasingly more effective and profitable.

Timing and Attention to Details

There is nothing more important than timing and attention to detail when waiting tables. It begins with getting ready on time. There needs to be a sense of urgency the minute a service employee walks in the door. Every detail must be finished and double-checked prior to opening for a shift. All work should be completed fully and accurately to ensure a successful meal period. If corners are cut or time is neglected, a shift can be chaotic and service will suffer. Every detail, regardless of how small, contributes to a positive guest experience. Table service itself should flow in a natural sequence and feel effortless. It takes training and practice to acquire the proper skills of timing during the dining experience. Observation skills can be extremely important while servicing a meal. It allows the server to accommodate a guest needs without verbal interaction.

Personality

A server must have a pleasant manner and truly enjoy people. He or she must be able to sustain a friendly demeanor with poise and self-confidence while under pressure. This will be discussed more in Chapter 7, Guest Communication.

Initiative

A server must take charge of his or her station (tables) and recognize when and what kind of service customers need and perform that service with a sense of urgency in every detail.

Positive Attitude

A positive or negative attitude affects performance. If one shows up for a shift in a bad mood, it is going to be a bad shift with bad customers and bad coworkers making bad tips. A positive "professional attitude" can generate positive, wonderful results.

Teamwork Ability

The server should be willing to work cooperatively with others in a fast-paced work environment that supports a common goal of providing the highest quality of guest service. Also supporting a mutual effort is completing all assigned work.

Good Manners

A server should have the understanding and ability to demonstrate the social skills of being polite, courteous, and respectful to coworkers and guests.

Professional Appearance

A server should maintain a professional appearance. Uniform should be clean, pressed, and fit properly. A server should practice good personal hygiene and pay attention to cleanliness of hair, fingernails, breath, and body odor. Excessive jewelry or body art (tattoos), although a personal statement, may not be appropriate in a conservative setting. Men should be clean shaven or maintain a neat beard and women should use natural makeup. Both men and women should not wear any fragrance. Professional appearance will be further discussed in Chapter 2, Professional Appearance.

Honesty

A server must have a strong sense of honesty when handling guest payment transactions, when sharing tips, and when equally sharing work responsibilities. Guests and fellow coworker must feel that they can trust and rely on a server. Many guests may feel uncomfortable turning over their credit cards to an unfamiliar server.

Sense of Humor

A good sense of humor is essential in order to survive the daily stresses of the job. When things seem to be getting a bit out of control, it is one's ability to step back and find humor in it all that helps to minimize the stress and tension.

Diversity Skills

The lifestyle, ethnic, and nationality mix of coworkers and the guests demands that the server have good cultural awareness.

Reliability

The server must always be on time for work, provide prompt service to guests, and complete all tasks, including opening, shift change, closing cleanup, and restocking service areas.

ADVANCEMENT OPPORTUNITIES

There is a basic hierarchy in a restaurant. This can vary depending upon the size of the organization and other services offered, such as banquets, room service, and outside catering. The chart in Table 1–6 reflects the organizational structure of a typical full-service restaurant.

Besides the positions listed in Table 1–6, there are a number of other lucrative career tracks that server skills can transfer to, such as those identified in Table 1–7.

TABLE 1–6
RESTAURANT ORGANIZATIONAL CHART

	Owner	
	General Manager	
	Department Managers	
	Assistant Managers	
Bar Manager	Dining Room Manager	Kitchen Manager/Chef
Bar Staff	Maître D'	Kitchen Staff
	Host Staff	
	Head Server	
	Servers	
	Busser/Server Assistant Staff	

TABLE 1–7
RESTAURANT-RELATED CAREER TRACKS

Private Catering
Lodging
Tourism
Personal Chef
Meal Replacement
Resorts/Spas
Nutrition/Health care
Food & Beverage Brokerage
Food & Beverage Distribution
Winery-Brewery-Spirits
Hospitality Equipment & Technology
Hospitality Internet Services
Hospitality Consulting
Customer Service Training
Hospitality Journalism
Retirement Living Facilities
Commercial Food Service

SUMMARY

The restaurant industry is an integral and growing part of American life, as shown by the impressive facts and figures that describe the industry. As a result, the number of opportunities for the professional server continues to grow. The level of income that a professional server can earn will be increased or decreased by the number of hours he or she is willing to work, and by the type of restaurant operation (ranging from the diner or deli, casual, family, or theme restaurant, to fine dining).

The nature of the work allows the server to develop and exercise entrepreneurial skills by offering a personalized service to customers. In addition, it advances one's marketing talents through the merchandising and upselling of food and beverage items.

The advantages of being a server are many and include the following: time flexibility to accommodate one's lifestyle; flexible income; high potential hourly earnings; career and job mobility; complimentary or discounted meals while at work; physical exercise to keep fit; and the opportunity to meet interesting people. The disadvantages often discourage people from entering the occupation, and include the following: working weekends, nights, and holidays; physical, mental, and psychological stress associated with the work; and the absence of good employee benefits.

The qualifications of a successful server include competencies in the following areas: product knowledge with a sound understanding of food and beverage items;

service knowledge in being able to provide each customer with a personalized service; a good sense of timing in serving the ordered items; a pleasant personality with a likable manner and positive attitude; the ability to support coworkers; a sense of humor coupled with the ability to handle the stress of the work; and an honest and reliable work ethic.

A wide selection of advancement opportunities exists within the restaurant industry, ranging from entry-level positions to actual ownership. For individuals with the interest, talents, and enthusiasm, along with the willingness to make a long-term commitment to the industry, the income and professional development can be excellent.

DISCUSSION QUESTIONS AND EXERCISES

1. Discuss the economic importance of the restaurant industry by identifying some statistics that were compiled by the National Restaurant Association.
2. Name the two sources of income for the professional server.
3. How does a career server earn an increased income?
4. What is the minimum wage for workers who receive tips?
5. After reading restaurant reality, do you agree or disagree with the servers that passed the guest by? Do you think servers typically make judgments about their guests?
6. If the average daily total guest-check sales for each server in a fine dining restaurant were $800 and a server worked 5 days, 40 hours per week at minimum wage with tip credit applied and earned a 20 percent tip average, what would be his or her annual income? Refer to Table 1.3, Potential Server Earnings.
7. Identify 10 factors that can affect a server's income.
8. What are the two critical variables that the server controls that directly impact his or her earnings?
9. Explain the entrepreneurial side of being a server.
10. List three reasons why a tip may be reduced or lost.
11. What are the trainable skills that a server should have?
12. If you were a guest what are the most important technical skills you would have liked a server to display?
13. How important do you think the desire to serve is?
14. Discuss several of the potential penalties for under-reporting tip income.
15. List 10 occupational advantages of being a server.
16. List 5 occupational disadvantages of being a server.
17. Describe at least 10 areas in which an individual should have competence in order to be a successful server.
18. Discuss potential career advancement opportunities for a server.
19. Identify several occupations to which server skills and training could be transferable and effectively used.
20. Discuss an example of personalized service that you have experienced or observed.
21. How much could a professional server earn by working in a fine dining restaurant where the average guest check is $50 per person? Assume the following: He or she works 5 days, 40 hours per week at minimum wage with tip credit applied, and serves an average of 60 people per shift. He or she also earns an average 20 percent in tip income.
22. Interview a server and ask what he or she likes and dislikes about the occupation. Write down the responses and report to the class.
23. How would you determine the amount of tip to leave a server?
24. Has your opinion of the server occupation changed after having read this chapter? If so, describe the change.

2

Professional Appearance

learning objectives

After reading this chapter and completing the discussion questions and exercises, you should be able to:

1. Understand the importance of good personal grooming standards.
2. Evaluate your own personal appearance.
3. Recognize that a well-groomed appearance is absolutely essential to project the image of good service, quality food, and a pleasant atmosphere.
4. Identify the personal grooming standards that are basic for servers.
5. Understand the value and importance of good body language, poise, and posture, and the positive impression that they create.
6. Know the importance of always wearing a clean fresh uniform each day.
7. Know what to look for when purchasing a quality pair of shoes for work.
8. Understand the importance of good server health.

It Begins With You

Your personal appearance will reveal to your customers much about your personality and attitude, because while you are in contact with your customers, they will be judging you, and what they see is reflected in your personality, your attitude, and your appearance. Remember, as a server, you are onstage at all times.

Sanitation is essential to all food service operations and every employee who prepares and/or serves food must meet the highest standards of neatness, cleanliness, personal hygiene, and good grooming. In order to prevent the contamination of food and food-contact surfaces, and the resulting potential transmission of food-borne illness, it is essential that servers observe strict standards of cleanliness, proper hygiene, and safe food handling. This is important at all times during their shifts, before starting work, or returning to work after breaks. A good appearance is necessary to project the image of good service, quality food being safely served, and a pleasant atmosphere. Your personal grooming takes into account more than just your uniform and your smile. It includes your hair, hands, teeth, posture, figure, and clothes. Customers do not know you and may unfairly pass judgment. This is a part of the job and must be understood and accommodations to the style of restaurant may have to be made.

Good grooming has many benefits and you, the server, benefit from all of them. The way to ensure good grooming is to go to a mirror and observe yourself very closely. Stand naturally. Look yourself over. Does your posture consist of a head held high with your chin parallel to the floor? Are your shoulders held up, back, relaxed, and your rib cage held high with the elbows slightly bent, and the hips tucked under? Are your knees relaxed?

How did you feel as you looked at yourself in the mirror? Did you feel good? Did it give you confidence in yourself? Did you appear to have poise and self-confidence? Make a note of your appearance and posture faults and work on correcting them.

Your appearance is your way of telling your customers how you value yourself. By being very critical of your appearance and taking the initiative to improve it, you are telling your customers, "I believe in myself." Personal grooming is as much a part of your personality as your feelings and actions. If you don't like what you see, improve yourself and your appearance by determining to work at it by making the necessary effort.

The principles for good appearance are the same for men and women. Taking proper care of oneself is essential, and devoting time to your appearance will add to your confidence and peace of mind.

GROOMING STANDARDS

Customers expect to see well-groomed servers just as much as they expect to see a clean restaurant. The well-groomed server conveys a professional image that supports an overall dining experience. A well-groomed appearance is absolutely essential to project the image of good service, quality food, and a pleasant atmosphere. Most restaurants are somewhat conservative and expect their server to reflect that image. Even though body art (tattoos) and piercings are popular and a form of self-expression, they do not project a conservative image. Excessive jewelry and body art should be covered up unless they support the restaurant's image.

The individual server has a significant role in the restaurant. The server is the only contact most customers have with the business aside from the food itself and perhaps the cashier. Therefore, the restaurant operator is challenged in setting forth and maintaining server standards that will help to ensure that customers feel comfortable and confident in returning to the restaurant.

Certain restaurant concepts in today's eclectic market offer a form of entertainment. Some of these concepts have impacted dress standards by providing uniquely designed uniforms that may serve as costumes. Servers may be allowed to have bold hairstyles and colors, and to wear excessive jewelry. However, these concepts are the exception, unusual and limited to a defined customer base.

The following is a list of personal grooming standards that are basic for servers.

Bathing and Deodorants Good personal hygiene begins with daily bathing and the use of unscented deodorants or antiperspirants. Offensive body odors caused by poor personal hygiene can cause coworkers and customers to complain to the management. Offended customers may choose never to return.

Hair Care The server should always have clean and fresh-smelling hair that is controlled in order to prevent hair from contacting or falling into food or onto food-contact surfaces. When hair is uncontrolled, it can be difficult to manage and distracting when serving food. Natural hair colors are pleasing and acceptable in contrast to bold unnatural colors that have the potential of projecting an image that may be displeasing to some customers. The professional server will have his or her hair styled professionally. The hairstylist will recommend a hairstyle that is becoming and easy to take care of. The hair should not be too long and preferably not go below the shirt collar. However, long hair should be restrained in a ponytail or hairnet. Servers should avoid fixing or touching their hair while in view of customers, and should wash their hands after coming in direct contact with their hair.

Skin Care If a server is having problems with skin—acne, or dry or oily skin—the server should take appropriate measures to control the trouble. Servers should never scratch dry or itchy areas of the body in view of customers. If the skin is dry, wash with a mild soap or cleansing cream. Apply a moisturizer to restore valuable lost oils and be sure to take care of chapped lips by using a lip balm. Proper care of the skin requires cleanliness and protection. Measures to prevent overexposure to the sun should be taken, such as using sunscreen. Men should be clean-shaven.

Cosmetics The proper use of cosmetics can enhance one's appearance; overuse can detract from it. Too much of certain kinds of cosmetics, such as body glitter, can "run" and get into one's eyes or food when the body heats up during a brisk shift. If the appropriate selection and application of cosmetics becomes a concern, the server should consult a cosmetic specialist.

Fragrances Fragrances may be offensive to some coworkers and customers, and actually be sickening to those who suffer from severe allergies; fragrances may conflict with the aromas of the food being served. Therefore these should not be used while at work.

Beards and Moustaches A well-shaped clean beard or moustache can be very attractive and can enhance a man's appearance, but it needs to be washed and trimmed daily.

Teeth and Breath Good oral hygiene is maintained by frequent tooth-brushing and flossing. A smile is always complemented by clean teeth and fresh breath. Breath fresheners should be used as needed. The chewing of gum should be avoided in order to maintain a professional image. Smoking should not be permitted during working hours. The smell of smoke in clothes and on one's breath can be offensive to guests. The time reserved for eating is during a lunch or dinner break; the server should never consume food in view of customers. If a server suffers during an allergy season, the coughing and sneezing must be controlled with the proper allergy medication. "A server cannot sucessfully work with a coughing and sneezing problem in view of customers." A server suffering from a cold or the flu should not be allowed to serve food, as colds and flu are contagious and unpleasant for customers.

Hands and Fingernails The hands of a server should always be immaculately clean. The server's fingernails should be smoothly filed and kept short and regularly washed with a fingernail brush. Clear polish or buffing can enhance fingernail appearance, versus striking fashion colors. A hand moisturizer should be used for dry hands and fingernails. Servers must thoroughly wash their hands and the exposed portions of their arms with soap and warm water for at least 20 seconds before starting work, during work as often as necessary to keep them clean, and after handling dirty dishes and utensils, eating, drinking, smoking, using the toilet, or after performing a nonfood-service activity. During busy periods when a hand washing sink may not be available, an alternative may be the use of a health department–approved hand sanitizer.

Foot Care The correct type of shoes will minimize foot fatigue. The server walks many miles during the course of each shift. Therefore, it is essential to have well-fitting and comfortable shoes in an acceptable style that is complementary to the server's uniform. Fashion shoes are not a good choice. Rubber heels and soles are best for reducing slips and skids on wet floors. Shoes should always be cleaned or polished and have clean laces. Foot powder or spray should be used during warm weather to prevent excess perspiration and odor. Clean socks for the waiter and clean hose for the waitress should be worn daily, free of runs, and in a color that complements the uniform. The server may also find comfort in wearing support hose designed to help relieve leg stress. Support stockings or hose are available in basic black, brown, and navy blue for men and in a variety of shades for women.

Jewelry The jewelry worn by a server should be simple and should not interfere with the performance of job functions. A plain watch, smooth ring, or small earrings are acceptable and reflect a conservative image. When jewelry is large, ornate, or dangling, it becomes awkward and potentially hazardous. Such jewelry may be displeasing to some restaurant customers. Body piercing and tattoos may also be displeasing to customers. Therefore, body piercing should be restricted and tattoos covered with clothing.

BODY LANGUAGE, POISE, AND POSTURE

Body language can convey positive or negative impressions. The way a server carries oneself creates a first impression for each of his or her guests. A server should always be aware of their nonverbal communication. It is very easy for a guest to read a server's willingness and enthusiasm to serve them, through their body language. A server should watch the placement of their hands, the expression in their eyes, and the expression on their face. A smile, good eye contact, and arms at their sides are all signs of potentially great service. A frown, eye rolling, and crossed arms are a sign of unwilling, insincere, and forced service. The guest's perception of a server is key to a pleasant dining experience; therefore, it is important to be aware of body language. Good body language, willingness to serve, and enthusiasm are positive attributes that lead to repeat customers.

Although servers may devote time and energy to daily grooming routines, they will not look their best unless strict attention is given to poise and posture. Poor posture can reduce a meticulous lady to a less-than-attractive figure and a good-looking man to a sloppy-appearing slouch.

The professional server is always on display and should stand and walk with poise and self-confidence. By moving more gracefully, confidently, and efficiently, the server will not only make a better impression, but will also conserve energy. The working day of a server is very tiring, and good posture can make long hours less tiring. Being able to walk quickly with an erect, well-balanced, controlled posture will create the impression of a confident, healthy individual. On the other hand, having a slouching, poor posture will create a bad impression with customers. The way that a server walks and carries him or herself is almost as important as the way he or she speaks and looks.

UNIFORMS AND APRONS

Most restaurants require that the server wear a special uniform and/or apron. Some uniforms and aprons are plain, while others are stylish and will accent the theme, décor, and colors of the restaurant, as shown in Figures 2.1a, 2.1b, 2.2a, and 2.2b. Some uniforms are as formal as a tuxedo or can be as casual as a pair of khaki pants, a polo shirt, and white sneakers. If the restaurant does not require a specific uniform or apron, the server should select a type of clothing that projects a professional image. It has been said that the clothes make the individual. With the server this is especially true. The clothing that a person chooses to wear may very well reflect his or her personality.

The server should have enough uniforms and aprons to allow for daily changes. If scheduled to work 5 days a week, then three uniforms and aprons would be appropriate, allowing the server to wear a clean uniform and apron each day. The server should never wear a uniform that is obviously soiled or stained, because food may be repeatedly contaminated by food debris or other soil from the uniform of the server. The uniforms and aprons should always be cleaned carefully. They should never be wrinkled, torn, or frayed. Having a clean fresh uniform and apron is, of course, essential to good sanitation. If the server lacks the ability to keep the uniform and apron looking professional, then he or she needs to find a good dry cleaner or launderer. Uniforms should fit properly and allow for comfortable movement. Also, the restaurant operator should establish a policy regarding the hem length of uniforms or shorts.

Uniforms help the customer identify who the employees are when they need assistance. They also add to the customer's perception of the cleanliness and organization of the server and the dining establishment overall.

Figure 2–1
(a) Solid Color Short Apron © Kurhan/Shutterstock
(b) Solid Color Long Apron © Mattomedia Werbeagentur/Shutterstock.

SHOES

Shoes are a significant part of the server uniform and should be selected for style, appearance, safety, and most of all total comfort. Shoes that have ergonomically designed shock-absorbent cushioned insoles, slip-resistant outsoles, and full-grain leather uppers are readily available and competitively priced, as shown in Figure 2.3. An investment in a pair of good-quality shoes pays for itself in a very short period of time. Sore feet can make a miserable shift and eventually lead to other physical problems, as well as increasing the potential for slips and falls. Two pairs of shoes are recommended for servers working long hours. One pair can dry out and air while the other pair is being worn.

Many restaurant operators have identified shoe stores in their communities that offer slip-resistant footwear for servers to purchase. Also, many have brochures, catalogs, and Internet sources available to allow servers to make their selections. The popularity of these types of shoes is rapidly growing as the number of slips and falls have been reduced in restaurants where employees are wearing slip-resistant footwear. Another benefit of this product is reduced stress on the feet and legs.

(a) (b)

Figure 2–2
(a) Theme Style Neck Tied Apron
(b) Theme Style Server Vest. Courtesy of Scorpio Apparel, Inc.

SERVER HEALTH

The health of servers is critical. No server, while infected with a disease in a communicable form that can be transmitted by foods or who is a carrier of organisms that cause such a disease, or while afflicted with a boil, an infected wound, or an acute respiratory infection, should work in a food service establishment in any capacity in which there is a likelihood of contaminating food or food-contact surfaces with pathogenic organisms or of transmitting disease to other persons.

Figure 2–3
Slip-Resistant Footwear. Courtesy of Shoes for Crews.

Disease transmitted through food frequently originates from an infected food service employee, even though the employee shows little outward appearance of being ill. A wide range of communicable diseases and infections may be transmitted by infected food service employees to other employees, and to the customer, through the contamination of food and through careless food-handling practices. It is the responsibility of both management and staff to see to it that no person who is affected with any disease that can be transmitted by food works in any area of a food service establishment where there is a possibility of disease transmission.

Servers should use gloves or tongs when handling any ready-to-eat food, which includes bread, lemons, salads, butter, or any other food that will not be cooked before the guest will eat it. The server should also be aware of the placement of their hands when carrying flatware, glassware, and china, which will be discussed in Chapter 3, Table Settings, Napkin Presentations, and Table Service.

SUMMARY

The server is in contact with customers at all times; therefore, his or her personal appearance is important. A good appearance is necessary to project the image of good service, quality food, and a pleasant atmosphere. The way to ensure good grooming is for the server to go to a mirror and observe him or herself very closely. Taking proper care of oneself is essential. The following list of personal grooming standards are basic for servers: bathing and deodorants, hair care, skin care, cosmetics, fragrances, beards and moustaches, teeth and breath, hands and fingernails, foot care, and jewelry.

The server should always convey positive body language, and stand and walk with poise and self-confidence. Poor posture detracts from the server's appearance. The way that a server walks and carries him or herself is almost as important as the way he or she speaks and looks.

Most restaurants require servers to wear a special uniform and/or apron. If the restaurant does not require a specific uniform or apron, the server should select the type of clothing that projects a professional image. The server should have enough uniforms to allow for daily changes. A clean fresh uniform is essential for good sanitation.

Shoes are a significant part of the server uniform and should be selected for style, appearance, safety, and most of all, total comfort. Slip-resistant footwear is increasingly popular, as the number of slips and falls have been reduced with these types of shoes. An investment in a pair of good-quality shoes pays for itself in a very short period of time.

Servers must always be in good health. No server, while infected with a communicable disease, should be allowed to work in a food service establishment in any capacity. The potential to contaminate food and food-contact surfaces, and to transmit the disease to other persons, is too great.

DISCUSSION QUESTIONS AND EXERCISES

1. What does a server's personal appearance reveal to customers?
2. How does a server ensure good grooming?
3. List and discuss 10 grooming standards that are basic for servers.
4. When might a bold hairstyle be acceptable for a server?
5. What should the server do when in doubt about the use of cosmetics?
6. Discuss the importance of good body language, poise, and posture.
7. What is the importance of body language? Name three positive and three negative nonverbal communication you have experienced in a restaurant.
8. What is an adequate number of uniforms for a server?
9. If a restaurant does not have a specific uniform, what type of clothing should the server select?
10. What should the server look for when purchasing a quality pair of work shoes?
11. If a server comes to work with a head cold, slight cough, and occasional sneeze, how should management respond?
12. Discuss a positive or negative grooming issue that affected your dining experience.
13. Name three restaurants within your community that are noted for a professional server staff and impressive server uniforms.
14. Visit a restaurant of your choice and observe the servers in relation to what you have learned in this chapter. Write a one-page summary of your observations.

3

Table Settings, Napkin Presentations, and Table Service

learning objectives

After reading this chapter and completing the discussion questions and exercises, you should be able to:

1. Understand, explain, and demonstrate a breakfast and lunch table setting before the meal and as the meal is served.
2. Understand, explain, and demonstrate a dinner table setting before the meal and as the meal is served.
3. Identify the most commonly used pieces of flatware and serving pieces.
4. Correctly handle flatware, glassware, china, and cups.
5. Understand, explain, and demonstrate the correct placement of wine, champagne, cocktail, and liqueur glasses.
6. Understand, explain, and demonstrate the correct placement of place mats.
7. Determine how many salt and pepper shakers to place at each table and when they should be removed.
8. Determine how many sugar and creamer sets to place on the table and when to place them, whenever coffee or tea is served.
9. Explain the different ways that bread and butter can be served.
10. Understand and demonstrate various napkin folds.

Server training begins with an understanding of correct table settings, and the correct way in which to handle flatware, glassware, china, and linen. The server must have the knowledge and ability to properly arrange table settings in a fast and efficient manner in order to keep pace with the demands of a busy restaurant. In time, the server will be able to immediately identify the most-used flatware and different serving pieces, such as a pasta spoon, lobster fork, or escargot tong. The server will also know how many salt and pepper shakers, sugar bowls, and creamers to bring to the table, as well as the restaurant's method of serving bread and butter.

Napkin presentations are elegant and impressive, and a professional server will have the opportunity to perform a number of different napkin folds. Therefore, he or she should be acquainted with the most popular folds and develop the ability to do them (Figure 3–1). Most restaurants will have identified one fold that they use consistently, but in response to customer's requests, may choose different folds for banquets or special events. There are some excellent napkin-folding books with many types of folds, as well as several websites that are helpful; www.napkin-foldingguide.com has a good selection of napkin folds with step-by-step instructions.

The professional server should also be acquainted with the five distinctively different methods of serving food, as many restaurants have developed a contemporary style of food service that shares various aspects from all five methods. There are technical aspects of the five services which define their uniqueness. In addition to table service, a server may have the opportunity to work in counter service, banquet service, or room service and should be knowledgeable in these types of service.

Salad bars, dessert tables, carts, and trolleys have become a significant part of many restaurants. The successful server understands their functions and setups, and how they have become part of the restaurant's service.

PLACE MATS

When place mats are used on rectangular tables, they should be centered between the fork and knife and approximately one-half inch from the edge of the table, as shown in Figure 3–2. For round tables, rectangular place mats should be placed so that the corners of the place mat are one-half inch from the edge of the table. Place mats of varying shapes and sizes, such as oblong, oval, or round, should be placed accordingly.

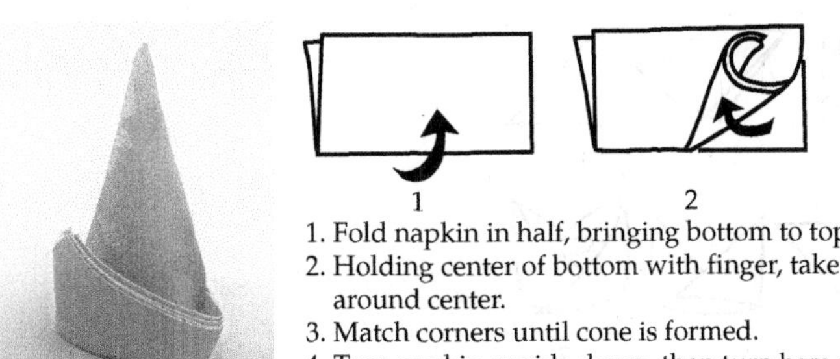

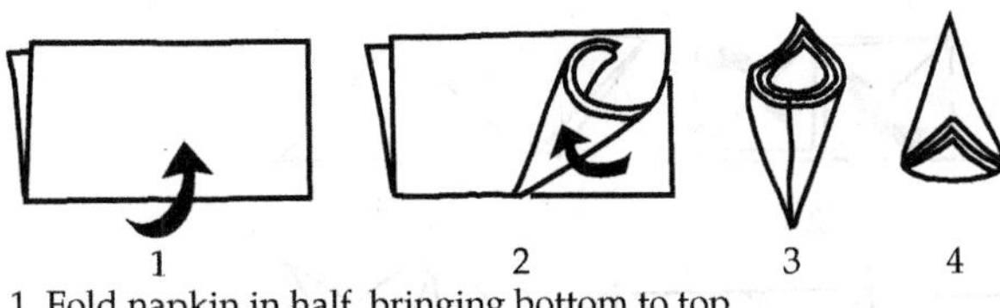

1. Fold napkin in half, bringing bottom to top.
2. Holding center of bottom with finger, take lower right corner and loosely roll around center.
3. Match corners until cone is formed.
4. Turn napkin upside down, then turn hem all around. Turn and stand on base.

Clown's Hat

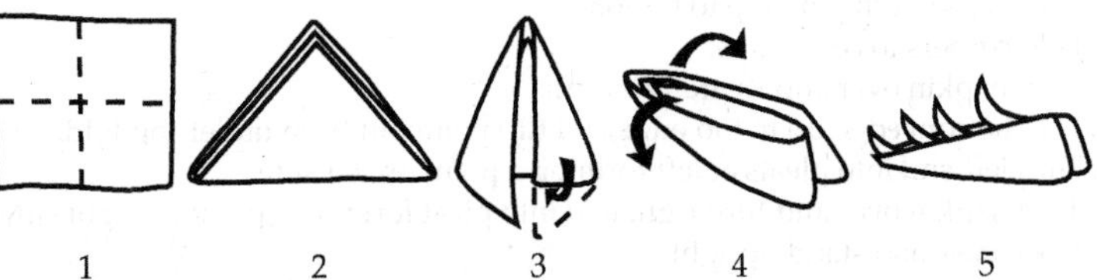

1. Fold napkin in half and in half again.
2. Then fold in half diagonally with points on the top and facing up.
3. Fold left and right sides down along center line, turning their extended points under.
4. Fold in half on long dimension with edges facing out.
5. Pull up points and arrange on a fabric surface.

Bird of Paradise

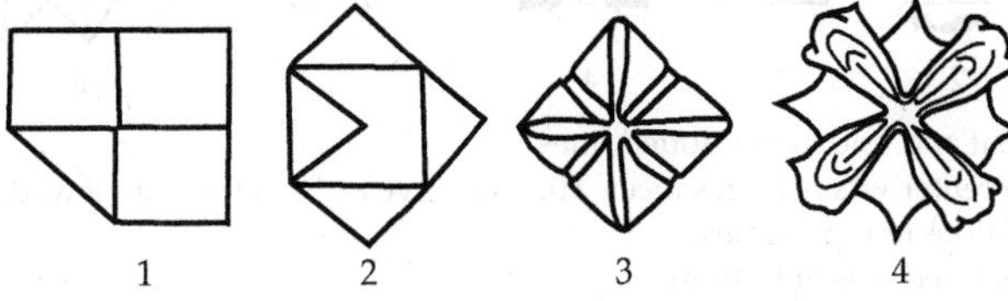

1. Fold all 4 corners of open napkin to center.
2. Fold new corners to center.
3. Turn napkin over and fold all 4 corners to center.
4. Holding center firmly, reach under each corner and pull up flaps to form petals. Reach between petals and pull flaps from underneath.

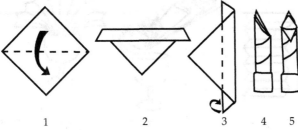

Rose

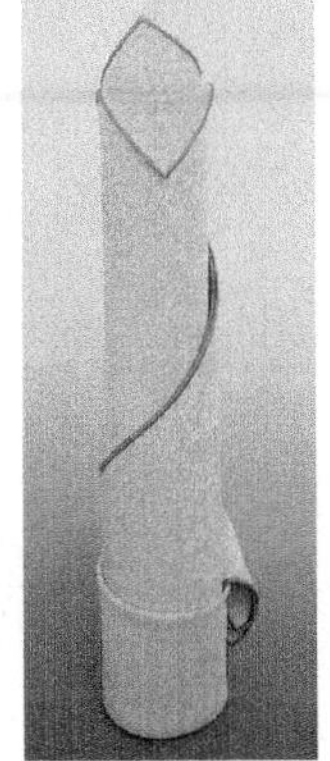

1. Fold napkin in half diagonally.
2. Fold down base 1/3 way.
3. Turn napkin over and roll from bottom to top.
4. Tuck corners inside cuff at base of fold and stand.
5. Turn one layer of point down and set on base.

Candle

Figure 3–1

Napkin Folds. Courtesy of Milliken & Company.

11. Explain and compare the five different methods of serving food, commonly referred to as service styles.
12. Explain how counter service functions and demonstrate different counter service table settings.
13. Explain the nature of banquet service and how a banquet menu is determined.
14. Understand and explain the service procedure for room service.
15. Explain the workings of salad bars, dessert tables, carts, and trolleys; demonstrate the correct way of using each.

SALT AND PEPPER, SUGAR AND CREAMER

Salt and pepper shakers should be preset according to the number of guests at each table, typically one set per four to six persons, depending upon the menu. As a general rule, they are removed after the main course and the same number of sugar bowls and creamers are placed just prior to coffee or tea being served (see Figure 3–3). It is important to recognize also that some restaurants may choose not to preset salt and pepper shakers, but to bring them to the table as needed.

Bishop's Mitre

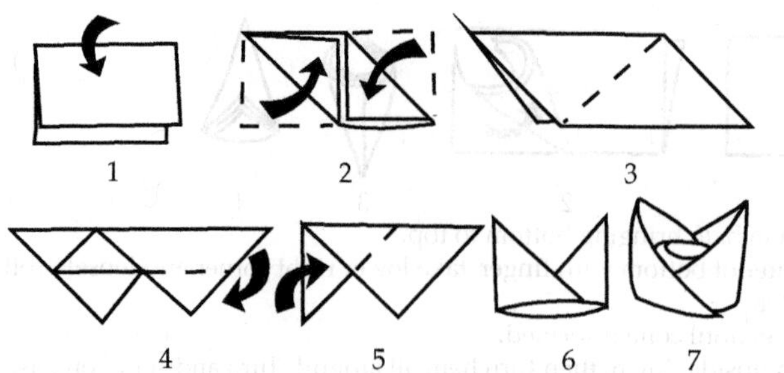

1. Fold napkin bringing top to bottom.
2. Fold corners to center line.
3. Turn napkin over and rotate 1/4 turn.
4. Fold bottom edge up to top edge and flip point out from under top fold.
5. Turn left end into pleats at left forming a point on left side.
6. Turn napkin over and turn right end into pleat forming a point on right side.
7. Open base and stand upright.

Oriental Fan

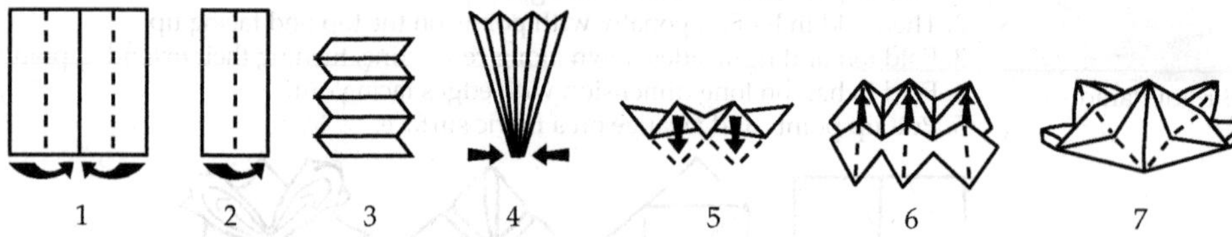

1. Lay napkin flat and fold along dotted lines.
2. Pick up from center where edges meet. This will give a "W" effect (if viewed from ends).
3. Pleat from bottom to top 5 times.
4. Grip from hemmed side at bottom.
5. Open accordion folds and pull down one side.
6. Repeat step 5 on other side.
7. Set napkin down and let fall into a fan shape.

Goblet Fan

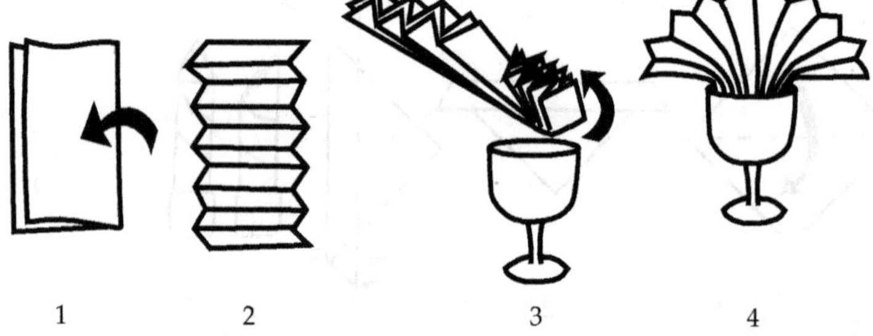

1. Fold napkin in half.
2. Pleat from bottom to top.
3. Turn napkin back 1/3 of the way on right (folded) end and place into goblet.
4. Spread out pleats at top.

Rosebud

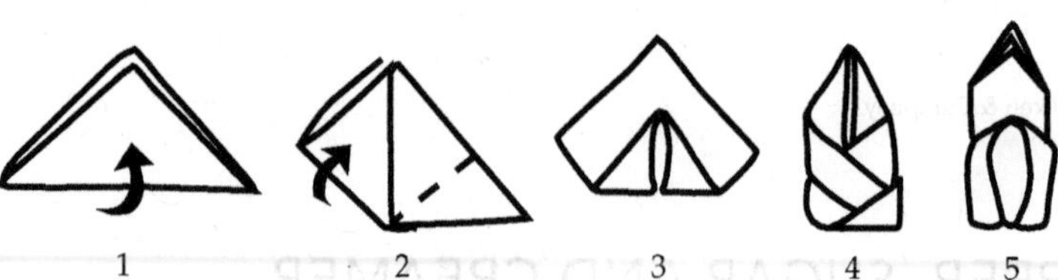

1. Fold napkin in half diagonally.
2. Fold corners to meet at top point.
3. Turn napkin over and fold bottom 2/3 way up.
4. Turn napkin around and bring corners together, tucking one into the other.
5. Turn napkin around and stand on base.

Figure 3–1 (continued)

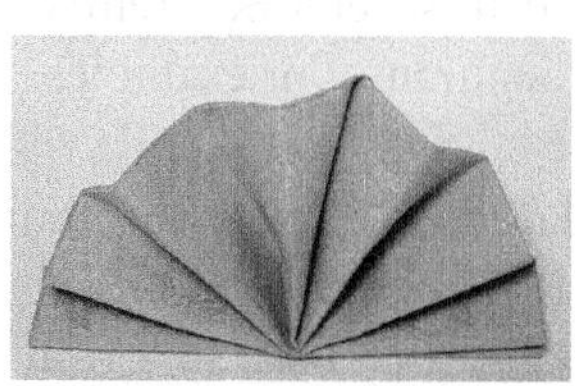

Land Windermere's Fan

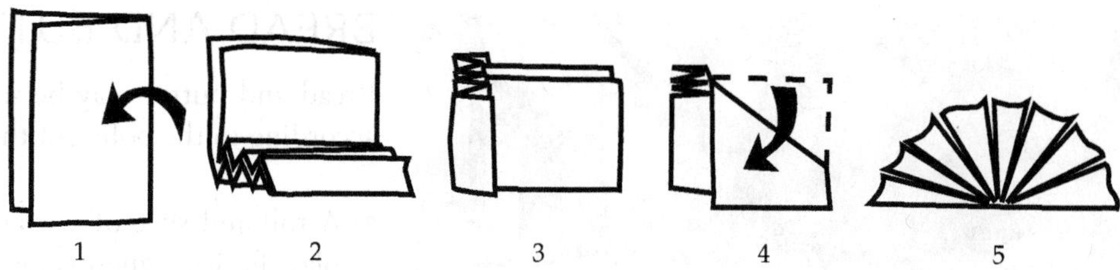

1. Fold napkin in half.
2. Starting at bottom, accordion pleat 2/3 way up.
3. Fold in half with pleating on the outside.
4. Fold upper right corner diagonally down to folded base of pleats and turn under edge.
5. Place on table and release pleats to form fan.

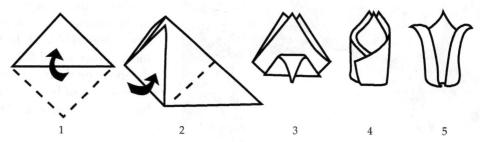

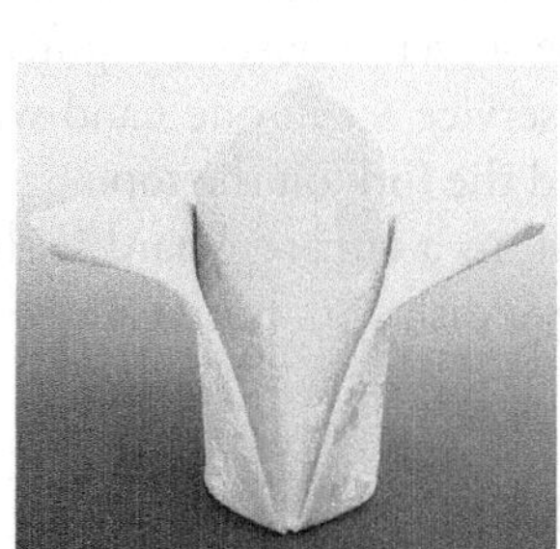

Cardinal's Hat

1 2 3 4 5

1. Fold napkin in half diagonally.
2. Fold corners to meet at top point.
3. Turn napkin over with points to the top, fold lower corner 2/3 way up.
4. Fold back onto itself.
5. Bring corners together tucking one into the other. Open base of fold and stand upright.

Pyramid

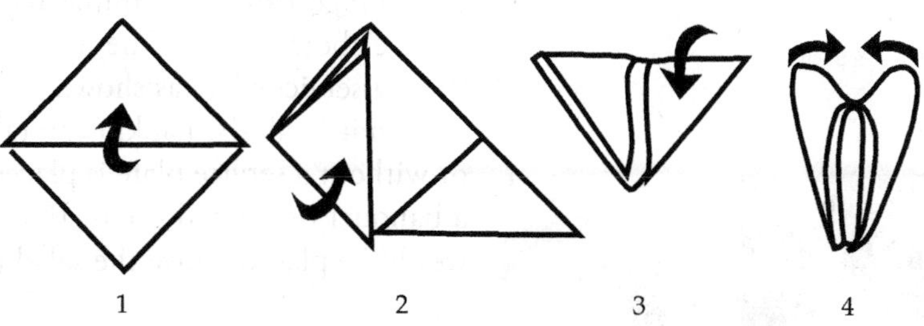

1. Fold napkin in half diagonally.
2. Fold corners to meet at top point.
3. Turn napkin over and fold in half.
4. Pick up at center and stand on base of triangle.

Crown

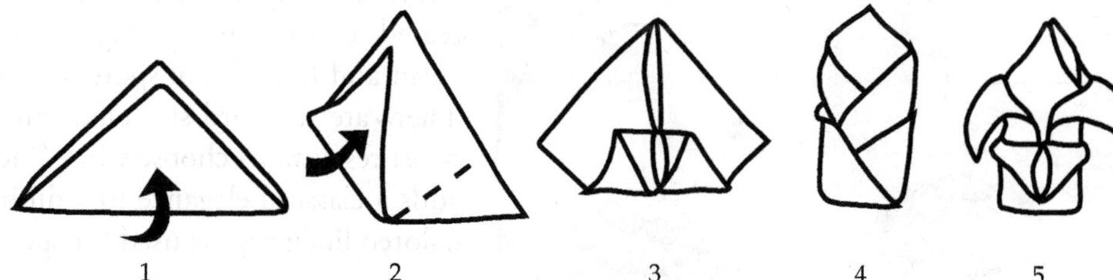

1. Fold napkin in half diagonally.
2. Fold corners to meet at top point.
3. Fold bottom point 2/3 way to top and fold back onto itself.
4. Turn napkin over bringing corners together, tucking one into the other.
5. Peel two top corners to make crown. Open base of fold and stand upright.

Figure 3–1 (continued)

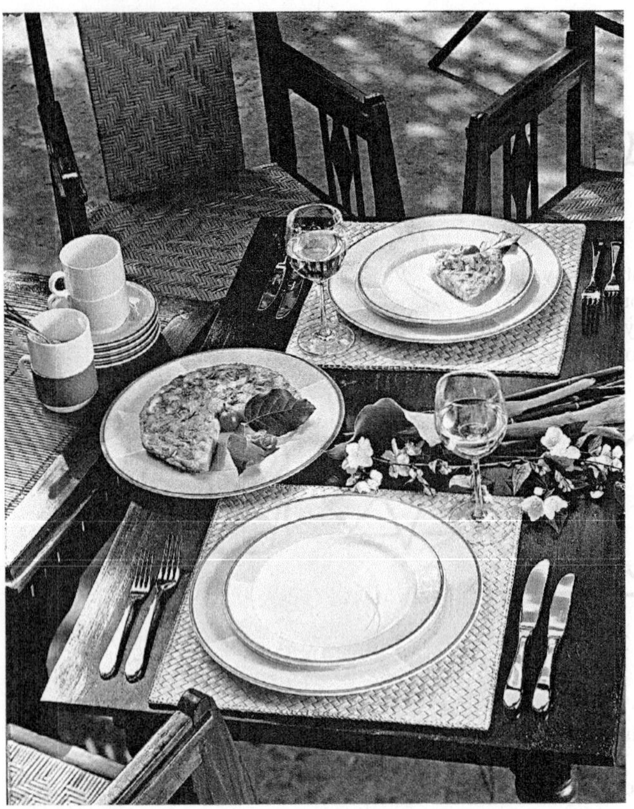

Figure 3–2
Place mats. Courtesy of Villeroy & Boch.

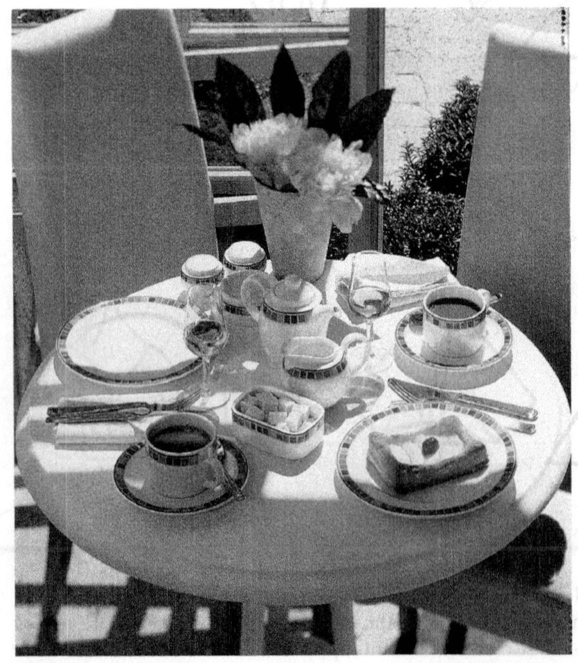

Figure 3–3
Salt and Pepper Shakers, Sugar and Creamer in Use. Courtesy of Villeroy & Boch.

BREAD AND BUTTER

Bread and butter may be served in several different ways, according to the policy of the restaurant. For example:

- A roll and slice of butter placed on a bread and butter plate for each guest prior to their arrival.
- Rolls in a basket and butter slices or balls in a dish for guests to serve themselves. The rolls may be served warm.
- Rolls and butter served to each guest by the server. This is typically done so that the rolls can be served hot. A server would use tongs or use the pincing method to serve bread in this manner. The pincing method requires a server to have a high skill level. If the server chooses the pincing method they would hold a service set in one hand with the spoon on the bottom and the fork on the top.
- A small loaf of bread served on a cutting board with a bread knife, accompanied by a dish with butter slices.

NAPKIN PRESENTATIONS

Napkins folded in a distinctive pattern can further add to the professional look of the table setting. Napkin folds can range from the simple flat fold to any one of the more elaborate folds. The napkin can be placed in the center of a service plate as shown in Figure 3–4. If a service plate is not used, the napkin can take its place. And a napkin with or without a service plate is placed on tables which are preset for a banquet or catered event. If a salad is preset, then the napkin would be placed above the salad plate.

TABLECLOTHS

Tablecloths should always properly fit tables and drape, approximately 1 inch above the chairs where guests will be seated. Before table settings are placed, the tablecloths must be clean and free of any spots or stains. The seam should face in. There are standard-size tables that require standard linen sizes. Most restaurants choose white linens for their tables; white linen adds a classical elegance to a dining room. Many other types of colored linen can be used for special occasions and for catering.

FLATWARE PLACEMENT

It is important that a server understands the correct placement of flatware on a table. There are certain guidelines to assist a server with this task. First and foremost, flatware is placed on a table so that the guest will use the flatware from the outside in. The first piece of flatware used is the flatware on the outside of the place setting. Forks are placed on the left of the place setting while knives and spoons are placed on the right; the blade of the knife faces in. In a banquet setting or prix fixe (fixed price) menu, the dessert flatware is placed on the top of the setting with the fork on the bottom and the spoon on the top. The handles face in the direction in which the flatware would be placed in the setting.

Certain seafood items such as mussels or oysters will require a cocktail or a seafood fork. This is a small fork that will allow the guest to remove seafood from the shell.

Figure 3–4
Napkin and Service Plate.

PRESET BREAKFAST AND LUNCH TABLE SETTING

The preset breakfast and lunch table setting is shown in Figure 3–5. The table setting includes a fork, knife, teaspoon, bread-and-butter plate, water glass, and napkin. The fork, knife, and teaspoon are set approximately 1 inch from the edge of the table. The blade of the knife is always turned inward toward the plate. The water glass is placed about 1 inch to the right of the tip of the knife, and the bread-and-butter plate is placed about 1 inch above the tines of the fork. The napkin is centered between the fork and the knife. There should always be approximately 12 inches between the fork and the knife, depending upon the size of the plate that will be placed between them.

When coffee or tea is served, the cup and saucer are placed to the right of the teaspoon, approximately 1 inch from the edge of the table with the handle angled at 4 o'clock (some prefer the handle angled at 3 o'clock). If breakfast toast or a lunch salad is served, the plate is placed to the left of the fork and approximately 1 inch from the edge of the table. When the breakfast or lunch plate is ready to be served, and the guest has removed the napkin, the plate is placed and centered between the fork and knife, approximately 1 inch from the edge of the table (see Figure 3–6). If side dishes are ordered, such as a side of pancakes with breakfast or onion rings with lunch, the dishes, along with any accompanying condiments, may acceptably be placed in a convenient location on the table when served.

Figure 3–5
Breakfast and Lunch Table Setting.

Figure 3–6
Breakfast and Lunch Table Setting as the Meal Is Served.

PRESET DINNER TABLE SETTING

The preset dinner table setting is shown in Figure 3–7. The table setting from left to right includes a salad fork, fork, knife, butter knife (or butter spreader), two teaspoons, bread-and-butter plate, water glass, and napkin. When a butter spreader is used, it could also be placed horizontally across the top half of the bread-and-butter plate with the blade turned inward toward the tines of the forks, or most often, parallel to the fork, the blade toward the left. The forks, knives, and teaspoons are set approximately 1 inch from the edge of the table. The blades of the knives are always turned inward toward the plate. The water glass is placed about 1 inch to the right of the tip of the butter knife, and the bread-and-butter plate is placed about 1 inch above the tines of the forks. The napkin is centered between the fork and the knife. There should always be approximately 12 inches between the fork and the knife, depending upon the size of the plate that will be placed between them. Formal dinner settings often include a decorative service plate, which will be removed and replaced with the actual plated entrée. At times, depending upon the menu, a salad plate or soup bowl may be set on top of the service plate, which is later removed with the salad plate or soup bowl.

Figure 3–7
Dinner Table Setting.

When coffee or tea is served, the cup and saucer are placed to the right of the teaspoons, approximately 1 inch from the edge of the table with the handle angled at 4 o'clock (some prefer the handle angled at 3 o'clock). When the salad is ready to serve, and the guest has removed the napkin, it is placed and centered between the fork and knife, approximately 1 inch from the edge of the table. When the dinner plate is ready to be served, and the guest is not finished with the salad, with the guest's permission, the salad plate is placed to the left of the forks. The dinner plate is placed and centered between the fork and knife, approximately 1 inch from the edge of the table (see Figure 3–8).

When an appetizer such as smoked salmon with caper dressing or soup such as consommé royale is served, it is placed and centered between the fork and knife, approximately 1 inch from the edge of the table. The appropriate flatware, such as a fish fork or soupspoon, is conveniently placed when the item is served, or the fish fork may be placed to the left of the salad fork and the soupspoon may be placed to the right of the teaspoon.

Bread baskets, butter plates, and side dishes, such as a side order of mushrooms, and condiments, such as Worcestershire sauce or Dijon mustard, may be placed in a convenient location on the table when served. It is best to place any jarred or bottled condiment on a small plate topped with a paper doily. This will allow the guests to easily pass the condiments to each other. The use of a doilied plate should also be applied to any items that more than one guest at the table will use—an example would be cream for coffee or butter.

The dessert fork and spoon are in place for when the dessert is served, as shown in Figure 3–9. The small dessert spoon (or demitasse spoon) may be used for dessert or for an intermezzo course, which would be served during an upscale dinner. The intermezzo is often served between salad and the entrée. The intermezzo typically consists of a small portion of citrus-flavored sorbet. The purpose of the sorbet is to cleanse the palate of strong flavors. The table setting also shows a napkin placed on a service plate. The number of courses in a given menu determines the number of forks, knives, and spoons that are selected for a preset table. Therefore, a seven-course meal may require five forks, four knives, a soupspoon, and three teaspoons. The rule to follow is that flatware is placed in order of usage from the outside inward.

Figure 3–8
Dinner Table Setting as the Meal Is Served.

Figure 3–9
Dinner Table Setting with Wine Glasses, Dessert Fork, and Spoon.

To be able to identify the most commonly used pieces of flatware refer to Figure 3–10, and for serving pieces refer to Figure 3–11 For safe and sanitary handling, the following procedures must be followed: Flatware should be held by the handles and never by the tines of a fork, the blade of a knife, or the mouth

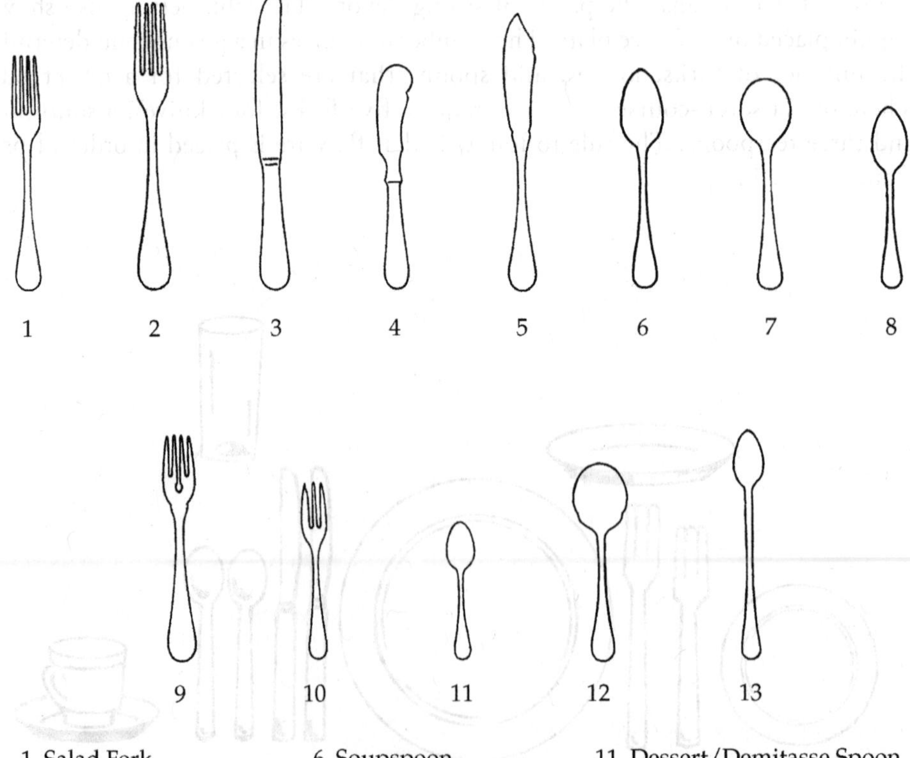

Figure 3–10
Commonly Used Flatware.

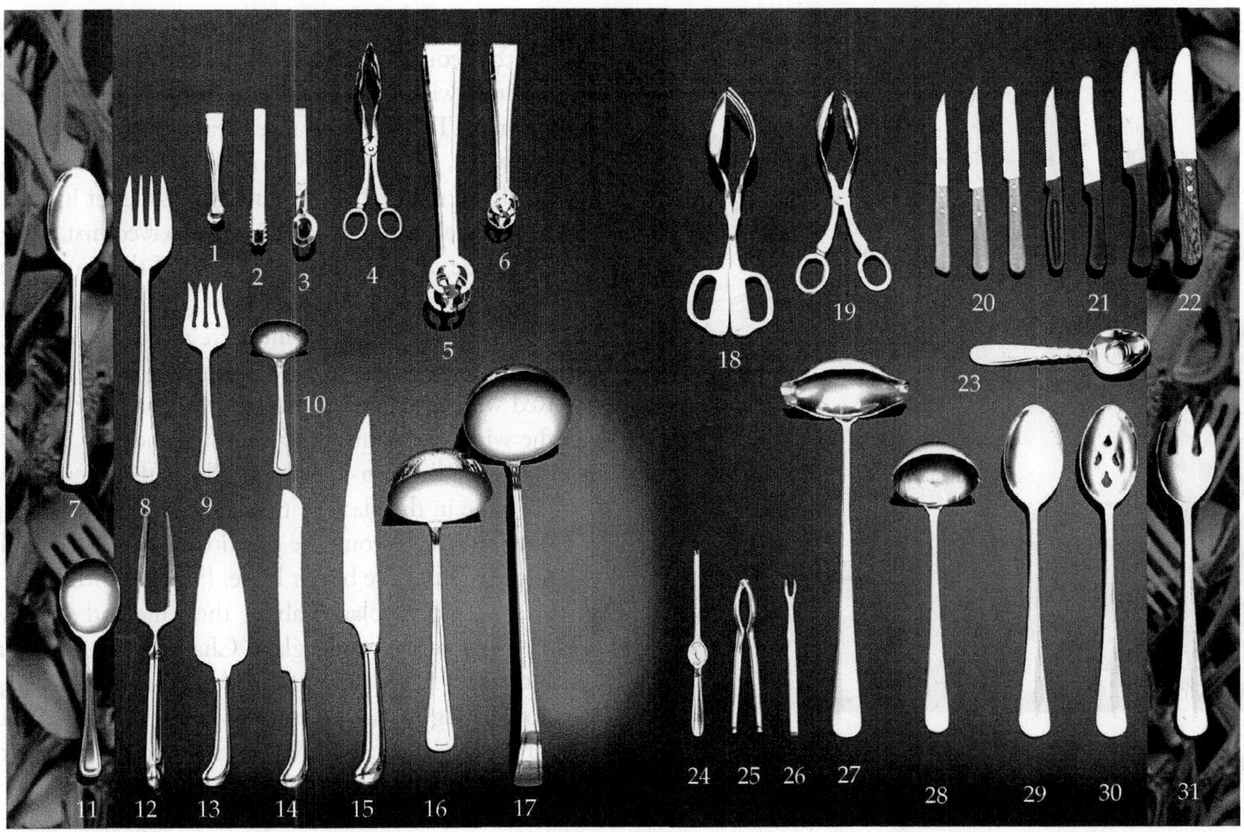

1. Sugar Tong
2. Ice Tong
3. Escargot Tong
4. Pastry Tong
5. Serving Tong
6. Tong
7. Banquet Spoon
8. Banquet Fork
9. Serving Fork
10. Gravy Ladle
11. Serving Spoon
12. Carving Fork
13. Cake Server
14. Cake Knife
15. Carving Knife
16. Soup Ladle
17. Punch ladle
18. Salad Serving Scissors
19. Salad Serving Scissors
20. Wood Handle Steak Knives
21. Plastic Handle Steak Knives
22. Large Wood Handle Knife
23. Pasta Spoon
24. Lobster Pick
25. Lobster Crack
26. Lobster Fork
27. Punch Ladle
28. Tureen Ladle
29. Buffet Serving Spoon
30. Serving Spoon, Pierced
31. Buffet Serving Fork

Figure 3–11
Serving Pieces. Courtesy of Oneida Foodservice Flatware.

of a spoon. Flatware should be spotless when placed on the table. Once the guest uses a piece of flatware for its intended purpose, it should be removed from the table. For example, when a guest has finished a salad, the salad fork and salad plate should be simultaneously removed. Glassware should be held by the stem or sides and never by the rim of the glass, and should always be spotless when placed on the table. Dishes should be held by placing the hand at the bottom of a dish with the thumb at the rim for balance, but never on the dish. Coffee cups should be spotless and held by the handle and never by the rim of the cup.

When a menu is predetermined, such as for a banquet or catered function, the tables are typically preset with the appropriate table settings to accommodate the menu and accompanying beverages, as shown in Figure 3–12. Additional information is presented in Chapter 10, Banquets, Catering, and Buffet Service.

WINE AND BEVERAGE SETTING

When wine is served, the water glass is moved above and slightly to the left of the knife. The wine glass is placed above and slightly to the right of the butter knife. Figure 3–9 shows a preset table, where two wines would be served during the meal. A wine would

Figure 3–12
Preset Banquet Table Setting. Courtesy of Villeroy & Boch.

accompany one course of the meal and a second wine another course. There are fine dining occasions when different wines are served with corresponding courses of the meal. Thus a five-course meal could have five different wines. At the completion of each course, that glass would be removed. The wine glasses are set in order of use. Therefore, if a white wine was served first, the glass would be positioned to the right of the butter knife. White wine glasses are normally taller and narrower by design. If the second wine were a red wine, the glass would be positioned above the tip of the butter knife. Red wine glasses are a balloon-like shape, which helps the wine to "breathe" by exposing more of its surface area. The balloon-like shape allows the guest to swirl the wine in the glass as it reacts with air. If champagne were served, it would be positioned above and slightly to the right of the butter knife. If served with wine, the glass would be placed above the wine and slightly to the right of the water glass. Champagne glasses are a slim flute-shape design, which keeps the champagne from losing its bubbles too quickly. Figure 3–13 shows different glass shapes. When a before-dinner cocktail or after-dinner liqueur is ordered, it would be served centered between the fork and knife, about 3 inches from the edge of the table.

TABLE SERVICE

There are five distinctive methods of serving food, often referred to as service styles: American Service, Butler Service, English Service, Russian Service, and French Service. The English, Russian, and French styles of service have changed over the centuries and evolved into different interpretations. Historical references correctly define these styles of service as they were originally set forth. Contemporary references are more focused on specific techniques that adapt the original definitions to what has transpired over the years.

Many restaurants have developed their own form of service that includes features from the different methods. This is often the result of a menu mix of international food items. The service style that a restaurant develops is one that will accommodate the menu, atmosphere, image of the restaurant, and nature of the clientele. What often develops are contemporary methods of serving food that are effective in meeting the individual restaurant's operational needs. These contemporary methods are a blend of one or more of the traditional methods, which fall into the following generally accepted definitions, combining some historical reference with a modern application.

American Service (Individual Plate Service)

This is the most popular type of service among today's restaurants. The service has been widely accepted because it is simple and quick, uses a minimum amount of serving equipment, and meets a wide variety of service needs, and a server can serve a station of many tables. The food is plated in the kitchen and individually served to guests, either at the guest's right with the right hand (traditional) or at the guest's left for left-handed servers, if desired. The guest's plate should be presented with the protein in front of the guest in the 6 o'clock position. Typically a server in a casual-style restaurant would be responsible for 4–6 tables and in an upscaled restaurant the server should have no more than four tables so that the attention to all service details can be obtained.

There is also a type of American plate service that is used in fine-dining restaurants, referred to as "team service." When applying this type of service, servers have specifically defined jobs to give broad coverage to the dining room. A service team can consist of three or more servers. There is commonly a front and back server and a server's assistant; there may even be a Sommelier who would be responsible for wine or a Barista responsible for specialty coffees, espresso, and spirited coffee drinks. Simply stated, the front sever is assigned all the tasks that require full guest contact; taking an order, making suggestions, and interacting with the guest so that all their expectations are met. The back server will pick up drinks from the bar, deliver food from the kitchen, and place any flatware that is necessary prior to each course being served. The server's assistant, often referred to as the SA, pours water, brings or serves bread, and removes soiled plates from the table. The advantage of this type of service includes constant attention to guests in the dining room. There is always at least one service person in the dining room that assists the guest and upholds all service standards. It is also the most sanitary way to serve guests—one service person handles clean plates and one handles soiled plates. When service teams are used, tips are usually divided among the team.

Figure 3–13
Glass Shapes. Courtesy of Stolzle Glassware.

Butler Service

This type of service is provided during a cocktail party or during the cocktail portion of a banquet or catered event. Hors d'oeuvres and/or light refreshments are placed on handheld trays and offered to guests by servers. The guest will serve themselves off of the handheld platter, using a cocktail napkin. This may also be referred to as "flying service" or "flying platters."

English Service

Formal English service is taken from the traditional service in English country homes where the head of the household acts as the carver and serves portions to family and guests with the assistance of servants. This type of service is often used in homes during holidays, such as Thanksgiving and Christmas. The head of the household (host) carves the turkey, ham, or roast and places an individual portion on each plate. The plate is then typically passed to another person (the co-host) who adds potatoes, vegetables, and other food items. Once the plate is complete, it is either served to a guest or given to the closest guests to be passed along to other guests. Soup is served in the same manner. That is, the host ladles soup from a tureen and either serves the guest or gives it to the closest guests to be passed along to other guests.

The professional (modified) application in the catering and restaurant environment adapts the above technique to a more formal presentation. The server presents a platter to the guest by the guest's left side and serves the food onto the plate by using a serving fork and spoon with his or her right hand—the Pincing (or Pliers) technique.

Russian Service

Russian service is sometimes referred to as silver service because there is an extensive use of platters and serving bowls which create a dramatic food presentation. Servers will serve guests from the platters onto their plates. Russian monarchy favored this type of service and introduced it to France. This service is not often used.

(a)

(b)

Figure 3–14
(a) Wheeled Guéridon or Flambé Cart. Courtesy of Lakeside™.
(b) Flambé Cart with Burner.

French Service

French service is reserved for very formal serving. Over time it has been modified and has come in and out of fashion. It is a service that requires special equipment such as a guéridon or flambé cart as shown in Figure 3–14. The guéridon is used so that a server can cook and plate food in front of the guest. This requires servers to have additional culinary skills such as sautéing and flambéing. This type of service takes a longer period of time to prepare and is associated with high-end dining where there is a limited amount of tables, creating an intimate dining-room atmosphere. The tableside service adds an element of showmanship which can be very impressive. Guests enjoy this element of French service and are willing to pay the higher prices to experience this show. Some fine-dining restaurants serve certain menu items from a cart, such as a Caesar salad or flamed desserts such as cherries jubilee.

Each type of service has its own application, style of restaurant, and advantages and disadvantages (see Table 3–1).

OTHER TYPES OF SERVICE

Several other types of service can be offered in conjunction with the restaurant's table service. They are counter service, banquet service, and room service.

Counter Service

This is a quick service and is generally found in diners, coffee shops, or old-fashioned soda fountains. The service is inexpensive and informal. The counter server will typically be assigned 12–18 seats depending upon the menu and how quickly the seats turn over. The table settings will vary from no setting at all until the customer arrives or orders, to a paper napkin with a fork, knife (blade turned toward fork), and teaspoon placed on top of the napkin and to the right of the counter seat as the customer would be seated.

TABLE 3–1
COMPARISON OF SERVICES

Type of Service	Who Serves	From What Side of the Guest	Food Presentation
American Service	An individual server is responsible for a set number of tables	The server traditionally serves their guest from the right side with the right hand or from the left side with the left hand	The food is plated in the kitchen on individual plates for the server to pick up, then serve their guest. Place the protein in the 6 o'clock position when applicable
Butler Service	A server presents a platter to the guests, then the guests serve themselves	In front of the guest	On a platter
Traditional English Service	The host carves and passes the plate to the co-host or closest guest		On platters or in soup tureens
Modified English service	A server presents a platter to the guest from the left, then uses the pincing technique to serve the guest	The guest's left	On platters or in soup tureens
Russian Service	A server serves guests from platters on to their plates	The plate is placed in front of the guest from the right with the right hand	First on a platter, then on a plate
French Service	A server prepares food tableside using a guéridon and serves to guests	Right from the right side	Comes out on guéridon or flambé cart and is cooked and transferred to plates

Or the table setting could include a place mat with the knife (blade turned inward), teaspoon to the right, a fork and napkin to the left. Water is placed above and slightly to the right of the tip of the knife and if coffee or tea is served, the cup and saucer or mug is placed to the right of the teaspoon with the handle angled at 4 o'clock. Condiments are usually within easy reach for the server, as are napkins, flatware, water glasses, ice, coffee cups or mugs, and tote boxes (bus tubs) for placing dirty dishes, flatware, glasses, and coffee cups or mugs. The bus tubs are usually placed under the counters. The service pace is typically fast and the server is required to be conscious of keeping the condiments full and wiped clean, maintaining an adequate supply of napkins, flatware, water glasses, and coffee cups or mugs. The tote boxes (bus tubs) need to be removed quickly to the dishwashing area and replaced with clean tote boxes. This may be either the server's responsibility or an assigned bus person's. The guest check is given to the customer face down once the meal is served. Due to the nature of the service, customer tipping usually ranges from 10 to 15 percent and in some cases 20 percent or higher.

Banquet Service

This type of service can accommodate any size group ranging from a dozen to an unlimited number of guests. Banquet service is most commonly used for large groups of people. The capacity of the banquet room will dictate the maximum number of people that can be served. A banquet menu can be limited and served quickly, or it may consist of several courses, elaborately presented and served. It may be a traditional breakfast, lunch, or dinner menu. The nature of the event typically influences the menu, such as a wedding reception, birthday party, anniversary party, Christmas or New Year's Eve party, bar or bat mitzvah, business awards luncheon, retirement dinner, or any other special occasion. Chapter 10 presents the details of banquets, catering, and buffet service.

Figure 3–15
Dessert Cart. Courtesy of Lakeside™.

Room Service

Many hotels and motels offer room service. The guests select from a room service menu and place their order over the telephone. The order is delivered to the room typically within 10–30 minutes from the time the order is placed. Delivery times can also be scheduled with advance ordering, such as for breakfast, which could be ordered the night before. The food is placed on a service tray or rolling cart and brought to the room from the kitchen by a server. Hot food plates are always covered to keep the food warm. The server has the added responsibility to double-check the order for its appearance and completeness along with bringing the appropriate condiments. When the server arrives at the room, he or she knocks on the door and announces, "Room Service." The server, once having been admitted to the room, will typically set the table and serve the food. The cost of the meal is usually charged to the room, with the guest signing the guest check and either writing in a tip amount or giving a cash tip to the server. The tip will generally be 20 percent or higher. There are some operations that identify an automatic gratuity (service charge) on the room service menu. It is also common for the house to retain a portion of this charge, thereby sharing the gratuity (service charge) with the room service server.

SALAD BARS

The server, once having taken the guests' food and beverage orders, invites them to visit the self-serve salad bar. On occasion, a guest may request the server to prepare and serve his or her salad with choice of salad dressing. Salad bars can be limited to lettuce and a few fresh vegetables to extensive offerings that include fresh fruits, sliced and grated cheeses, a variety of prepared salads, anchovies, pickled herring, seasoned croutons, bacon bits, assorted crackers, and bread sticks. The server keeps the water glasses full and serves the guests' beverages while the guests are eating their salads. When the meal is ready to be served, the server removes the salad plates and forks, if the guests are finished.

Figure 3–16
Pastry and Dessert Cart. Courtesy of Lakeside™.

DESSERT TABLES, CARTS, AND TRAYS

Desserts can be attractively presented and displayed in several ways. Dessert tables are typically set up for guests to serve themselves. Desserts may be plated or dessert plates may be at the dessert table for guests to serve themselves. A dessert cart, as shown in Figure 3–15 with a display of desserts, is rolled to the side of the table by the server and offered for guests' selection. A dessert and pastry cart, as shown in Figure 3–16 has a larger capacity to display a greater variety of desserts that may include pastries, fresh fruits, and soft cheeses. A smaller variety of dessert offerings may be shown to the guests on a handheld tray using the visual aid sales technique. When the server rolls the dessert cart or walks the tray through the dining room, they are enticing guests who are eating their meals with the possibility of dessert.

SUMMARY

Server training begins with an understanding and demonstrated ability to prepare correct table settings for breakfast, lunch, and dinner, prior to and as a meal is served. Also, the correct sanitary handling of flatware, glassware, and cups must be understood and adhered to at all times. A server, with experience, will be able to quickly identify the most commonly used flatware and serving pieces, along with the correct number of salt and pepper shakers and sugar and creamers to bring to a table. The different ways of serving bread and butter should also be understood.

Napkin folding is an integral part of a server's functions; therefore, the server should be acquainted with the most commonly used napkin folds and have a demonstrated ability to perform the folds.

There are five distinctively different methods of serving food. These methods are often referred to as service styles, and are as follows: American Service, Butler Service, English Service, Russian Service, and French Service. It is important to recognize that many restaurants have developed their own service style that includes various features from the different methods. This is typically done in order to accommodate the menu, atmosphere, image of the restaurant, and the nature of the clientele. Therefore, many contemporary service styles have evolved in today's restaurant environment. Other types of service include counter service, banquet service, and room service.

DISCUSSION QUESTIONS AND EXERCISES

1. Demonstrate, with the use of tableware, the correct breakfast and lunch table setting before the meal and as the meal is served.
2. Demonstrate, with the use of tableware, the correct dinner table setting before the meal and as the meal is served.
3. Demonstrate the correct placement of a dessert fork and spoon for a preset dinner table setting.
4. Where possible, lay out on a table a variety of the most commonly used pieces of flatware along with various serving pieces and identify each one by actual use.
5. Demonstrate, with the use of tableware, the correct way to handle flatware, glassware, dishes, and cups.
6. Demonstrate the correct placement, with the use of wine, champagne, cocktail, and liqueur glasses, before, during, and after a meal is served.
7. Describe the shape of a champagne glass, white wine glass, and red wine glass.
8. Demonstrate the correct placement of the place mat with a lunch table setting.
9. How many salt and pepper shakers would be placed on a table set for eight people? Explain the general rule regarding the number of salt and pepper shakers to be set on a table and when they should be removed.
10. When would sugar and creamers be placed on a table? How many would normally be set?
11. Explain three different ways that rolls and butter could be served to guests.
12. Practice folding five different napkin folds and explain a setting they could be used in.
13. Define the five different methods of serving food and give an example of where each service would be used.
14. Where is team service used and how does it work?
15. Explain how a guest orders and receives their order using counter service.
16. Demonstrate different counter service table settings.
17. List several occasions that would require banquet service.
18. Explain the service procedure for room service.
19. Explain the workings of salad bars, and dessert tables and carts.
20. Visit a restaurant of your choice, observe and evaluate the type of service method in use and write a one-page summary of your experience.

4
Serving Food and Beverages

learning objectives

After reading this chapter and completing the discussion questions and exercises, you should be able to:

1. Describe the 25 tips for proper table service.
2. Explain and demonstrate the procedures to follow when serving guests seated at a booth or next to a wall.
3. Explain and demonstrate the correct procedures for plate handling.
4. Describe and demonstrate the correct way to hold and serve a dish to a guest.
5. Explain and demonstrate the correct way to hold and serve beverage glasses, wine glasses with stems, cups, and mugs.
6. Describe the correct procedure to follow when serving wine.
7. Explain what additional items to bring to the table when serving specialty foods, such as lobster.
8. Describe the correct way to prepare a finger bowl for use.
9. Explain the different ways that crumbs and food particles can be cleared from a table.
10. Understand, explain, and demonstrate how to correctly load and carry trays, such as the large oval, small rectangular, and round beverage tray.

A restaurant's table service is developed to meet guests' expectations and designed to anticipate guests' needs. The particular demands or needs of the menu and dining room facility are also taken into consideration when selecting the type of service to use. Each restaurant will follow the method best suited for its particular dining room setting and layout; this can be defined as *protocol* for that restaurant. An example of a restaurant's particular protocol could be the type of service it uses or the way it places an order in the kitchen. Some restaurants use guéridon service, for example, to execute tableside service, whereas another restaurant would not use guéridon service because it does not have the space necessary to move the cart around the dining room. Another example of protocol would be to circle the woman's seat on the guest check to assure that they would be served first. A restaurant server must learn to follow the serving protocol exactly so that service will be uniform throughout the restaurant. This chapter presents the basic service techniques that have been adopted at many restaurants throughout the country.

In addition to protocol, there are certain practices that are considered basic etiquette. This means that it is always appropriate and desirable to practice these things. Some basic etiquette guidelines would be to serve women before men and the guest of honor before the host. These basic etiquette guidelines are based in tradition but are still truly appreciated by many guests, who consider etiquette an important part of dining room service in any type or style of restaurant. See more about etiquette that follows in the section titled "Twenty-Five Tips for Proper Table Service."

During breakfast, fast and efficient service is essential; many guests are in a hurry. Service at breakfast may be limited to juice, toast, and coffee, or it may include a complete breakfast of bacon, eggs, hash brown potatoes, and a side order of pancakes. Breakfast can be a difficult meal to serve with guest satisfaction; because this is the one meal of the day that many guests prefer to be prepared exactly like it is prepared each morning in their own home. To fully understand and replicate a home-cooked breakfast for their guest, a server must listen carefully and ask appropriate questions when necessary. There are many ways eggs can be cooked as well as different types of toast, therefore each breakfast can be customized for the guest. A breakfast server must practice excellent listening skills to re-create the guests' breakfast for them exactly the way they like it prepared. In addition, breakfast foods cool quickly so it is imperative the order is taken and delivered to the guest in a timely manner.

At lunch time it is also essential to serve guests as quickly as possible. Many times they have only 30 minutes in which to eat and get back to work. As a result of these time restrictions many restaurants offer special lunch menus that are quickly and easily prepared. These time-sensitive lunches are very popular for business lunch guests. A guest, however, may want to order in courses. If an appetizer is ordered, such as a cup of soup or salad, place it in front of the guest as soon as possible. As quickly as possible, after the first course is cleared, serve the entrées and side dishes. If the guest orders nothing but a sandwich and beverage, whenever possible serve the beverage first. It is acceptable to serve them together if they are served in a hurry. A server must practice his or her interpersonal skills, such as maintaining eye contact when listening to a guest so that the guest's service expectations are met and to be able to ask the right questions that can lead to not only meeting guests' expectations, but also exceeding them.

In contrast, guests may want to linger over coffee or dessert after lunch to discuss business or celebrate a special occasion. Therefore, the server needs to exercise good judgment when asking whether a guest has any time restriction. It is very disappointing to a guest with no time restrictions to feel rushed. The professional server is able to accommodate guests in a hurry, as well as those who do not want to be rushed. Most importantly a professional server should possess the skills necessary to determine the diverse needs of their guests.

Dinner is generally more leisurely and allows the server to give guests special attention. However, at times guests may be attending an event later in the evening or have another engagement, and they may want to eat quickly. Therefore, the server should inquire as to the guest's time frame for dinner. Often, dinner begins with a cocktail or two. The courses may include an appetizer, salad, soup, entrée, and a side dish. Bread and butter should be served with the salad or brought to the table immediately following the order. Coffee, espresso, or tea should be offered as well as dessert. The dessert can be ordered from a menu, a dessert tray, cart, or guéridon. When dessert is served, beverage refills should always be offered. After dessert the guest may want an after-dinner drink or spirited coffee.

As the guest check increases, guests' expectations will also increase. The more a guest spends on a meal the more he or she will expect from a server. This of course is true of most consumer goods and services. Therefore each shift will have a skill base necessary to meet the guests' expectations at that meal period. For example, it would not be expected that a breakfast server would have extensive knowledge of wines and spirits but it would be imperative that they know the many different ways eggs could be prepared. A lunch server would be expected to understand and explain basic cooking techniques such as sauté, grilling, and poaching but may not be expected to prepare a table side dish. A dinner server would have to have a broad and extensive knowledge of food, food preparation, food service, wines, spirits, etiquette, protocol, and possibly tableside cooking techniques. The dinner meal period is the one that the guest would typically spend the most money and expect to dine more leisurely. Because of all these factors a guest's expectations for dinner are the highest.

Identifying the different serving needs at each of these meal periods helps to deliver the best possible service for the guests. A professional server will "read the needs" of their guests and exceed their guest's expectations. Each meal time is unique and offers challenges for a server. By hiring well for each meal period and matching the server's skills to the meal-period requirements, a restaurant can have happy guests who return to the restaurant more often and even recommend the restaurant to friends. Table 4–1 presents server skills needed for different meal periods.

11. Understand, explain, and demonstrate the basic technique for carrying multiple plates.
12. Recognize and define serving priorities and the importance of correct timing.
13. Explain how to handle difficult situations that a server may encounter.
14. Understand and explain the function of a server's assistant.
15. Know and explain how a bussing cart should be equipped.
16. Understand and explain the procedures to follow in order to properly bus a table with the use of a cart or with the use of a tray.

TABLE 4–1
SERVER TRAITS

Meal Period	Important Traits And Skills
BREAKFAST	• Morning Person • Good Listening skills • Fast • Efficient • Cheerful
LUNCH	• Read the need of the guest • Good Communication Skills • Timely • Efficient • Friendly Personality
DINNER	• Confident • Knowledge of various types of food • Knowledge of food preparation • Wine and Spirit Knowledge • Good Observation Skills • Listening Skills • Service Experience • Out going personality

TWENTY-FIVE TIPS FOR PROPER TABLE SERVICE

Professional servers traditionally serve food and beverages according to the following general rules and techniques:

1. Serve all dishes with the right hand, approaching the table to the right of the guest or from the left side with the left hand. This avoids the server's arm crossing over the guest. Serving in this manner helps avoid accidents caused by a guest hitting a server's arm when they are trying to serve.
2. Serve liquids (beverages and soups) before solids. Serve with the right hand and to the right of the guest. A guest should have a beverage before food, whenever possible.
3. Serve everyone at the table the same course at the same time, but serve a woman or older guest first as a matter of etiquette. When there is more than one woman or older guest present, serve the woman or older guest on the host's right first. Then continue serving around the table clockwise, serving the host last. Treat children the same as adults, but serve them first if the parents request they be served first. The host or hostess may or may not be predetermined. The host or hostess typically would be the person who made the reservation. A professional server will always be aware of the host of the table and take great care to follow the guidelines for proper etiquette. The host or hostess will be the person presented with the check upon conclusion of the meal.
4. Check the table setting for each guest to make sure that he or she has the necessary flatware for each course being served before they serve the food. Flatware is to be held by the handles, never by the tines of a fork, the blade of a knife, or the mouth of a spoon. Preferably, flatware should be carried on a tray or plate, not in a server's hands. The flatware should be clean and spotless. If water spots repeatedly occur, there may be a final rinse problem with the dishmachine that can be corrected. The manager should be informed of the problem.

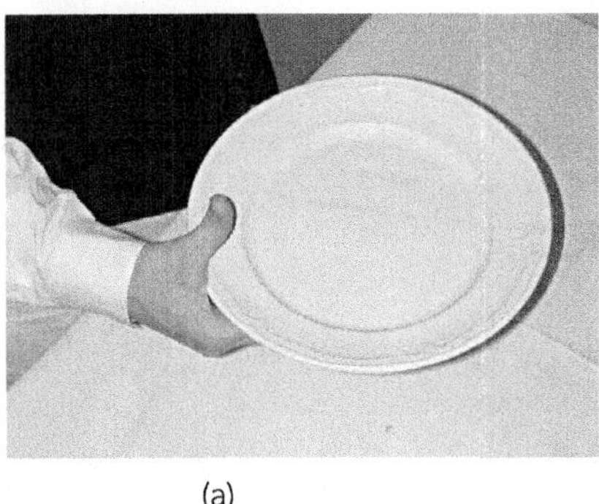
(a)

(b)

Figure 4–1
(a) Plate-Handling with thumb up
(b) Plate-Handling with thumb to the side of the outer rim. Courtesy of the Federation of Dining Room Professionals.

5. Remove dishes and flatware from the right when each course is finished, using the right hand; then serve the next course from the right using the right hand. Exceptions to this rule are as follows:
   a. When it will be inconvenient to the guest.
   b. If the guest is leaning to the right to talk with another guest.
   c. When serving a guest seated at a booth or next to a wall.
   d. If there is a bread-and-butter plate on the right of the guest.
6. Serving guests seated at a booth or next to a wall requires the server to stand at the end of the booth or table and serve the guests seated farthest away first. Therefore, the guests seated on the right would be served with the left hand and the guests seated on the left would be served with the right hand. This reduces the possibility of the server accidentally elbowing a guest. Refilling water glasses or coffee cups may require the server to pick up the glass or coffee cup to be able to pour safely.
7. Serve all dishes by placing the thumb up or to the side of the outer rim of the dish and never inside, as shown in Figure 4–1 a and b. Be careful never to serve a chipped or cracked dish.

Depending on the style of the restaurant a server will have to transport plates to the guest's table. They may use a large oval tray or they may hand-carry multiple plates as a function of service. There are several methods to hand-carry plates. Hand-carrying plates is a skill that many restaurants expect their servers to use. It can be intimidating at first but it easily can become a skill that a server can master. In one hand a server will hold three plates; one will balance on the pointer finger and the second finger next to the pinky, the second on the thumb and pinky, and the last on the large middle finger below the other two plates (Figure 4–2). The server could also hold the fourth plate in the other hand. The way you choose to transport a plate to the guests table will be influenced by several key factors. If the plate is hot a server should use a service towel so they do not burn their hand. The plate should be carried so that it is placed down in front of the guest as intended by the chef. Traditionally the protein or main item should be in the 6 o'clock position when presented to the guest. A server may have to adjust how they serve a guest if there is an obstacle in their way.

When the chef decides on plate presentations they should understand the impact this will have on the servers' techniques as well as the guests' first impression. One of the best plate presentation practices dictates that no decoration shall ever extend to the edge of the plate on the rim. This is where the server must place their fingers when serving. If a chef decorated the rim of a plate with paprika or chocolate powder to add

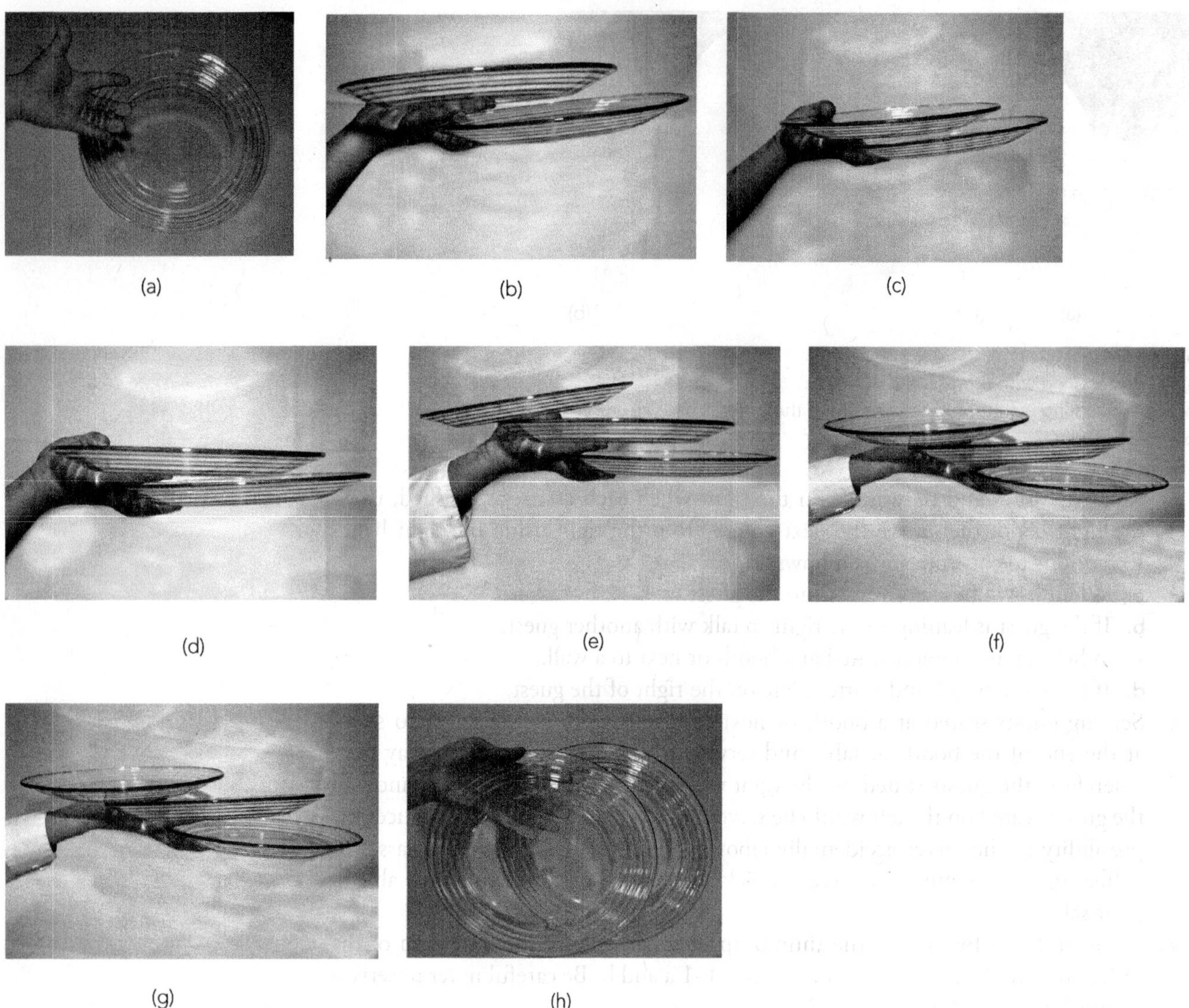

(a) (b) (c) (d) (e) (f) (g) (h)

Figure 4–2
(a) Clear Plate Holding, Four Fingers, (b) Two Clear Plates Held in Hand, Fingers between Plates, (c) Two Clear Plates Held in Hand, Thumb on Top, (d)Two Clear Plates, Thumb on Top, Fingers in Middle and Bottom, (e) Three Clear Plates, Fingers between all Plates, (f) Three Clear Plates, Top Plate Balanced on Top of Thumb, (g)Three Clear Plates, Top Plate Balanced on Top of Thumb, and (h)Two Clear Plates, Photo with Palm up. Gerald Lanuzza.

color, for example, it is inevitable that the server will leave an unattractive finger print after carrying the plate to the guest.

8. When serving beverages it is important to never place your fingers near where a guest would drink. There are many different types of glasses each type requires a different service procedure.
   a. Stemless glasses, such as a highball glasses or a stemless wine glass, should be carried by the base.
   b. Any stemmed glass, including a stemmed water glass or a wine glass should be carried by the stem.
   c. A coffee mug should be carried by the handle and placed in front of the guest with the handle in the 4 o'clock position.
   d. A coffee or tea cup with a saucer should be carried by the saucer and should be placed in front of the guest with the handle in the 4 o'clock position; a teaspoon should be placed to the right of the guest or on the saucer.

9. When serving coffee, fill the cup or mug two-third full to allow the guest to add cream and sugar, if that is their preference. It is the protocol of most restaurants to offer coffee refills. The server should first make eye contact with the guest and ask them if they care for more before refilling their coffee. It is always best to serve hot beverages such as coffee or tea in a warm cup or mug to maintain the temperature. To protect the guest from being splashed with a hot beverage, place a service towel, or a clean folded napkin, between the guest and the hot beverage. The pot used for the refills would be in the right hand and the service towel in the left. This creates a barrier between the hot liquid and the guest.
10. Wine service is an important part of a meal and great care should be taken when serving a bottle of wine. After the host orders the wine it should be presented to them by showing them the label. The server should then recite the name, vintage, producer, classification, and type of wine for their approval. The bottle is then opened and served to the host first by pouring about 1 ounce for tasting. Once the host has approved the wine, it is poured for other guests, filling each glass half way full, beginning with the female guests, then male guests, with the host being served last. If the wine has been selected prior to the meal, as in the case of a banquet, serve the wine just before the main course. If more than one wine is served, serve the appropriate wine just before its designated course. Refer to Chapter 6 for additional information about serving wines and wine temperatures.
11. Follow the protocol of the restaurant when serving rolls, breads, or crackers. When serving rolls or bread in a basket, the basket should be lined with a napkin.
12. When handling butter, use a fork, ice tong, or spoon.
13. When serving relishes, pickles, olives, or cheese, serve with a fork or spoon.
14. Salads as a separate course are served directly in front of the guest. If the guest desires to finish his or her salad with the entrée, then the salad should be placed to the left of the fork before the entrée is served. A side order salad or other sides would automatically be placed to the left of the fork when served.
15. When serving an appetizer, place them directly in front of the guest. If guests are sharing an appetizer, be sure to bring an additional fork or spoon and appetizer dish. Some guests may appreciate having the appetizer split in the kitchen and served separately.
16. When serving specialized foods, such as lobster, bring a lobster cracker, fork, and pick, and an empty plate for the lobster shell. Place the lobster cracker to the left of the fork and the lobster fork and pick to the right of the teaspoon. If a pick is not used, place the lobster cracker to the right of the lobster fork. Place the empty plate for shells above and slightly to the left of the lobster plate. Place the dish of melted butter above and slightly to the right of the lobster plate.
17. Formal dining sometimes includes the use of finger bowls at the end of a meal with shellfish or finger foods. Place a small bowl filled with warm water on an underliner (small plate) garnished with a lemon wedge to the left of the guest. Extra napkins are also provided for guests to wipe and dry their hands. Hot towels or a packaged moist towelette may also be used.
18. When serving steaks or fish, place the steak knife or fish knife to the right of the knife (or butter knife), followed by the teaspoon.
19. Always ask the guest if he or she would like any condiments that might accompany the meal, such as ketchup, mustard, Dijon, Worcestershire, or steak sauce. The appropriate way to serve condiments would be on an underliner, a small plate with a doily.
20. Know the restaurant's policy regarding extra servings, so if a guest requests an extra portion, such as an additional serving of bleu cheese salad dressing or an additional slice of toast for breakfast, you will know how to respond (including any additional charges).

21. Clearing can be tricky; some guests like their plates cleared immediately and others want a server to wait until all guests finish. It is best to ask the guest if you may clear their plates. The use of observation can also be helpful. Look for flatware which is placed in the closed position to know if the guest is finished. The closed position is when both fork and knife are laid across the plate on the right side. If a guest is resting, the knife would be laid across the right side of the plate and the fork across the left. Dirty dishes should be taken to a side stand, a tray on a tray stand, or directly to the dishwashing area, and never scraped or stacked in front of guests.
22. Smoking is prohibited in most restaurants, but certain circumstances or events may allow the privilege for smokers. Therefore, when an ashtray is in use and needs emptying, simply remove it and replace it with a clean ashtray. Remove the ashtray slowly so ashes will not blow out, or cover the ashtray with another one held upside down over it (capping), being careful not to clang them together to avoid chipping and unnecessary noise. Then remove both of them and replace with a clean one.
23. Completely clear all dishes, glasses not in use (leaving the water glass), salt and pepper shakers (if not normally left on the table), and condiments before serving dessert.
24. Tables should be cleared of all crumbs before presenting the dessert menu or serving dessert. This is done by using a crumber (handheld scraper), a mechanical handheld vacuum, or a clean napkin. When using a napkin, it should be tightly folded or rolled, then remove crumbs or food particles by sweeping onto a plate, small tray, or into another napkin, not into the other hand.
25. Desserts may be ordered from a dessert menu or selected from a dessert tray, cart, or pastry and dessert cart. After the guest has indicated a choice of dessert, the server should appropriately serve the dessert from the kitchen, tray, or cart. Place the dessert in front of the guest along with the dessert fork or spoon to the right of the dessert.

LOADING AND CARRYING A TRAY

There are various types of trays in general use, such as the **large oval** for bigger loads, **small rectangular**, and **round beverage trays**. Large oval trays are used when there are tray stands or side stands available to the server so that he or she can put the tray down before serving the guests. Rectangular trays are used for smaller amounts of food or for glasses. The round beverage trays are used for serving wine and cocktails. Restaurants that expect servers to handle full dinners for large parties generally use trays and tray stands. As a rule of professional service, a tray should not be placed on guest tables.

The following procedures should be followed when loading and carrying an **oval tray**:

- Make sure the tray is clean, top and bottom.
- Unless the tray has a nonskid surface of cork or similar material, cover the inside of the tray with a damp service cloth to prevent dishes or glasses from sliding.
- In most serving situations, hot and cold items will be loaded on the tray. Position on the tray is not determined by order of loading, but by the need to:
  a. Balance the tray.
  b. Keep hot foods away from cold foods.
  c. Preserve the food's attractiveness for the guest.
- Load the center of the tray first, and then work toward the outer edge.
- Load larger, heavier pieces toward the center of the tray or at the edge of the tray nearest the shoulder when carrying.
- Load lighter, smaller pieces toward the edges of the tray.

- Do not stack or overlap hot dishes with lids on cold dishes, or cold dishes on hot dishes.
- Keep plates with sauces or liquids level with the tray to prevent spillage.
- Do not place appetizers, soups, or cups on underliners (small plates) or saucers on the tray, but stack all underliners and saucers separately.
- Place coffee and teapot spouts away from food and plates, but not hanging over the edge of the tray.
- When stacking dishes with covers, do not stack more than 4 high or attempt to carry more than 16. It is possible to carry 5 stacks of 4 each, if done carefully.
- Never overload a tray. This will cause breakage as well as a possible accident or personal injury and loss of the food spilled.
- Balance the tray before lifting.
- Lift with your legs not your back to avoid possible injury
- Keep open dishes away from the side that will be nearest the server's hair.
- Leave one hand free to carry a tray stand.

An **oval tray** is carried on the server's shoulder, and it must be lifted to shoulder height. Since a tray may be fully loaded with covered dishes, it can be extremely heavy; therefore, it must be lifted properly according to the following procedures:

- Make sure the tray is properly loaded.
- Position the tray so that one side of the oval extends 5 inches off the service table, side stand, or tray stand in which the tray rests.
- Drop into a squat position by bending completely from the knees to get under the tray.
- Firmly place one side of the shoulder underneath the edge of the tray and slide the shoulder side hand toward the bottom center of the tray as the tray is being slid off the table or stand, as the other hand grasps the outer rim to steady the tray (see Figure 4–3).
- Stand up, keeping the back as straight as possible, using the legs to do the lifting; then the tray can be properly carried, as shown in Figure 4–4.

  Note: The server should never attempt to lift more than he or she is comfortable handling, nor should the server ever try to lift the tray to the shoulder using only the arms. This can result in twisted back muscles.

- Once the tray has been brought to the table, place the tray on a side stand or tray stand by keeping a straight back and again using the legs to drop into the squat position so that the tray can be slid onto the stand. Remove dishes evenly from the tray to ensure the tray remains balanced on the stand, as you serve the guests.

Figure 4–3
Preparing to Lift a Tray.

Small rectangular trays are widely used in high-volume, limited-menu restaurants. They are used in some cocktail lounges, especially when the need to use all available space for seating leaves no room for side stands or tray stands.

A rectangular tray cannot be loaded as heavily as an oval tray, but a full breakfast or lunch for two people can be accommodated if properly loaded. The following procedures should be followed when using a rectangular tray:

- Make sure the tray is properly loaded and balanced.
- Slide the tray broad side forward onto the left forearm.

Figure 4–4
Properly Carrying a Tray.

- Hold the upper left arm close to the body.
- Use the right arm to carry a tray stand.
- Once the tray has been brought to the table, properly place the tray on the tray stand and serve the guests.
- When serving guests with the tray in the carrying position, unload it first from one side and then from the other in order to maintain balance.

Round beverage trays are best carried with the palm of the hand underneath and in the center of the tray, as shown in Figure 4–5. This enables the server to maintain balance and compensate for weight shifts while serving beverages. The tray should also be held close to the body to prevent spills or accidents.

When serving, slowly lift the glasses or bottles from the tray. If the tray starts to tip, quickly return the glass or bottle that caused the shift in balance. Then carefully slide the hand underneath the tray to the area that needs support, and resume serving. A good technique to keep the load steady is to make sure all items are clustered together and touching, as shown in Figure 4–6. This stabilizes individual items (tall beer bottles and wine glasses) and minimizes the possibility of a single item losing balance and knocking over the rest to the load.

CARRYING GLASSES

It is good service practice to carry glasses on a beverage tray when serving and clearing a guest's table as shown in Figure 4–7. Another method which applies to transporting stemmed wine glasses to a table is hand-carrying. It is possible for a well-trained server to carry many wine glasses to the table in one trip. It is very common for a server to carry as many as eight glasses at one time. The size of the bowl of the wine glass and the size of the server's hand will dictate the amount of glasses a server can safely carry to the table (Figure 4–8—three glasses; Figure 4–9—four glasses; Figure 4–10—five glasses). Advanced glass-carrying skills are easily learned and then mastered with adequate practice. However, when the potential for slippage exists, the server should only use one hand to carry glasses.

Figure 4–5
Properly Carrying a Round Beverage Tray.

SERVICE PRIORITIES AND TIMING

Service priority and timing are among the most important skills for a server to possess. It is a skill that is developed through experience, and is sometimes difficult to train because it requires critical thinking skills and good judgment on the part of the server. Before we begin to discuss service priority and timing, it would be beneficial to ask some relevant discussion questions.

Figure 4–6
Items Clustered Together.

Figure 4–7
Carrying Glasses on a Beverage Tray.

SERVICE PRIORITY AND TIMING QUESTIONS

1. If while helping a guest at the hostess stand, the phone rings, typically another restaurant associate will pick up the phone. Is this a good idea?
2. When a server is seated with multiple tables at one time a server should make brief contact with each table then proceed to take the orders as the tables are ready. This is an example of good communication skills. True or False?
3. When a server goes to a side-stand it is important for them to think of the needs of all their tables and pick up what is necessary for them in one trip. True or False?
4. A server should serve an appetizer and entrée at the same time because most guests are in a hurry. True or False?
5. A server should refill water before serving hot food that is ready in the kitchen. True or False?
6. The key to excellent service is observation; a server should be looking at their tables and anticipating their needs. True or False?
7. The first impression of the guest is important; when the restaurant is busy, it is always best to acknowledge a guest for a few seconds and then tell them you will be right with them. True or False?

The host or server should always greet, welcome, and, if it is the protocol of the restaurant, serve water to guests within seconds from the time they are seated. The server should be alert and attentive at all times and constantly aware of what is happening at his or her tables. This is accomplished by frequently looking at different

Figure 4–8
Server Holding Three Wine Glasses.

Figure 4–9
Server Holding Four Wine Glasses.

Figure 4–10
Server Holding Five Wine Glasses.

tables and making eye contact with guests, even when engaged in taking an order or serving. Other tables may simultaneously need water or coffee refills, or may be ready to order dessert. Therefore, the server needs to cultivate service priorities and timing that convey a sense of urgency. This can be accomplished by developing the following techniques:

- Always make trips count. Never go empty-handed. The efficient server takes something that has to be delivered or removed from guest tables; for example, delivering an order from the kitchen to one table and removing dishes from another table to prepare for dessert. This saves time and energy and increases the speed of service by focusing upon efficiency and not wasting steps.
- Hot foods should be served the moment they are ready. The aroma, sizzle, and intensity of certain foods, such as soups, seasoned sauces, steamed vegetables, and steaks, only last a short time and make up part of the guest's dining pleasure. Conversely, cold foods, such as seafood appetizers, fruit salads, or parfaits, must be served cold.
- After placing the guests' orders with the kitchen, promptly serve rolls and butter, appetizers, salads, soups, and/or drinks. Some restaurants have a policy of serving water as soon as guests are seated. Guests appreciate quick service and like to have enough time to finish one course before the next course arrives.
- Serve all the guests at the table the same course at the same time, without long lapses of time between courses. There is a delicate balance between not rushing guests and preventing them from fidgeting and getting impatient between courses. A constantly observant server will be able to maintain the appropriate service timing.
- Pivot point service is a designated starting position with all orders served clockwise from that point. Servers should mentally number the positions at their tables with the designated starting pivot point and then go around the table

clockwise as orders are taken. This allows the server to identify what each guest has ordered. The pivot point could be the party's host or, as with booths, the first person seated on the left and closest to the aisle. Also, guest checks may provide table diagrams to assist in taking orders, as shown in Figure 4–11. When serving the food order, never ask guests what they have ordered. Be accurate and correct when taking the order and exact when delivering it.

- Keep water glasses refilled at all times. To some guests, nothing is more disturbing than to have an empty water glass. It is essential to check water glasses each time the server visits the guest, for any reason. For example, check water glasses when serving salads; when serving hot foods; when about halfway through with the meal; when suggesting dessert; and when serving dessert. Knowing which glass to fill first is important: a wine glass or coffee cup would be refilled before a water glass, for example.
- While it is important to follow the basic rules and techniques for proper service, successful servers focus on smooth, efficient serving procedures that are convenient for the guest, and that do not interrupt the guest's comfort. Also, remember that serving gracefully takes poise and know-how, and it brings pleasure and satisfaction to both the server and the guests.
- When taking orders, ask if the guests prefer individual checks or one check for the group. Never keep a guest waiting for the check. When presenting the check, place it in the center of the table face down, unless one of the guests has specifically asked for the check, or unless it was obvious when the orders were placed who would be paying. As soon as a credit card or money has been placed next to the guest check, the server should quickly process and return the credit card slip with the card and a pen or the change to the guest. The experienced server uses an inexpensive ballpoint pen and removes the cap. This reduces the possibility that the absent-minded guest will place the pen in his or her pocket. The process for guest check payment should always be quick. If it is slow or delayed, guests may be displeased. Guest check processing and payment will be further discussed in Chapter 7, Guest Communication.
- Occasionally, guests take a leisurely approach to leaving after their meal. This may be acceptable when the restaurant is not busy, but when the table is needed for the next party, the guests may need a gentle hint that it is time to leave. The server may ask if the guests would like anything else, or start clearing the dessert dishes and glasses, thanking the guests and wishing them a pleasant evening.

Table diagrams assist in taking orders and serving correct meal to each guest.

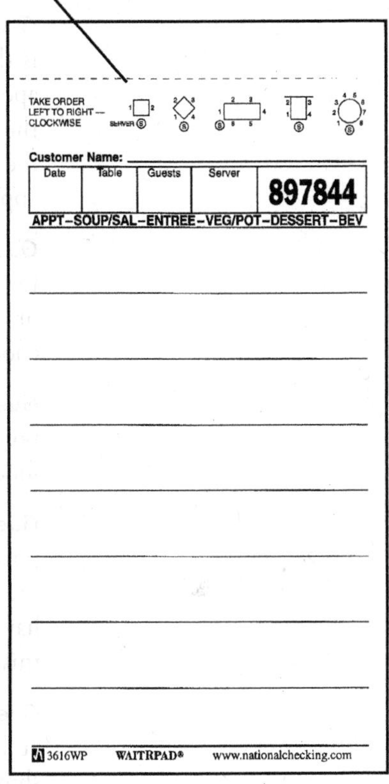

Figure 4–11
Guest Check, WaitRPads®. Courtesy of National Checking Company.

HANDLING DIFFICULT SITUATIONS

Difficult situations with guests arise occasionally in most restaurants. The initial reaction to a difficult situation may be defensive anger or frustration. This reaction could cause the restaurant to lose valuable customers. It is best to maintain a positive attitude and to resolve the incident as quickly and efficiently as possible. The server is typically the person who has to deal with and solve guest problems and complaints. The server needs to be confident of his or her abilities and remember that customer satisfaction comes before anything else. The server needs to be empowered to solve difficult situations and also have the support of management.

The following are examples of situations that occur most often, along with suggestions for effectively solving them.

Guest Receives Food Not Up to His or Her Expectations A good policy to maintain is that the "guest is always right." Food should be substituted or exchanged with an apology. The fact that the food is just right by the restaurant's standards is immaterial; the guests should have it the way they want it. This, of course, does not mean that the restaurant will change its basic recipe for each guest, a fact that most guests will appreciate.

Guest Complains That Food Is Cold or Undercooked The server apologizes and immediately remedies the problem by returning the food to the kitchen to be warmed or fully cooked, and quickly returns when the food has been properly warmed or cooked.

Guest Says Food Is Overcooked or Burned The server should follow the restaurant policy for how to handle this type of problem. A substitution may be offered or the food item can be replaced.

Guest States That the Portion Size Is Too Small If the server recognizes that the portion is smaller than normal, the server should apologize and immediately take the guest's plate back to the kitchen for the correct portion amount. Most restaurants have standard portion sizes and a manager is the best person in the restaurant to address this issue.

Guest Says That the Order Is Wrong When this occurs, it is not important who is at fault; what is important is to apologize and promptly correct the mistake. The error should be reported to the manager and the manager should be asked to visit with the guest to resolve the problem.

Guest Would Like a Baby Bottle Heated Although this may be inconvenient, do not give the guest the feeling, either by words or actions, that it is inconvenient or too much trouble to have the bottle heated. Be cheerful about doing it.

Guests Allow Their Children to Wander the Floor Children should be asked to return to their table, or brought back to the table for adult supervision. Quite simply, the children would be at risk of getting knocked over, accidentally tripping a server, or annoying other guests.

Guest Is Very Dissatisfied with Food and Does Not Want to Wait for a Replacement Apologize sincerely and suggest another entrée that is already prepared or is easily and quickly prepared. If the guest refuses, call the manager for help. The best decision may be not to charge the guest for the meal.

Guest Complains that Food Is Undercooked, Although It Is Half Eaten Apologize and offer to return it to the kitchen for additional cooking. If the guest refuses, some restaurants authorize the server to offer the displeased guest a complimentary dessert.

Guests Order Together and then Want to Pay Separately Do not become annoyed by this request, and by all means do not ask them to pay together and then figure it out themselves. Chapter 7 demonstrates a point-of-sale (POS) system that can quickly adjust to this type of situation.

Server Forgot to Enter the Guest's Order to the Kitchen This might happen during a very busy shift where the server forget to enter an order at the POS terminal. When it is discovered, the server should immediately place the order with the kitchen. Alert the kitchen and the manager of the problem. Then explain and apologize to the guest for the delay. Sometimes a free drink, appetizer, or beverage refill is necessary, if the server is authorized. This may appease the guest and salvage a tip.

Guest is Unhappy and Has a Bad Opinion of the Food and Service Always call for the manager when something like this happens. A third person often will be able to rectify the situation better than the server. Guests need to be satisfied before leaving the restaurant.

Guest Is Intoxicated Inform the manager and bring coffee to the guest. If the guest becomes loud, obnoxious, or abusive, the manager may ask the guest to leave or may have to take other measures in having the guest escorted out of the restaurant. With the increase of liquor liability and laws passed specifically affecting alcohol service, the responsibility of monitoring alcohol service many times falls directly upon the server. The server should be completely informed about the legal statutes and house policies regarding intoxicated patrons. This is further discussed in Chapter 6, Wine and Beverage Service.

Too Many Guests Are Seated in a Server's Section When this occurs, and the server can't adequately handle the situation, the host or manager should be informed. Perhaps another server could be assigned to help, or the hostess or manager could step in to help. The mistake would be to try to serve more people than the individual server can effectively handle. The guest will not be pleased and the server's tips will suffer.

Guest Leaves Shopping Bag or Backpack in the Aisle The server needs to politely suggest that the guest move the bag or backpack out of the way of traffic to avoid possible trips or falls.

Server Spills Food or Drink on the Clothing of a Guest When a spill accident occurs, the server should react immediately by doing the following: Apologize and be certain that the guest was not hurt; assure the guest involved that the restaurant will clean the garment or replace it if necessary; replace the item that was spilled and alert the manager; and clean up the mess as quickly as possible.

Food Is Slow Coming from the Kitchen Occasionally a kitchen may be temporarily backed up with orders. When this occurs, the server should explain the reason to guests—for example, a large party just arrived, or a tour bus just dropped off a large group. Most people are understanding and patient if they know why they have to wait and if they are not forgotten. The server needs to keep the rolls and butter replenished, water and beverage glasses full. If the delay is prolonged, some restaurants have a policy of providing guests with complimentary beverages, appetizers, or desserts.

Server Is Informed that the Kitchen Is Out of the Food Item Ordered When this happens, the server should apologize to the guest for the inconvenience and suggest some comparable choices. It may be necessary to return the menu for the guest to review. Once the kitchen has run out of an item, the servers should be informed immediately. This will avoid or minimize the possibility of having to disappoint a guest once having placed the order versus being told ahead of time that the item is not available.

Foreign Object Found in the Food by the Guest This is among the worst possible situations. If a guest finds a piece of metal or glass, a Band-Aid, a bug, or anything else that would be dangerous and unappetizing, the server needs to immediately apologize and remove the plate, inform the kitchen and the manager, and return with fresh food for the guest. Most restaurants have a policy of not charging the guest for the meal along with offering the utmost apology for the unfortunate occurrence.

Guest Complains about the Food, Having Eaten Most of it Apologize and try to satisfy the guest in a reasonable manner. If that is not possible, the manager should be asked to resolve the situation. Some guests are never satisfied, and some are attempting to get a free meal. They still have to be treated with respect and dealt with fairly.

Guests Leave Without Paying Check with the cashier to be certain. Act quickly and inform the manager who in turn should follow them to their car, getting their license plate number. If they are not yet at their car, the manager should approach them and ask whether they paid, being polite but firm.

restaurant reality: complaints are not always reasonable but always have a solution.

Ms. Kane was a young and enthusiastic restaurant manager in a large four-star hotel in a beautiful city near the sea that attracted tourists from all over the world. She worked very hard and had a true understanding of hospitality. Despite her long hours she always arrived at work with a cheerful disposition. She truly liked to see her guests happy and went out of her way anytime she could.

Tourist season was in full swing, the hotel was booked solid for three consecutive weeks, and all managers were working long hours and six-day workweeks. Ms. Kane was in the middle of her second long week when she recognized a table of guests in the restaurant. They have eaten in the restaurant three out of the four days since check-in at the beginning of the week. She approached the table and asked if they were enjoying their meal and more importantly their stay in the hotel. Their response was very complimentary and Ms. Kane was delighted. She excused herself as the guests' next course arrived. The restaurant was busy but everyone in the dining room looked as though they were enjoying themselves. Ms. Kane checked on other tables and helped her staff with anything that they needed. Time was flying by as it does in a busy restaurant. Ms. Kane noticed the regular customers finishing their dessert and she walked toward their table to say good-bye. While she was saying good-bye to her guests, a server approached the table and asked for help. Ms. Kane excused herself and went to another table where the server was having difficult time with a guest. Ms. Kane introduced herself and asked what she could do for the guests. At this time the gentleman sitting at the table in a loud voice bellowed "These are the most uncomfortable #$@^ chairs I have ever sat in my entire life, something needs to be done about it immediately." Ms. Kane was flabbergasted; she had never heard such a vulgar complaint about the restaurant's very expensive chairs. She composed herself and knew she had her hands full. She told the guest that she would be right back. She gathered six throw pillows from the lounge area and raced back to the restaurant. She offered the guest one, then two, then three of the pillows. He was NOT satisfied. She offered him four then five. He positioned himself in the chair and finally he was comfortable. Ms. Kane smiled broadly. Her server looked at her from across the room and thanked her. The guest was happy the rest of the night and everything went smoothly.

Ms. Kane felt good about the outcome of the complaint. She knew that the chairs were designed and chosen for the restaurant for their elegance and comfort but she kept it to herself. It was more important to Ms. Kane to display true hospitality then if the guest's complaint was valid. The guest may not always be right but they must always be satisfied.

Steps to Resolve a Complaint

1. LISTEN—the most important step in solving a difficult situation is to allow the guest to feel they have an opportunity to explain themselves. Many guests want to be heard first and foremost.
2. UNDERSTAND—a guest wants you to understand why they are upset. Showing understanding can diffuse a difficult situation. Understanding the exact problem is very important for the future so allow the guest to completely explain themselves.
3. APOLOGIZE—let them know you are sorry for the things that you have control over. Be sincere.
4. RESOLVE—each guest will need or want something different from you. The ultimate goal is to get the guest to return and have a better experience. So make sure you know exactly why they are unhappy and then try and match the solution to the complaint.

TABLE BUSSING

Being a server's assistant (SA) or busser, is an excellent opportunity to learn the restaurant business thoroughly. Because of the wide variety of duties, the bus attendant can learn about waiting on tables, cooking, dishwashing, food preparation, and a variety of other areas—a little about every job in the restaurant. The bus attendant of today is often the server of tomorrow and the managers of the future.

Bussing is a very demanding job; it requires someone who can work quickly. The server's assistant or busser must be able to perform under pressure when the restaurant is extremely busy and fast-paced. The server's assistant or busser should be in excellent physical condition and should want to be of service to people. He or she should always be courteous and respectful to guests and other staff members.

Since the busser is an assistant to just about every employee in the restaurant, he or she may take orders from the servers, host or hostess, cooks, and management, as well as the guests. During rush periods this may become frustrating. In the restaurant business it seems that everything happens at once, and this is a time when teamwork is essential. Through training and experience the bus attendant will be able to learn the order in which to perform tasks, always doing things that directly affect the guest first, working with speed and efficiency.

The personal appearance of the server's assistant or busser is very important. Since the job puts the attendant in direct contact with guests, he or she must be neat, well groomed, and professional at all times. The same grooming standards that were discussed in Chapter 2 for servers apply to the server's assistant or busser.

Throughout the restaurant industry a common goal is to provide guests with quality food and good service, in a clean and sanitary environment. Therefore, the role of the server's assistant or busser is critical in providing good service and in working to maintain a clean and sanitary restaurant. The best habit that the server's assistant or busser can develop is to clean as he or she works. The key is not to wait until later to clean and straighten but to consistently do it as part of the work.

CUSTOMER COMPLAINTS—A UNIQUE OPPORTUNITY FOR THE SERVER

Stephanie A. Horton, CMP, a professional speaker/trainer/author in hospitality sales and service, and founder of Pacific Rim Protocol Server School in Seattle, Washington, offers the following advice to servers.

It is so easy to say, "turn lemons into lemonade" or "kill them with kindness." In this crazy business of hospitality, sometimes things go wrong. It is nobody's fault; there is just that moment when people, air, and food connect, then boom—something happens. Unfortunately, we cannot simply disappear (which seems like a pretty good idea sometimes)!

Your sense of humor is your finest attribute when an awkward situation looms. Remember, you can and you will get through it, because you are a hospitality professional. Then relax and enjoy the positive impression you have made! Now is the time to shine!

Listen to the parties involved, without interrupting. People need to "vent" when a situation occurs. Smile and focus entirely on the guest. Do not look around. Do not appear distracted. Empathize and acknowledge the complaint. Use words like, "I understand. You are absolutely right. Thank you for bringing this to my attention." Put yourself in their shoes. How would you react in the same situation?

Make sure your body language is "in sync" with what you are telling the guests—no crossed arms, sighing, shifting from foot to foot, or hands in pockets—all communicate negativism.

Do not argue. Whatever happens, resist the urge to defend yourself or the restaurant. The guest does not need to know how short on staff you are, or how the new oven just blew up. The guest is there for a relaxing, stress-free experience. All the guest cares about is what you are going to do about the problem!

Take action, fast! The guest needs to know that you can make something happen. Clarify with management in advance how much you are empowered to change. Can you bring a complimentary beverage or appetizer while the guests are waiting? If there is a breeze, perhaps a different table is in order, etc. Do something now! If you must get the manager—ask your team for help. Of course, jump in if one of your associates needs a hand. Once a problem has been solved, do not bring it up again or draw further attention to the situation. It is best forgotten!

Guests appreciate a server who takes action with a positive attitude. They are very understanding and forgiving, as long as their situation has become a priority. Take responsibility, and make something happen. You will be remembered for it!

The manager explains general housekeeping duties and assigns specific responsibilities to the server's assistant or busser for each meal period during the day. Bus attendants may keep service stands equipped and tidy, replenishing supplies and ice, rolls, coffee, and other items as needed so that servers can serve guests quickly. The server's assistant or busser works quietly, talking to others only when necessary and then in a low voice. This contributes to quiet and dignified service and in maintaining good guest relations.

As soon as guests leave, the tables must be cleared. During the meal hours other guests are often waiting for tables; they are hungry and sometimes impatient; therefore, the bus attendant needs to act immediately in clearing and preparing tables. This can be accomplished by bussing with a cart or tray.

Bussing with a Cart

Typically a bus cart is used in casual fast-paced restaurants. Using a cart to bus tables is the fastest, most efficient method of bussing. It is essential that the cart is clean, polished, and well stocked. It should have three or four shelves equipped with two clean tote boxes (bus tubs), with or without a flatware compartment, and two clean cloths, one dampened with a sanitizing solution and one dry. Some carts may also have a refuse bin attached. Refer to Figure 4–12 for an example of bussing carts.

The upper shelf of the cart may have a flatware bin (tub) filled with clean flatware. The top shelf may carry place mats and/or clean tablecloths and napkins.

Using a bussing cart allows the server's assistant or busser to clear and clean a table and then set it up immediately. To properly bus a table, the following procedures should be followed:

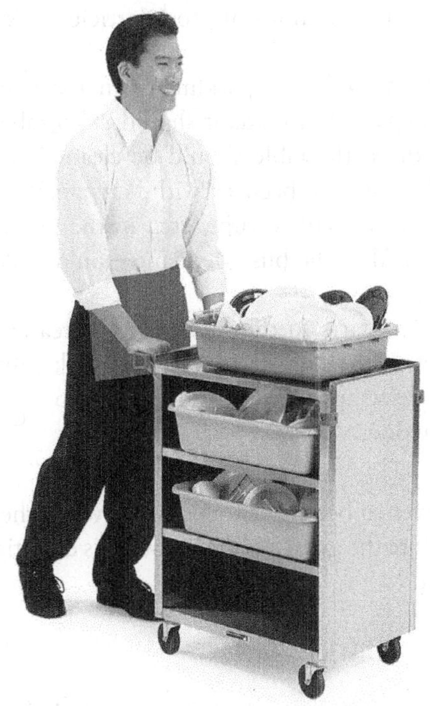

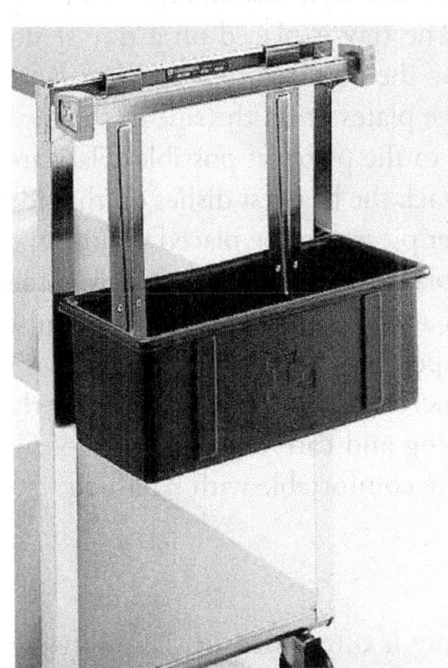

Figure 4–12
Bussing Carts. Courtesy of Lakeside™.

- Pick up all flatware by the handles first, and place in a separate container.
- Put all paper and waste in a separate section.
- Put all "like" items together (e.g., glasses with glasses).
- Do not touch parts of dishes or flatware that may have come in contact with the guest's mouth. Avoid exposure to possible germs by picking up cups by the handles, glasses at the bottom or by stems, and flatware by the handles.
- Soiled napkins and place mats are rolled up and placed on the cart.
- Place condiments such as Dijon, Worcestershire, or steak sauce on the bottom shelf of the cart.
- Wipe off table, chairs or booth, table condiments (ketchup and mustard), etc. Remove crumbs or food particles by sweeping them onto a plate or into a

napkin, not into the other hand. Do not allow crumbs or food particles to fall on the floor.

- Before leaving the table, check to see that the table has sparkling clean and filled salt and pepper shakers and sugar containers. Bus attendant should clean table, chairs, or booth if needed. The floor around the table should be cleaned and vacuumed if needed. Check to see that the table has been set with flatware, place mats, and/or clean tablecloths, napkins, glasses, coffee cups, etc., in the proper places according to the restaurant's policy. Also, the bus attendant should make sure the chairs are straight and in order.
- Server's assistant or busser should take bus carts to the dishwashing area and separate items in preparation for washing. The flatware goes in presoak tubs, glasses and cups go in racks, and dishes are scraped and placed together by size. Trash should be placed in the proper container.
- Work fast and efficiently.

Tables properly set up will enable the server to better serve the guests when they arrive. It is preferable to have the table set up before the guest sits down, but it is essential to have the table set up before the order is taken.

Bussing with a Tray

Using a tray to bus tables would be used in many different-style restaurants, including some fine-dining restaurants and banquet settings. The tray is placed on a tray stand next to the table to be bussed. The dishes are stacked on the tray according to size—large plates together, small plates and saucers on top of large plates or on the side of the tray, glasses and cups around the edge of the tray as close to the plates as possible. Flatware should be placed together along the side of the tray. Stack the heaviest dishes on the side of the tray that will be carried on the shoulder. Lighter pieces can be placed around the edge. Soiled napkins and place mats are rolled and placed on the tray, unless it is the policy of the restaurant to place napkins and place mats on a separate tray. Care must be taken not to accidentally wrap any flatware in paper or it will end up in the trash instead of the dishwashing machine. Follow the procedures listed above to properly bus a table. Then lift the tray according to the loading and carrying steps previously discussed, remembering never to lift more than you are comfortable with handling.

Setting Up with a Tray

Setting up can be done with a tray. A rectangular tray is often used in the following manner. A linen napkin can be unfolded on the tray to serve as a liner. Clean flatware (forks, knives, and spoons) is spread on the tray. Glasses and napkins are also included. This allows the server or server's assistant to quickly set up tables. All tables should be set up as soon as they are bussed.

Additional Server's Assistant's Responsibilities

The focus of the server's assistant or busser is to do his or her best to keep the restaurant in top operating condition. Some additional responsibilities are as follows (Note: Porters may also be employed to perform some of these tasks.):

- During meal periods keep an eye on the floor. Crumbs and food particles should be swept up immediately with a small mechanical sweeper. Napkins, flatware, a piece of food, or any litter should be picked up as soon as it is seen.

ng procedures should be smooth, effi- nient for the guest; never keep a guest ck.

sight of the fact that the customer is If customers are not happy and satisfied not return tomorrow. Even worse, they ersuade friends to stay away, too. One functions is to create and maintain the e guests. When a guest complains about server needs to understand the complaint take care of it immediately. Most com- e handled through the server or the man- a guest is dissatisfied, first and foremost o be heard. Good listening skills will help resolve the complaint in an effective and timely manner. Several of the most common difficult situations that might occur in a restaurant are discussed in the chapter along with solutions and corrective actions.

The server's assistant or busser has an important function in every restaurant. The most important duty is to please the guest. Nearly everything that a server's assistant does is aimed toward that goal either directly or indirectly. "Clean as you go" is one of the best habits that a server's assistant can develop, as this always contributes to a clean and efficient restaurant. The server's assistant or busser is responsible for bussing and setting tables, replenishing supplies at the server's stand, and performing other responsibilities as assigned by the restaurant manager.

DSSION QUESTIONS AND EXERCISES

No actual restaurant dining room setting or mock setould be used in order to allow the student to demate procedures, techniques, and functions that were ented in this chapter. Students can be asked to escr what they feel is excellent service.

xplain and demonstrate the general rules and techques of proper table service.

hen there is more than one woman or older guest sent at a table, whom would you serve first as a ter of traditional etiquette?

should children be treated when being served?

t should the server do if he or she continues to water spots on the flatware?

n the procedure to follow when serving guests th or next to a wall.

nd demonstrate the procedures for correct dling.

d demonstrate the correct way to hold dish.

demonstrate the correct way to hold erage glasses, wine glasses with stems, mugs with and without saucers.

cedure to follow when serving coffee or here guests are seated close together?

dure to follow when wine is being

11. What additional items are brought to the table when specialty foods such as lobster are served?
12. How is a finger bowl prepared for use, and when should it be used?
13. Explain the ways that crumbs and small food particles can be removed from a table.
14. Explain or demonstrate the correct way to load and carry a large oval tray.
15. Explain or demonstrate the correct way to load and carry a small rectangular tray.
16. Explain or demonstrate the correct way to load and carry a round beverage tray.
17. Explain the correct procedure for carrying multiple plates. Demonstrate the basic technique.
18. Identify and discuss six techniques that a server could develop to help improve serving priorities and timing.
19. Discuss how the following difficult situations could be handled:
    - Guest receives food not up to expectations.
    - Guest complains that food is cold or undercooked.
    - Guest says food is overcooked or burned.
    - Guest states that the portion size is too small.
    - Guest says that order is wrong.
    - Guest would like a baby bottle heated.
    - Guests allow their children to wander the floor.

- Spilled liquids should be cleaned up as soon as the spill occurs. If an area with a spill must briefly be left unattended, be sure that a chair or some other obstacle is placed over it so that no one will slip. Most spills can be soaked up quickly with a clean dry towel.
- All rugs and carpets should be vacuumed before and/or after meal periods, but never during a busy time. Vacuuming near guests should be avoided. The noise and activity can be irritating.
- Restrooms need to be checked periodically for cleanliness and supplies. Restrooms may need to be cleaned after every meal period, and soap, hand towels, and toilet paper replenished.
- Keep high chairs wiped clean with a safe sanitizing solution.
- The bus cart should be clean, orderly, and properly stocked with table setup supplies, such as forks, knives, spoons, napkins, place mats, etc., ready to go into use.
- Server stand trash must be emptied periodically and replaced with a new trash bag liner. The station must be well equipped with supplies, and replenished with ice, rolls, coffee, and other items as needed.
- Salt and pepper shakers, sugar bowls, and table condiments (ketchup and mustard) are checked and refilled as needed between meal periods.
- Some dining rooms have table candles that need to be lit before the dining room opens and checked throughout the evening.
- A salad bar or dessert table may need to be checked and refilled frequently.
- In addition to meal-period responsibilities, the manager will assign and schedule daily and weekly housekeeping and cleaning duties. Most of these assignments should be scheduled so that the entire restaurant receives a thorough cleaning once a week. This means washing windows and cleaning all the small cracks and crevices where soil and food particles can accumulate.

In carrying out responsibilities within the restaurant, the server's assistant or busser will often be dealing with guests. Server's assistants should be familiar with all menu items in case a guest asks a question. Courtesy is the key to good guest relations. If a guest requests some service from the server's assistant, such as a water refill, it is important that the server's assistant take care of it right away. If the request is for food or something that the server's assistant cannot deliver, the guest should be advised that the server will be informed without delay.

Restaurants have their own procedures for service but there are basic steps of service that can be applied to any style restaurant.

Basic Steps of Service

1. SIDE WORK
   - Follow side work instructions completely
   - Closely pay attention to the details in each task to allow for maximum readiness
   - Check all details on each table in the assigned station
2. CHECK WRITING or computer transmission (discussed in Chapter 8)
   - You must fill out the top of the check completely—date, table number, number of guests, and server name
   - Quantities are on the left
   - Seat numbers are on the right
3. BEVERAGE SERVICE—carried on a tray
   - Make eye contact when taking orders
   - Use protocol when taking orders, serving, and refilling.

- Beverage trays are held in the left hand
- Beverages are served with the right hand

4. TAKING THE ORDER
   - Make eye contact
   - Use protocol and etiquette
   - Follow the lead of the guest. Some guests want to order an appetizer while deciding on an entrée; others prefer to order all courses at one time.
5. ADJUSTMENT OF SILVERWARE
   - Adjust flatware after an order is taken
   - Check the status of silverware often
   - The guest should have the appropriate flatware before the food item is served
6. SERVE FIRST COURSE
   - Use etiquette and protocol
   - Serve from the right with the right hand
   - Quality-check with your guest by asking, "Are you enjoying your meal? Is everything OK?"
7. CLEAR FIRST COURSE
   - Ask the guest if they are finished before clearing their plate. Check to see if flatware is in the closed position.
   - Clear each guest using etiquette and protocol
   - Take out everything that is not needed
   - Think about your next move to serve an entrée
8. SERVING THE ENTRÉE
   - Use protocol and etiquette
   - Serve from the right with the right hand
   - Check back with your guest shortly after entrée is served. Ask them if they are enjoying their meal. Check-back should be within two minutes or two bites.
9. CLEARING THE ENTRÉE
   - Use protocol and etiquette
   - Clear the entrée plates, one person at a time.
   - Clear the bread basket and the salt and pepper shaker
   - Crumb the table
10. DESSERT SERVICE
    - Tell the guests about the dessert, present the menu or present the dessert cart
    - Offer coffee
    - Provide the appropriate flatware
    - Serve dessert
    - Present check then take payment
11. FAREWELL
    - Thank the guest for coming into the restaurant
    - Invite them back again
    - Bid them farewell

THE BARTENDER/SERVER

Many restaurants are experiencing an increase in the number of meals being served at their bars. A guest may be alone or with one or more friends that are drawn to the bar atmosphere for the possible view or just the "energy" of the bar itself. It may represent a faster service or simply an active setting that guests find enjoyable along with having the opportunity to, perhaps, share a brief conversation with the bartender. Some restaurants have guests that repeatedly sit at the bar for lunch or dinner because they find it to be a comfortable place. Guests enjoy the bar atmosphere many times because they are interested in sporting events which are on the bar's television. The bartender should know the restaurant's menu and be fully trained in basic service, including flatware placement, all types of beverage service, and dessert service.

Professor James Reid, Hospitality Management Program, New York City College of Technology, has worked many years in the hotel and restaurant industry, and has served as director of training and development for the New York Waldorf Astoria Hotel and general manager of food and beverage operations at the Sheraton Manhattan. He offers the following observations:

> Bartenders are most often excellent listeners and communicators with likable personalities. So it is not uncommon to see guests frequenting a bar for more than just an alcohol beverage. And with more restaurants currently making their complete menu available at the bar it is no surprise that this has become a growing area of business.
>
> The experienced bartender has the ability to connect with guests in a casual way that can foster the good feelings that are associated with a friendship. When that relationship is supported with outstanding customer service it becomes a winning formula for repeat business and generous tips. During the peak lunch and dinner time periods the seats at the bar can turn very quickly with guests that have the need for fast service. When this fast turnaround occurs and the bar operation is staffed with professional bartenders/servers and server's assistants/bussers, the tip income can be substantial.
>
> The hotel and restaurant operators that have identified this as a growing trend within their establishments are inviting bartenders to join their server-training programs to advance server skills at the bar. Bartenders also join in menu sampling/tasting sessions just as dining room servers join in wine sampling/tasting in order to become more knowledgeable to better serve their guests. It's all about superior guest service in the hotel, restaurant, and the bar.

SUMMARY

The general rules and techniques of proper table service are presented in 25 detailed procedures that apply to most restaurant operations. The correct methods of loading and carrying various trays are explained; every server should be competent in these methods.

The server needs to cultivate service priorities and timing that convey a sense of urgency in meeting the need of the guests. They must also follow what is called *protocol* of the restaurant which encompasses the procedures that work best in the style and layout of the restaurant. This is accomplished by developing techniques that include the

- Guest is very dissatisfied with food and does not want to wait for a replacement.
- Guest complains that food is undercooked and it is half eaten.
- Guests order together and then want to pay separately.
- Server forgot to turn in the guest's order to the kitchen.
- Guest is unhappy and has a bad opinion of the food and service.
- Guest is intoxicated.
- Too many guests are seated in a server's section.
- Guest leaves shopping bag or backpack in the aisle.
- Server spills food or drink on the clothing of a guest.
- Food is slow coming from the kitchen.
- Server is informed that the kitchen is out of the food item ordered.
- Foreign object is found in the food by guest.
- Guest complains about the food, having eaten most of it.
- Guests leave without paying.

20. Define some of the functions of a server's assistant.
21. How should a bussing cart be equipped?
22. List the procedures for properly bussing a table.
23. Explain how a server's assistant or busser would use a tray to bus a table.
24. How would a small rectangular tray be used in the process of setting up tables?
25. Identify seven server's assistant responsibilities.

5
Service Readiness

This chapter introduces the new server to service preparation techniques that will help in providing the best in guest service; for the experienced server, it will reaffirm the importance of service readiness.

The server has many duties and responsibilities; once having mastered them he or she can provide the ultimate in service. Many times the server is the only individual who comes in contact with the guest; therefore the guest expects the server to be fully knowledgeable about menu items and restaurant operations.

The server is responsible to ensure that everything needed to serve guests efficiently is done before the guests arrive and after the guests leave; this is commonly referred to as opening and closing *side-work*. Side-work is assigned to each server and should correspond to the station or tables that they will be serving during their shift. Opening side-work helps the servers prepare themselves for their shift. Closing side-work helps the restaurant prepare for the next shift.

In addition to side-work there are ongoing duties during service that helps the restaurant run smoothly. This includes a detailed organization of each station and work area so that the server is better organized and able to provide quick and efficient service.

The server's efficiency will be measured by the care he or she takes in performing those duties before guests arrive, during the meal service, and at the close of the server's shift. Additionally, *side-work* includes housekeeping chores that will ensure that every aspect of the restaurant is clean and spotless at all times; these can be done weekly or even monthly. It also includes a detailed organization of each station and work areas so that the server is better organized and able to provide quick and efficient service.

learning objectives

After reading this chapter and completing the discussion questions and exercises, you should be able to:

1. Explain how dining room stations are assigned.
2. Define zone coverage.
3. Define *mise en place* and know the responsibilities that accompany it.
4. Understand the importance of side-work.
5. Identify the items that are typically included on a service stand.
6. Define the basic steps and safety issues associated with closing procedures
7. Explain the visual elements of a successful menu.
8. Relate what the server needs to know in order to help guests make the best selection.
9. Identify the differences between a breakfast, lunch, and dinner menu.
10. Describe an à la carte menu.
11. Explain what a table d'hôte menu includes.
12. Recognize the importance of server knowledge in wine selections.
13. Describe the purpose of "menu meetings."
14. Discuss the things that a server should learn about a menu in order to answer a guest's questions.
15. Understand dining room do's and don'ts

RESPONSIBILITIES THAT SUPPORT GOOD SERVICE

The host, maître d', or manager divides the dining room into work areas known as stations. The stations may vary in actual number of tables but each usually has approximately the same number of seats. Most restaurants have a diagram of the dining room showing each station according to a number, such as #1, #2, #3, #4. A number is assigned to each table. A server is assigned to a station and is responsible for a list of opening side-work duties at that station to prepare for serving guests. The server must also maintain that station during the shift (the meal period) and be certain to follow the list of closing side-work duties at the end of the shift.

Many restaurants rotate station assignments on a regular basis, even daily. The typical restaurant may have certain areas that are more desirable because of a view or location within the restaurant. Therefore, the station will generate more activity due to guests' requests. Some stations may include booths or counters, or private dining areas that can seat groups up to 12 or

Figure 5–1
Service Stand. Gerald Lanuzza.

more at one table. New, contemporary-designed restaurants have often achieved ideal seating throughout the restaurant. For those guests who request the same server, seating is usually not a concern. New servers are often assigned to smaller stations or a station with less activity as they gain experience and confidence in handling larger numbers of guests and moving at a faster pace. Some restaurants have permanent station assignments for servers with seniority or for all servers based on good performance reviews.

As the dining traffic winds down, the number of servers on the floor is reduced. Terms used for this are *phasing* or *cutting* the floor. Zone coverage comes into play, as the remaining servers pick up tables in addition to their assigned station. In some instances, the manager will close areas of the dining room to seating and seat only in areas where there is a server available.

The French term *mise en place* is occasionally used in fine dining restaurants and means "put into place." It refers to the preparation steps from the kitchen to the dining room in terms of being prepared, with everything in place before service begins. Specifically, each server is responsible for his or her assigned station and should check it thoroughly with a visual inspection before guests are seated, during the shift, and at the end of the shift. Looking from top to bottom includes a quick glance up at the ceiling—a cobweb or birthday balloon may need to be removed; ledges may need to be dusted or a foreign object removed; light bulbs may need to be replaced. Shelves should be stocked with appropriate serving supplies; counter tops and tabletops should be immaculately clean with spotless table settings; table bottoms should be completely free of any gum or sticky substance; chairs, booths, booster chairs, and high chairs should be wiped clean and free of any crumbs, food particles, or grease. The floor should be swept or vacuumed and always safe, with nothing that a guest could slip on or trip over.

OPENING SIDE-WORK

The importance of opening side-work duties cannot be overemphasized. Many times up to half of a server's time will be spent on these items, which help to ensure better service for guests. This preparation always pays off during rush periods. It can

TABLE 5–1
OPENING SIDE-WORK

	M	T	W	TH	FR	SA	SU
STATION 1 Make coffee and tea (using diagram in pantry) Fill creamers and place in refrigerator Place 4 underliners next to coffee machine Stock all coffee cups, saucers, and spoons							
STATION 2 Restock all paper products Put ice in all bins Fill the pepper grinders Polish water glasses; leave in racks							
STATION 3 Organize the pantry (see diagram in pantry) Stock coffee and tea in drawers Cut 4 lemons (see diagram in pantry) Turn bread warmer on, then stock bread in warmer							
STATION 4 Polish flatware; fold napkins Clean and stock trays and tray jacks Fill sugar caddies, salt and pepper shakers, and stock condiments on shelf							

make the difference between efficient and inefficient service. Most restaurants have a checklist of side-work duties, as shown in Tables 5–1 and 5–2. It is important to recognize that most restaurants will have side-work duties that are somewhat standard within the industry, along with duties that are unique to the individual restaurant.

TABLE 5–2
CLOSING SIDE-WORK

	M	T	W	TH	FR	SA	SU
STATION 1 Return all coffee cups, creamers, and saucers from the dishroom Wipe all trays with sanitizer and stack to dry Wipe down shelves and drawers in beverage station. Remove glass mats and run through the dishwasher							
STATION 2 Clean coffee and tea machines Wipe walls and sweep floor in service station Clean coffee pots and tea pitchers							
STATION 3 Wipe the back of all chairs in the dining room Wipe the legs of all tables in the dining room Vacuum the dining room Stock all miscellaneous items							
STATION 4 Clean all high chairs and booster seats							

Servers must fully understand that side-work must be entirely completed in a timely manner. It is inappropriate for servers to complete side-work after the guests arrive. It is also unprofessional for a server to be catching up on side-work instead of giving the guests undivided attention. The sense of timeliness is a must for anyone who wants to be a successful server. A server should avoid the appearance of being rushed when guests are coming into the restaurant to dine. All side-work should be completed before the restaurant opens for business.

Each restaurant varies in what supplies are in inventory and what is kept at each service stand. Figure 5–1 shows an example of a typical service stand. The server should check that the correct items in the correct amounts are in a service station before the shift begins. If items are low or out they should quickly be replenished. Proper planning helps to eliminate wasted time in having to fetch items during rush periods. The work area should be arranged to allow for the maximum efficient service with the minimum amount of wasted time, energy, and effort. Everything should be easily accessible. This will reduce or eliminate the amount of unnecessary bending, reaching, twisting, and stretching. Utensils and supplies should always be kept in the same place at all times and returned to the appropriate place after each use. This allows the server to pick up items without deliberate thought or effort during rush periods, increasing efficiency and conserving time and energy. The service stand will typically include some or all of the following items:

Beverages: ice, water pitchers, glassware, straws, coffee, tea bags, teapots, cups, saucers, cream, half-and-half, sugar, honey, soft drinks, lemons, and limes.

Flatware: salad/dessert forks, dinner forks, knives, steak knives, teaspoons, soupspoons, iced tea spoons, serving spoons, ladles, tongs, and seafood (cocktail) forks.

Condiments: ketchup, mustard, Dijon, Worcestershire sauce, A-1 sauce, Tabasco sauce, salt, pepper, sugar, and sugar substitute.

Breakfast: jams, preserves, and syrups.

Bread, Butter, and Crackers: bread, rolls, crackers, bread and cracker baskets, bread plates, and butter pats.

Linens: tablecloths, place mats, napkins (linen or paper), beverage napkins, children's bibs, and bar towels.

Miscellaneous Items: pens, peppermills, corkscrew, bottle opener, food-to-go containers, and guest check trays or holders.

The functionality of side-work coincides with the nature of the shift. The tasks, while similar, can vary in details from shift to shift; for example, baskets for jams and preserves during the breakfast shift could be used for bread or rolls at lunch or dinner. Servers will be assigned specific tasks for each shift to make the transitions smooth and efficient. Each restaurant will have guidelines for side-work, with some more formal than others. Assignments might be delegated by station or by the sequence in which servers start or end their shifts. In the long run it takes organization and teamwork to get all the bases covered throughout the day's shifts.

Typical issues which may occur when *side-work* is not completed are as follows:

1. During the lunch rush on a hot day, the iced tea runs out because the opening side-work function of brewing a 4-gallon backup was not completed.
2. The guest wants A-1 steak sauce but it was not stocked in the service station the night before, so the server has to run to the storage room to get it and to bring out the correct number of backups.
3. The server is getting three waters for a table but the glass rack was left empty in the service station. The server responsible for ongoing side-work during the shift

is not paying attention to stock levels, not to mention whoever took the last glass and did not replace it with a full rack.

4. The guest tries to use the pepper mill but it is empty. The server from the preceding shift did not complete the side-work of refilling all the pepper mills.
5. A guest orders coffee but all the creamers are empty because the server responsible for filling 12 only filled 6.

CLOSING PROCEDURES

These procedures are basically the same as the *mise en place* steps described under the subject of dining room preparation, but somewhat in reverse. Ultimately the goal is to restock everything used and to clean the restaurant. Food and beverage products should be placed in their appropriate storage locations. Close attention should be paid to food storage safety. Primary attention should be given to securing the facility regarding safety issues: fire, water sources, security, and especially safe food storage. Again, these tasks would be assigned as described previously.

THE MENU

The menu is the focal point of a restaurant operation. It is the number one selling tool, and the first thing that a guest reads when determining what to order. Therefore, the menu should look attractive, use color appropriately, and reflect the quality and style of the restaurant. When a menu is professionally designed it can further support the restaurant's general appearance and ambiance, thus creating a positive first impression. It is important that the menu is easy to read and has clear descriptions of the menu items. When selecting a menu type-font the restaurant should consider the clarity and size of the font for easy readability. If a menu is soiled, frayed, bent at the edges, or poorly printed and hard to read, it can create a negative first impression. Therefore, the menu should always be prepared, designed, and printed in the best possible manner to achieve its intended objective; it should always be crisp and clean when presented to the guest. Before the meal shift begins a host or maître'd should look carefully through each menu and dispose of any menus that are unacceptable.

Common menu designs are bi-fold, tri-fold, or a one-page menu which always lays open in front of the guest. Each menu design has its advantages but all menus are a sales tool to entice guests to order. The most profitable menu items are placed on the menu where they will be noticed and ordered by guests. The guest's eyes naturally go to the top and bottom of menus and to the right of a bi-fold menu. Special items are often highlighted by the use of colorful, creative fonts or boxes so that they stand out and are recognized as special. The way prices are placed on a menu is also very important; for example, if prices are placed in a column it makes it easier for a guest to look for the least expensive item—although some menus have prices following the description of each of the menu items. A restaurant will choose a menu design which best suits its needs. Menus can be an expensive item for a restaurant to purchase so they must be carefully designed and well taken care of by the restaurant's associates.

Although management can produce an effective menu, the individual who really determines the effectiveness of the menu for the guest is the server. It is up to the server to see that the guest understands what is on the menu. The server should be able to answer any questions the guest may have about menu items. Many guests rely on the server to offer suggestions that will enhance the enjoyment of their meal. A server should be comfortable with this task since it is a sign of menu mastery and effective training. Using sales techniques to sell the menu is one of the most important tasks the professional server has.

The server needs to be very familiar with the menu in order to guide and help the guest in making a selection. The server needs to know important details about each and every item on the menu—for example, the method of preparation, the major ingredients, and when and if substitutions are allowed. Furthermore, the server should know how to pronounce all of the words on the menu and be able to interpret them for their guest. Many restaurants have menu-training programs to ensure that each server understands and is able to communicate the menu to the guests. Basic verbal and written tests are used to gauge the server's understanding of the menu. This is an excellent and affective training program for any style restaurant.

Breakfast Menu

Most restaurants have a separate breakfast menu, unless breakfast is listed and served 24 hours a day or all of the hours that the restaurant is open. Generally the menu consists of two sections. The first lists a combination of food items served at fixed prices, and the second lists items that may be ordered individually, as shown in Figure 5–2.

Lunch Menu

The lunch menu may have food categories such as appetizers, soups, salads, sandwiches, several complete entrées, desserts, and beverages. The menu selection typically includes several price levels, which are planned to cater to the wishes of different customer categories. Many restaurants feature special lunches, such as the business lunch, lunch special, chef's suggestions, manager's special, or *du jour* (of the day) menu. These items can be printed on a daily menu, restaurant reader board, or announced to guests when they are handed the menu by the host or server. It is important that the server practices good communication skills when reciting any special menu items. Figure 5–3 is an example of a typical lunch menu.

Dinner Menu

The dinner menu has an appetizer section and may list prices for complete dinners that include soup or salad and the entrée. There may be choices, of a starch, such as mashed, baked, French fried potatoes or rice, along with a choice of vegetables and possibly a selected seasonal vegetable offering. Also, the menu may have à la carte appetizers or add-ons that are individually priced, such as a signature soup or fresh sautéed mushrooms. Complete à la carte menus are becoming more popular; this type of menu allows the guest to order the exact side dishes that they like. The menu has a protein section, a starch section, and a vegetable section, from which a guest will select each item separately. Some guests may select one side, while some may select several. Some fine-dining restaurants offer a table d'hôte menu or chef's tasting menu that includes a complete meal from appetizer to dessert for a predetermined price (Figure 5–4). A restaurant may also offer early bird specials in the late afternoon, with menu entrées reduced in price or a few different entrées offered at a price lower than normal. A restaurant may also feature dinner specials that could include chef creations or the fresh fish catch of the day. The host or server normally announces these items when the menus are handed to the guests, or the items may be listed on a reader board. Figure 5–5 is an example of a dinner menu.

Wine List

Wine continues to grow in popularity and many restaurants have excellent selections of wine. Wine lists are typically organized several ways. A wine list can be organized according to the style of the wine, which means the wines are in categories such as red white, rose sparkling, dessert, and fortified. A wine list can be organized according to

Stone Cup Roasters Fair Trade Coffee

Plain'Ol Joe	$2.50	free refills
Espresso	single$1.75	double $2.25
Cappuccino	$3.95	16 oz.
Café Latte	$3.65	16 oz.
Café Mocha	$3.95	16 oz.
Espresso Con Panna	$2.75	
Macchiato	$2.25	
Shot in the Dark	$3.25	
Frappebeano ~ Blonde or Brunette		$4.50 (frozen drink)
Xtra Espresso Shot	.50¢	
Syrup Shots	.50¢ caramel • chocolate • vanilla • hazelnut • raspberry	

Sugar Free syrups available for all above flavors

Decaf available for all choices

Hot Tea (Honey and Soy Milk $.50 extra)

Organic Chai Latte - Caf or decaf	$3.95 16 oz. only
Tea Rex Jasmine Green Tea	cup $2.75
English Breakfast Tea	cup $2.75
MateVana (Herbal)	cup $2.75
Assorted Bija Decaf teas	cup $2.75

Soda/Tea $2.00 (free refills)

Coke • Diet Coke • Sprite • Gingerale • Soda Water
Mello Yello • Barq's Root Beer • Pink Lemonade
Organic Passion Fruit Iced Tea • Zada Jane's Classic Southern Sweet Tea

Juices $2.25 small $3.25 large

Organic Orange Juice • Organic Apple • Grapefruit
• Organic Cranberry • Pineapple • Tomato • V8

Grandma Zada's "TLC" Biscuits or Fresh Bread Breakfast Sandwiches

One Big'Ol Fluffy TLC Biscuit	95¢
plus choice of Cheese	$1.45
plus one Happy Egg	$1.95
plus one Happy Egg and cheese	$2.45
plus one Protein and Cheese	$3.50
plus one Protein, one Egg, and choice of Cheese	$3.95
with Herb Gravy	$2.25
with Herb Gravy plus Sausage or Soysage	$3.95

Now featuring

Delicious and Local Grateful Growers Pork Products for an additional $1.50

Figure 5–2
Breakfast Menu. Courtesy of Zada Janes.

Breakfast Time Plates

The Zada Janer 28205 Basic Breakfast $6.95
two Free Range happy eggs any style with choice of one protein, and one carb, plus toast or TLC biscuit

Grande Quande $8.95
basic breakfast plus one big fluffy pancake

Booker T.'s East Side Hasher...................................... $7.95
a bed of sweet potato hash browns topped with two Happy Eggs frittata style with your choice of local Grateful Growers pork sausage, turkey sausage, or soysage, then covered with melted cheddar cheese and green onions - choice of toast or TLC biscuit

Bunny Rancheros $8.95
two of your choice happy eggs atop black beans, home fries, your choice of: chorizo, turkey sausage, local Grateful Growers pork sausage, or soysage, or Chipotle chicken topped with a pepper jack cheese queso sauce, guacamole, salsa verde and sour cream - served with warm flour tortillas

Pinckney Street Pancakes $7.25
three big and fluffy buttermilk pancakes served with honey butter and syrup, plus choice of one morning side (gluten-free pancakes available upon request...add $2.00)

Michael T.'s Amaretto French Toast $7.95
two thick and hearty fresh challah slices dipped in vanilla and amaretto batter, served with orange butter and toasted almonds plus choice of one mornin' side

Another Green World Breakfast Salad $7.95
relax and start the day with a green mind - organic field greens tossed with our sun dried tomato vinaigrette, (on the side) topped with applewood smoked bacon or marinated tofu, plus Herb's roasted potatoes, tomatoes, and one happy egg over easy - served with toast or TLC biscuit

The East-Western $7.25
organic tofu seasoned with yellow Indian curry and scrambled with sauteed mushrooms, green peas, fresh spinach, tomato and carmelized onion - served with toast or TLC biscuit

** Local Grateful Growers pork sausage for an additional $1.00*

** To help us better serve you. Please note 18% Gratuity for 6 or more. No separate checks*
** Please be considerate of people waiting during our busy hours on Saturday and Sunday*

Thank you

Figure 5–2 (continued)

the region or place that the wine comes from—for example, Champagne, Bordeaux, Burgundy, Alsace, and Rhone Valley; another way is to list based on the place of origin—France, Germany, Italy, the United States, or New Zealand. A wine list could be organized by how it tastes; a younger market will embrace and understand and appreciate this organizational method. The wine list will describe the flavor of the wine, such as dry, fruity, full-bodied, light, heavy, or smooth. Some restaurants will employ a sommelier whose responsibilities include dealing with all aspects of wine and the wine list. The sommelier would be responsible both before and during service for the wine and wine list. Before service the sommelier would select the wines for the list, order the wines, inventory the wines, and educate the servers on the wine list. During service the sommelier would help the guests select the appropriate wine for their meal. The wine list may also include a list of domestic and imported beers. The host or server will present the wine list to the guest along with the menu. The server should be knowledgeable about the wines and be able to suggest appropriate wines (or beers) to accompany the guest's meal, as discussed in Chapter 6, Wine and Beverage Service.

Dessert Menu

The dessert menu is typically presented in a way that is very enticing to guests. The description of each dessert item can tell a tale of great delight, and may include photos of the items as they look when served. The menu may be separate or part of a lunch and dinner menu as shown in Figure 5–6.

THE GUEST AND THE MENU

Guests naturally feel that the server should be able to answer their questions about the menu, such as, "What are the ingredients in a certain menu item or entrée? What does it include? How is it cooked and plated and how long will it take to prepare?" A guest may even ask how to pronounce the name of a menu item or sauce if the menu uses unfamiliar vocabulary. Therefore, the server is expected to have a comprehensive knowledge of the restaurant's menu, being able to answer questions and offer suggestions. Appendix A, Common Menu Terms, lists many of the most commonly used terms to describe menu items and cooking procedures.

When new menu items and/or terms are introduced, the server should be eager to learn about them. The restaurant owner or manager should also schedule time for "menu meetings," informing the servers about the new items, and the daily specials that may be offered. These meetings usually take place 15–30 minutes before the meal period. This is a good time to allow the servers to taste any new menu items or the special of the day. This is an opportunity to have the kitchen and service staff communicate with each other and to discuss each other's needs. This is an important training tool which will give each server a personal reference for the restaurant's menu items, thereby making them an informed and enthusiastic salesperson.

If a guest wants only a light meal, the server should know the menu well enough to suggest an appropriate item. The same is true for guests who say they are very hungry and want a full-course dinner. Also, if the guest is in a hurry, the server should be able to suggest an item that will not take much time to prepare, which means that the server should know how much time it takes to prepare each item on the menu.

There are special types of menus that restaurants may choose to offer. A restaurant may want to participate in programs that identify the healthy choices on its menu. These programs list nutritional values, and grams of fat and sugar. There has been an interest by many restaurants to have smaller portions and healthier food items in response to guests' requests. In recent years there has been concern about large portions and unhealthy fats such as trans-fat.

LUNCH MENU

STARTERS

Pimento Cheese Dip with Kettle Chips $4.25

Traditional Hummus garnished with a Tomato & Cucumber Salad served with Grilled Pita $5.25

Soul Rolls – Collard Greens & Smoked Turkey Spring Rolls served with Chili Sauce $6.25

SALAD BOWLS

Savor Salad- Mixed Greens, Tomatoes, Cucumbers, Shredded Carrots & Chick Peas $5.50

Wedge Salad with Iceberg Lettuce, Candied Pecans, Bacon & Bleu Cheese Crumbles $7

Mediterranean Salad –Mixed Greens, Tomatoes, Cucumbers, Artichoke Hearts, Kalamata Olives, Feta Cheese & Croutons Served with Greek Dressing $8

Cobb Salad-Mixed Greens, Avocado, Bleu Cheese, Turkey, Eggs, Bacon &Tomatoes $8.50

House made Dressings

Balsamic Vinaigrette, Ranch, Bleu Cheese, Basil Vinaigrette, Greek & Honey Dijon Vinaigrette

Add: Scoop chicken salad $ 2 Seasoned Sliced Chicken Breast $3 Pan Seared Salmon $5

THE BURGER

8 ounce Ground Sirloin Burgers or 8ounce Ground Turkey Burger Served on a Kaiser Roll $7.50

Build Your Own:

Apple Wood Smoked Bacon, Caramelized Onions, Sautéed Mushrooms, Pimento Cheese add $1

Bleu Cheese, Cheddar or Swiss add $.50

Adam Bomb Burger – Cajun Rubbed, Grilled Tomatoes, Pepper Jack Cheese, Smeared with a Roasted Red Pepper& Caramelized Onion Aioli $9

SANDWICHES – Served with 1 Side and a Dill Pickle Spear

Grilled cheesy pimento on white or wheat $5.50

Farmers Market- fresh mozzarella, tomato & basil drizzled with balsamic reduction on focaccia$7.50

Veggie Voodoo – Grilled Portobello, Squash, and Zucchini with Tomato, Pesto & Pepper Jack on a baguette $8

So Club- turkey, ham, bacon, lettuce & tomato on white or wheat $8.50

Mojo Marinated Chicken Breast Sandwich with Avocado Spread on a Sesame Bun $8.50

Pesto Chicken Salad with grapes and toasted pecans on Multi-Grain Roll $8.50

Pulled BBQ Chicken Sandwich with Cole Slaw on a Onion Bun $9.00

Cuban – Roasted Pork, Smoked Ham, Swiss, Pickles & Dijon Mustard on Cuban Bread $9.00

Seared & crack peppered Salmon B.L.T. on Focaccia $10.50

ENTREES

Grilled Meat Loaf with a Tangy Pepper Relish served with Two Sides $9.00

Sweet Chili Glazed 6 ounce Salmon Filet served with Two Sides $11.50

Carolina Shrimp & Andouille Sausage Gravy over Yellow Stone-Ground Grits $12.50

Check with server for today's blue plate specials & house made desserts

Casserole of the Day Small Savor Salad Black-Eyed Pea Salad

Kettle Chips Seasonal Fruit Salad Cole Slaw

For parties of 8 or more an18% Gratuity will be added

Sales tax is included in all prices

Please advise server of food allergies or diet restrictions, we will make every attempt to accommodate.

Figure 5–3

Lunch Menu. Courtesy of Savor Cafe and Catering.

entree

Roasted Langdon Farms Veal and Morel Mushroom Reduction 28
with morel mushrooms, mascarpone polenta and saffron carrots

Grilled King Mackerel Steak 24
with young asparagus and chile-rubbed sweet potato chips

Garden Mountain Farms New Lamb Fillet and Mint Infusion 34
with baby summer vegetables, jersey royal potatoes and girolle mushrooms

Rainbow Meadows Farm Duck Medallions 26
with baked figs and truffled mashed potatoes

Pan Seared Diver Scallop 20
with melted leeks and fennel, roasted chile potatoes and orange buerre noisette

Coastal Striped Bass Meuniere 24
with haricot verts, truffled potato croquette and saffron mornay sauce

Langdon Farms Certified Angus Fillet Rossini 30
with potato-leek gnocchi and truffled foie gras demi-glace reduction

Maple Brined Rainbow Meadows Farms Quail 20
with baby carrots, minted jasmine rice and curried pear chutney

Rainbow Meadows Farm Rabbit Saddle Roulade 26
with spinach mousse, pappardelle pasta and wild mushroom jus

Fairfax/Lewis Farm Center Cut Pork Chop 26
with garlic penne pasta, sautéed spinach and balsamic-onion marmalade

Spicy Red Snapper Fillet en Papillote 22
with onions, garlic, habanero peppers and sweet potato frites

Molasses Glazed Pork Loin 24
with steel-cut oat risotto with baby peas and Pecorino cheese

Fairfax/Lewis Farm Paprika-Garlic Roasted Chicken Quarter 22
with caramelized broccoli and wild mushroom pilaf

The Bridge Tender signature

Hickory Smoked Fairfax/Lewis Farm Chicken Quarter
with jicama slaw, golden raisin and carrot quinoa and apple-cider aioli

26 per guest

The Bridge Tender tasting menu

An exclusive four course offering thoughtfully designed by our Executive Chef to provide the ultimate dining experience. Paired with a glass of 2006 Baglio di Pianetto Piana del Ginolfo Viognier.

Sweet Potato Beignet
golden-brown and slightly sweet beignet with Indigo Farms sweet potatoes and sheep's milk Ricotta cheese

Haricot Vert, Petite Artichoke and Wild Mushroom Salad
extra-fine haricot verts, baby artichokes, wild mushrooms and shallots garnished with chervil and artichoke crisps and dressed with an aged balsamic vinaigrette

Butter Poached Lobster with Crispy North Carolina Soft Shell Blue Crab
gently poached Maine lobster tail accompanied by a fried North Carolina soft shell blue crab and served with saffron new potatoes, broccoli rabe and buerre blanc

Espresso Panna Cotta
silky vanilla espresso panna cotta with Berry Tyme raspberries

75 per guest

Figure 5–4
Dinner Menu with Menu Tasting. Courtesy of the Bridge Tender.

Appetizers

Fresh Oysters on the Half Shell
Six oysters shucked to order. Ask your wait person for species. Market Price/Availability

Fresh Northwest Oyster Shooters $1.25/each

Fresh Manilla Steamer Clams
Steamed in garlic, butter and white wine. Market Price/Availability

Razor Clams
Lightly breaded and grilled, fresh in season. $6.95

Fried Calamari
Calamari rings and tentacles flash fried and tossed in a lemon butter sauce. $7.95

Cajun Popcorn
Bay shrimp in a cajun breading, served with cocktail sauce and a lemon wedge. $6.95

Fresh Salmon Nuggets
Fresh salmon fried golden brown in dill tempura. $5.95

Escargot
Sauteed in garlic, white wine and butter. Served with dipping croutons. $7.95

Shrimp Cocktail
Bay shrimp served with cocktail sauce and a lemon wedge. $6.95

Crab Cocktail
Dungeness crab served with cocktail sauce and a lemon wedge. Market Price/Availability

Fresh Stuffed Mushrooms
Mushroom caps with bay shrimp, baked with sherry and cheese, topped with fresh scallions. $6.95

Fresh Sauteed Mushrooms
Whole button mushrooms sauteed in madeira wine, garlic and butter. $5.95

Fresh Cut Vegetable Crudite
With dipping sauce. $4.95

Baked Brie with Roasted Garlic
Served with dipping croutons. $5.95
With pesto 6.95
With bay shrimp 8.95
With dungeness crab 10.95

Conch (konk)
Pounded thin like abalone, lightly breaded and grilled. $7.95

Steak, Veal, Chicken & Pasta

6 oz. Filet Mignon
Choice cut 6 oz. steak char-broiled to your taste and served with madeira mushrooms and bernaise sauce. $16.95
- With sauteed prawns $21.95
- With grilled razor clam $18.95
- With pan fried oysters $18.95

10 oz. Choice New York Steak
Center cut steak char-broiled to your taste. $17.95

One Pound Porterhouse
Pressed with green and black peppercorns, char-broiled to your taste, and topped with whiskey mustard sauce. $19.95

Veal Tenderloin
Lightly breaded then seared and topped with madeira mushrooms, dungeness crab, and hollandaise sauce. $17.95

Rack of New Zealand Lamb
Char-broiled to your taste. $19.95

Boneless Pork Loin
Oven roasted with rosemary and juniper, sliced and served with black currant sauce. $14.95

Chicken Breast
Boneless and skinless chicken breast char-broiled, or ask your server for our nightly chicken special. $12.95

Seafood Fettuccine
Bay shrimp, dungeness crab, sea scallops, and fresh fish in white sauce. $15.95

Fettuccine Alfredo
Fettuccine alfredo-style or tossed with olive oil, garlic & parsley. $10.95

Vegetable Fettuccine
Fresh seasonal sauteed vegetables served in alfredo sauce or tossed with olive oil, garlic & parsley. $12.95

Vegetarian Platter
Fresh steamed seasonal vegetables, parmesan baked tomato, dill tempura onion rings & artichoke hearts with house potato or rice pilaf. $13.95

Desserts

We feature fresh homemade desserts.

Selected Child's Portions $8.95 • Corkage Fee $7.00 • Split Dinner Charge $5.00
To serve you better, one check will be written for parties of 7 or more.

Child's Price | Corkage Fee | Split Dinner

Figure 5–5
Dinner Menu. Courtesy of Deschuter River Trout House Restaurant.

See our reader board for tonight's special selections.

All entrees served with your choice of homemade Soup or House Salad, Chef's Vegetable, and our fresh baked bread.

Choice of Rice or Potato of the Day (except pasta dishes).

Add-ons → *Add shrimp for 2.50 or crab for 3.50 to your House Salad.*

When we advertise "fresh fish," it is fresh fish!

Signature Dinners

Dan's New York Steak, 10 oz. Center cut choice New York steak stuffed with dungeness crab, char-broiled, and topped with madeira mushrooms, and bernaise sauce.	$20.95
Mixed Grill Venison, lamb rack, prawn saute, and razor clam with whiskey mustard sauce.	$22.95
Fresh Blackened Salmon Fresh salmon filet with blackening spices pan seared, then baked and served with a tequila-lime-sour cream sauce.	$16.95
Fresh Stuffed Northwest Rainbow Trout Rainbow trout stuffed with bay shrimp and dungeness crab, then baked.	$16.95
Fisherman's Stew Prawn, scallop, fresh fish, clams, mussels, dungeness crab, and bay shrimp served in a rich tomato broth.	$19.95
New Zealand Venison & Prawns Medallions of venison and prawns sauteed with whiskey mustard sauce.	$20.95
Tournedos of Beef with Prawns & Artichoke Two petite cuts of filet mignon char-broiled to your taste and topped with artichoke bottoms, prawns, and bernaise sauce.	$21.95

Fresh Seafood & Shellfish

Fresh Salmon Filet Your choice of char-broiled, grilled, poached, or baked.	$15.95
Fresh Baked Stuffed Salmon Salmon filet stuffed with bay shrimp and topped with a rosette of red wine butter.	$17.95
Halibut Your choice of char-broiled, grilled, poached, or baked. Fresh "in season".	$15.95
Fresh Grilled Northwest Rainbow Trout	$12.95
Fresh Northwest Cod or Red Snapper Poached, baked or lightly breaded and grilled.	$13.95
Fresh Northwest Sole Lightly breaded and grilled or baked. Market availability.	$14.95
Prawns, Scampi Style Sauteed with white wine, lemon juice, garlic, capers and butter.	$17.95
Fresh East Coast Sea Scallops Baked in a mornay sauce.	$15.95
Prawn and/or Scallop Saute Sauteed with garlic, white wine and finished with a creamy lemon-butter sauce.	$16.95
Fresh Northwest Oysters Lightly breaded and pan fried.	$12.95
Fresh Manilla Steamer Clams Steamed in garlic, butter, and white wine.	Market Price/Availability
Razor Clams Lightly breaded and grilled. Fresh "in season".	$15.95
Seafood Combination Plate Fresh pan fried oysters, grilled razor clam, and prawn saute.	$16.95
Conch (konk) Pounded thin like abalone, lightly breaded and grilled.	$14.95
Lobster Tail Baked with white wine and butter.	Market Price/Availability
Fried Calamari Calamari rings and tentacles flash fried and tossed in a lemon butter sauce.	$14.95
Shrimp Louie Chef's selection	$13.95
Crab Louie Chef's selection	Market Price/Availability

All fresh seafoods are susceptible to market availability and price.

Figure 5–5 (continued)

In addition to healthy menus there may be a separate children's menu. If there are children seated at their table a server should inquire if the guest would like to see the children's menu. A children's menu will have food items that appeal to kids. They are items that may also have quick preparation times so that small children can be served first. In addition, a restaurant may have selected child's portions from the regular menu at a special price. If a child orders an expensive item from the regular menu, the server should get a parent's approval by asking if this is all right. Parents usually appreciate this. If it is not all right, the server should be prepared to quickly suggest another item or two from which the child can choose.

There has been an increase in allergies; guests will ask servers many questions about ingredients to avoid an allergic reaction. Some of the most common allergies

Chocolate Hazelnut Terrine
orange puree, chocolate cake powder, hazelnut praline ice cream 12

Italian Zeppoli Doughnuts
lemon curd 9

Granny Smith Apple Bread Pudding
roasted vanilla scented apples, butterscotch ice cream 9

Pineapple Sorbet
pineapple puree, tuile cookie 10

Dark Chocolate Ice Cream
chocolate sauce, almond sugar cookie 10

Artisan Cheese Plate
humboldt fog goat, brillat-savarin triple cream
point reyes blues 10

please allow 8-12 minutes on baked items

Pastry Chef / April Harris

Figure 5–6
Dessert Menu. Courtesy of Artisanal.

are seafood, dairy, nuts, and flour. These ingredients are widely used in many menu items. A server should be aware of these ingredients and should always check with the kitchen to make sure that the ingredients are not present in a guest's food. It is easy to make some adjustment to accommodate the guest. When transmitting a check to the kitchen make it clear that the guest has an allergy to a specific item. It is always a good idea to double-check with the kitchen to make sure they leave off that ingredient. When serving the guest their meal, repeat to them that the ingredient has been left out of their food. For example, if the guest is allergic to dairy you can say, "Club sandwich no cheese." This was an easy accommodation that will help illustrate good customer service. It is important to have an allergy statement on a restaurant menu. A common restaurant allergy statement would be, "We will try and accommodate allergy needs, please inform your server if you have an allergy need." A menu may also have a statement about undercooked or raw foods: "Consuming raw or undercooked meat or seafood may be hazardous to your health."

Some menus may include a short history of the restaurant, the chef's background, the origin of some of the house specialties, historic sites, and information about the community that may be of interest to tourists, and perhaps a list of nearby recreational areas or activities. The server should be able to answer any questions that a guest may have about such things. Some local and regional tourist associations offer complimentary maps for restaurants to give guests. This allows a server to offer additional service and help.

If a server cannot adequately answer a guest's questions about the menu, it weakens the guest's confidence in the server and reduces the opportunity for the server to suggestively sell other menu items, such as wines, appetizers, salads, and desserts. The server may be reduced in the guest's mind to just an order taker. Therefore, the opportunity to increase guest sales and tips is lost. Some questions that a server may need to be prepared to answer are as follows:

"How is the pork tenderloin prepared?"
"What does the balsamic basil dressing taste like?"
"What is in the Satay sauce?"
"Can I substitute onion rings for French fries?"
"What is the difference between a New York Steak and a rib eye?"
"What is in the béarnaise sauce?"
"What are capers?"
"How do you pronounce 'gazpacho'?"
"What type of oil do you use for frying?"
"Flan sounds good, what is it?"
"Do you have a vegetarian entrée alternative on your menu?"
"How long will it take for the rack of lamb to cook?"

THE SERVER AND THE MENU

The guest assumes the server knows everything about the menu. Therefore, the server should take the initiative to master the menu in order to be prepared to answer questions and give explanations. Here are some tactical points to consider when learning a menu. Refer to the dinner menu in Figure 5–4 and Figure 5–5.

1. Learn the menu by categories. That is, know where the signature (house specialty) items, appetizers, salads, sandwiches, entrées, features, à la carte items, beverages, and desserts are located on the menu. As you respond to a menu item question, point to the specific item on the menu. As you read, the guest will "read along," following your finger as it moves across the menu description. Reading the menu description eliminates the potential of describing the item incorrectly, and through repetition, the server gradually gains a confident and comprehensive knowledge of the menu.
2. Learn what items include soup and/or salad and the cost of the add-on items, such as adding shrimp or chicken to the house salad that may be included with a dinner entrée. Know the add-on (additional) charge for items.
3. Learn what (if any) beverages have complimentary refills, such as soft drinks or iced tea. Also, there may be a corkage fee when a guest brings in a special bottle of wine or champagne to be served with dinner.
4. Learn cooking and preparation times. Since each item on the menu takes a different amount of time to cook, it is important to keep guests informed. An easy tip to remember is that items such as thick meats require lower heat and a longer

time to cook than pasta items, for example. Also, the degree of doneness of meats can change the cooking times, such as a steak cooked rare in 10 minutes or well done in 20 minutes. A server can quickly learn the cooking and preparation times through experience with the kitchen.

5. Learn that sandwiches and hamburgers often automatically include some or all of the following ingredients: lettuce, tomato, onion, mayonnaise, pickles, and mustard. Many people do not like some of these ingredients and become irritated when they find them on their sandwiches. Therefore, identify when and if these ingredients are automatically included with sandwiches and hamburgers. If they are, mention it to the guest at the time the order is placed. The guest may choose not to have some of these ingredients or may prefer to have them served separately.
6. Learn the ingredients of sauces and be able to describe their flavors. If a guest seems unsure about a sauce, offer to have the kitchen put it in a cup to be served on the side.
7. Learn the restaurant standard for the varying degrees of doneness in meat. Then be able to describe the degrees of doneness by color, such as the following:
   Rare—brown, seared crust with cool red center.
   Medium Rare—brown, seared crust, warmed through with a red, warm center.
   Medium—outside well done, dark brown with reddish pink hot center.
   Medium Well—outside dark brown, inside cooked through with little juice left.
   Well Done—outside black-brown and inside brown throughout with no pink.
8. Learn the portion sizes of menu items; for example, three large pancakes as big as the breakfast plate, shrimp cocktail served with five jumbo shrimp, broiled lamb chops with a serving of three 4-ounce lamb chops, or a hot fudge sundae with two large scoops of vanilla ice cream. A guest who expects a different portion size may be either disappointed or overwhelmed. Therefore, you should be prepared to describe the portion size when asked by the guest or when you anticipate the need to do so. For example, you should know that a full-size sub sandwich is 12 inches long. If a guest states that he or she is full from dinner but can't pass up that hot fudge sundae, it may be appropriate to describe its size, two large scoops of vanilla ice cream. You do not want the guest complaining, "Why didn't you tell me it was so big?"
9. Learn what appetizers and entrées can be split for guests. Also, inform the guest if there is an additional plate charge when providing this service. An example might be when two guests are splitting an entrée, such as a 10-ounce halibut steak, and they prefer not to split the baked potato, but request an additional potato. An additional charge of $5 may be appropriate.
10. Learn the restaurant's policy and pricing for extra portions and substitutions. It is not uncommon for guests to request extra portions, such as double the cheese on a cheeseburger, or to ask for a substitute, such as cottage cheese for French fries. When this occurs, the extra charge for the double portion of cheese may be $1. The restaurant may have limits as to what will be allowed when substituting, and may not allow onion rings to be substituted for French fries. Therefore, the restaurant should identify the most commonly asked questions regarding extra portions and substitutions and have a clear policy for servers to follow. When a guest makes an out-of-the-ordinary request, you should make every effort to accommodate the guest, but you should first ask the manager for a decision.
11. Learn where to access information for recipe ingredients and cooking methods. Guests with dietary restrictions will expect the server to be able to answer their questions. They may have concerns about oils, butter, fats, sugars, dairy, and low-calorie ingredients, as well as foods that may be fried, grilled, or sautéed. Also, people on

vegetarian diets will be very specific about not wanting any food item that contains animal or animal by-product. Ask the owner or manager where this information is available. Some restaurants may have it implemented into a point-of-sale (POS) system as product management software, as discussed in Chapter 8. At the touch of a button, you would find a list of recipe ingredients, cooking methods, and nutritional information, in addition to other related information, which could be printed on the POS printer and given to the guest. There are various types of recipe management software that can also generate the same information. A restaurant that does not have the technological advantage will have to rely upon the cooks and chef to be able to answer recipe-ingredient questions.

12. Learn the restaurant's cooking methods for various menu items, as guests will expect you to be able to describe those methods. The following is a list of common cooking methods:

    Baked—food is cooked in an oven with dry heat.

    Boiled—food is cooked in boiling water.

    Braised—a combination of dry and moist heat; usually cooking meat in a small amount of liquid in a covered pan, allowing the meat to cook in the moisture created from its own juices.

    Broiled—quick cooking by direct flame or heat. (Note: *Pan broiling* is cooking in a hot frying pan or on a griddle without the addition of fat.)

    Fried—food is cooked in hot oil or fat. Food is *deep fat fried* when it is placed or immersed in oil or fat at a sufficiently high temperature to brown the surface and cook the interior of the food. *Pan frying* or *sautéing* is done with a small amount of hot oil or fat in a pan, to which the food item is added.

    Grilled—food is cooked with oil or fat on a griddle, or cooked over hot coals (*charcoal grilled*).

    Poached—food is covered in water or other liquid and simmered.

    Roasted—food is cooked in an uncovered pan without moisture in an oven using only dry heat (similar to baking).

    Sautéed—a food item is browned and cooked in a small amount of hot oil or fat in a pan.

    Simmered—food is immersed in a liquid and slowly cooked over low heat.

    Steamed—food is cooked in steam.

13. Learn the definitions of the menu terms that name or describe food items and cooking procedures. Also, the pronunciation of the terms should be correct and adds flair to the merchandising description. Refer to Appendix A, Common Menu Terms.

SUMMARY

The server has responsibilities that support good service. The server is responsible for a list of opening duties at his or her assigned station to prepare for serving guests. The server must also maintain that station during the shift and be certain to follow the list of closing duties at the end of the shift. These duties are commonly known as side-work. The side-work includes housekeeping chores to ensure that every aspect of the restaurant is clean and spotless at all times. Each restaurant differs in what is kept at each server station, but the server should be certain that the correct items in the correct amounts are there before the shift begins, and again at the end of the shift.

The menu is the focal point of a restaurant operation. It should be well designed and project the image of the restaurant. The server needs to be totally familiar with each item on the menu, so that he or she can answer questions the guests may have regarding the ingredients, preparation, cooking time, and pronunciation of a menu item or a sauce.

Generally there is a different menu for every meal, such as breakfast, lunch, and dinner, along with a wine list. Menus are priced à la carte, with a separate price for each separate item and also as full dinners, which usually include a soup or salad and the entrée. A table d'hôte menu includes a complete meal, from appetizer to dessert, for a fixed price.

The server can quickly learn a menu by remaining alert, attentive, and focused upon the following: Learning the menu by categories, that is, signature (house specialty) items, appetizers, salads, sandwiches, entrées, features, à la carte items, beverages, and desserts; learning what items include soup and salad, and the cost of add-ons; learning what (if any) beverages have complimentary refills; learning cooking and preparation times; learning the ingredients that automatically come with sandwiches and hamburgers; learning the ingredients of sauces and being able to describe their flavors; learning the restaurant standard for the varying degrees of doneness in meat; learning the portion sizes of menu items; learning what appetizers and entrées could be split for guests; learning the restaurant's policy and pricing for extra portions and substitutions; learning where to access information for recipe ingredients and cooking methods; learning the restaurant's cooking methods; and learning the definitions of the menu terms that name or describe food items and cooking procedures.

DISCUSSION QUESTIONS AND EXERCISES

1. When a host, maître d', or manager divides a dining room into work areas, what are those areas known as?
2. Explain zone coverage.
3. What does the French term *mise en place* mean and what does it specifically refer to?
4. Explain the importance of side-work.
5. How should a service stand work area be arranged?
6. List five different categories of items that a service stand typically includes and give examples within each category.
7. Give two examples of what can happen when side-work is not done.
8. What is the goal of an effective closing procedure?
9. What are the visual elements of a successful menu?
10. What should the server know about the menu in order to help guests make the best selection?
11. Why is the placement of items on a menu important?
12. Describe the differences between an à la carte menu and prix fixe menu.
13. Why would a server need to know anything about wines?
14. List five things that a guest could possibly ask the server about the menu.
15. What would be discussed at a menu meeting?
16. If a child orders an expensive item from the normal menu, how should the server react?
17. What happens when a server cannot adequately answer a guest's questions about the menu?
18. List 10 things that a server should learn about a menu in being prepared to answer a guest's questions.

6

Wine and Beverage Service

Beverage service is an important aspect of an enjoyable dining experience. There are many types of beverages that enhance a guest's dining experience. The server needs to acquire the basic knowledge of the various wines, liquors, and brands and types of beer; in addition the server needs to know the proper way of serving each of them.

A meal can begin with a guest's favorite bottled water, a tasty cocktail, a special bottle of wine, and end with the perfect cup of coffee or espresso. Each type of beverage requires a server to be knowledgeable in several key areas. The server should know the origin of the beverage, the proper technique to serve it, the correct serving temperatures, the glassware or china it should be served in, and most importantly the responsible way to serve alcohol beverages.

learning objectives

After reading this chapter and completing the discussion questions and exercises, you should be able to:

1. Understand the legal responsibility when serving an alcohol beverage.
2. Understand the importance of wine temperatures and the recommended serving temperatures of various wines.
3. Describe how and when to use an ice bucket.
4. Understand and explain the correct way to present, open, and serve a bottle of wine or champagne.
5. Explain the process of decanting wine.
6. Identify the correct wine and beverage glass.
7. Understand that the climate in which grapes are grown affects the taste and color of wine.
8. Recognize the popular varieties of red and white wines along with some of their characteristics.
9. Understand when fortified wines would be served and why they are often used in cooking.
10. Describe the process of making vodka and the names of several popular vodka drinks.
11. Relate the origin and production process of Bourbon, Scotch, Tennessee whiskey, blended whiskey, and Irish whiskey.

RESPONSIBLE ALCOHOL SERVICE

A serious responsibility comes with the privilege of having a liquor license issued by a State Liquor Control agency that authorizes a business to sell alcohol beverages within strict governing laws. Therefore, it is in every restaurant's best interest to be vigilant in protecting that license. Stringent standard operating procedures are necessary to prevent the loss of the license and to protect against lawsuits that could financially devastate the business.

Dram Shop liability refers to a body of law that governs the liability of bars, taverns, restaurants, and other establishments that sell alcohol beverages to visibly intoxicated persons or minors who may cause death or injury to third parties (persons not having a relationship to the bar) as a result of alcohol-related car or other type accidents. *Dram shop* is a legal term referring to a bar or establishment where alcohol beverages are sold. The name *"Dram Shop"* originated with reference to a shop where spirits were sold by the dram, a small unit of liquid.

Legally, those who serve alcohol beverages are increasingly being held to the *Prudent Person Rule*, which specifically asks, *"What would a prudent person do in this or a similar situation?"*

The basic answer to the question is that a prudent or responsible person would not serve alcohol to someone who is intoxicated. Nor would a prudent person allow someone who is visibly intoxicated to drive a vehicle anywhere.

Management proves that it is a responsible provider of alcohol beverages in several of the following ways:

1. *Set and enforce a house policy that specifically states the house rules concerning visibly intoxicated persons.* Management writes the house policy indicating how employees are to behave in given situations of alcohol beverage service. The house policy would be posted in a conspicuous place in order to allow access for everyone to read the policy.

2. *Support an alcohol beverage server training program for beverage managers and all servers.* A certified alcohol server training program is available from the National Restaurant Association Educational Foundation. Other alcohol server training programs may be available in various states. Rules governing alcohol beverage service are set forth by individual State Liquor Control agencies. Everyone involved with the preparation and service of alcohol beverages should go through an alcohol server training program before beginning to work in a beverage operation. Information about the National Restaurant Association Education Foundation alcohol training program is provided on the following website: www.nraef.org—*ServSafe Alcohol® Responsible Alcohol Training*
3. *Review reports from POS (point-of-sale) systems which may provide information regarding the number of items sold, specific quantities, dates, and times.* This keeps management informed of any irregularities or out-of-the-ordinary occurrences that may give cause for concern which might result in additional or renewed alcohol server training.
4. *Complete an Incident Report for any problem occurring with a customer.* This is a form used to record incidents that occurred in serving or denying service to customers.
5. *Possibly the best defense, as part of a third-party liability claim, if ever sued, is to complete an Incident Report.* The Incident Report is used to record a description of any episodes that occur and is signed by the person reporting the incident, employee(s) involved, manager, and any witnesses. The report effectively documents irresponsible behavior and helps an establishment avoid a lawsuit. Figure 6–1 is an example of an Incident Report.

Figure 6–1
Incident Report.

Incident Report

Date: 01/11/XX　**Shift:** 5:00 PM to 1:00 AM

Reported By: Rick V., Bartender　**Manager:** Harry M.

Employee(s) Involved	Position	
Betty S.	Server	
Customer(s) Involved	**Address**	**Phone #**
David D.	?	?
Witnesses	**Address**	**Phone #**
Fred W.	123 Central Ave, City, State, ZIP	(555) 555 - 5555

Description of Incident

Drink order refused to David D. who was acting belligerent and appeared visibly intoxicated. Server tried to call a taxi but customer refused any help and would not give address or phone number. David D. left.

12. Explain the process of producing brandy.
13. Name several popular drinks made with gin.
14. Identify several drinks made with rum.
15. Describe the process of producing tequila along with popular drinks made with tequila.
16. Identify popular liqueurs (cordials), and explain their characteristics.
17. Understand and explain the difference between beers, lagers, and ales.
18. Judge the quality of beers.
19. Describe malt liquor.
20. Define saké and explain how it is made.
21. List the recommended temperatures for serving beers, lagers, ales, and dark beers.
22. Correctly serve bottled water.
23. Understand and explain the various types of coffee roasts.
24. Describe how a French Press is used to make coffee.
25. Understand how espresso is made and explain how a caffé latte, cappuccino, and mocha are prepared.
26. Recognize some of the many coffee and alcohol combinations.
27. Describe how tea is prepared and served.

Responsible alcohol service begins with the server verifying that the person ordering the alcohol beverage is of legal age. For proof of age, servers should accept only stand-alone identification, such as a valid driver license with photo, passports, military identification, or state-approved identification. The responsible server takes this task seriously and checks identification for all their guests. They realize that this is an important part of their server duties and ensures a pleasant dining experience for their guests.

Servers should always be conscious of taking good care of their guests and protecting them from the effects of alcohol misuse. Along with being a legal obligation, responsible alcohol service constitutes good business, and is the "morally correct" thing to do. Therefore, the server should be aware of the number of drinks a guest has been served, and should know and recognize the signs of visible intoxication. The server should have a brief chat with the guest before serving, and at each visit to the table determine if the guest is intoxicated or at risk of intoxication because of mood, fatigue, medications, or changes in behavior.

Wine Service

Many customers and restaurateurs alike feel intimidated by the mystique of formal wine service. Distinctive techniques and flair of service are as abundant as talented wine servers. However, the true key to serving a bottle of wine to a guest is as simple as knowing a few basics. Once these are mastered, a server can slowly develop the time-honored panache (skills) of the great sommeliers of the world.

History tells us that humans have been offering and accepting wine since the beginning of documented time. Cave and tomb drawings, spanning ages, depict man in the company of a jug of wine. These early peoples did not have the glassware from which to sip nor the bottles to house wine in, but their traditions, superstitions, and earthenware amphorae (jars) and cups were the precursors to the service we offer today.

Wine has always been a great partner for food but in recent years the interest in wine and the number of wine enthusiasts have increased dramatically. Many people have become interested in wine as a hobby or have embraced wine for its newly discovered health benefits which make wine and wine service an important addition to servers training. Guests will come to a restaurant with various levels of wine knowledge; therefore the more prepared the server becomes the greater the level of service to the guest.

The server should be able to offer help when needed and listen carefully to more experienced guests who know what they want. Inexperienced guests may not order wine because they feel they may make a mistake. The professional server needs to be familiar with the restaurant's wine list and be able to explain their selections to guests with limited knowledge or answer complicated questions from more sophisticated and educated guests. Furthermore, for the guest to thoroughly enjoy the wine, it must be served properly.

PROPER TEMPERATURES FOR SERVING WINES

Serving wines begins with the knowledge of serving temperatures, which is as important to a server as it is to a wine steward and a chef. A bottle of overchilled wine will mask desirable or undesirable qualities of the wine instead of highlighting the best that the wine has to offer. A wine that is too warm may taste heavy and lack finesse, creating an unpleasant experience for the guest. The vapors that are released from wine vary depending on its relative volatility. Red wine has higher molecular weight than white and is therefore less volatile. The aromatics of a red wine require a warmer room temperature

TABLE 6–1
WINE SERVING TEMPERATURES

Dessert and Sparkling Wines	40–45°F
White Wines, Roses, Sherries, and Champagnes	45–50°F
High-Quality Dry Wines, Light-Style Reds	50–55°F
Lighter-Style Reds	55–60°F
Full-Bodied Reds	60–65°F

to vaporize the wonderful aromas that are desired. Because lighter white wines and rosés are more volatile, they release their perfume at a much lower temperature. This requires chilling whites and serving reds near a cellar temperature which is 55–65°F. We sometimes refer to red wines being served at room temperature, which is hard to calculate due to climatic and seasonal differences. For example, room temperature in May in Florida varies from the cooler room temperature at the same time of year in Vermont. A restaurateur needs to consider this when serving and storing wine.

Different types of wines benefit from different serving temperatures. By adjusting wine service temperatures it allows the wine to show its best characteristics. The best wines are wines that are balanced. A great wine can be a wine that has some sweetness, some acidity, and if it is a red wine some tannins, or a wine that the guests prefer and enjoy with their meal. Wine is very subjective; therefore a server must communicate and listen to their guests. Each guest has their own personal taste in food and wine. Asking a guest what type of wine they prefer at home is an excellent way for a server to understand what style of wine that guest would enjoy. In addition, it is very important to know what type of food the guest has selected from the menu. Heavy wines are not recommended with light food because they can, in fact, overpower the food and disguise the flavors intended by the chef.

Generally speaking, white wines and sparkling wines should be served between 45° and 50°F. Dessert wines should be served slightly cooler at 40–45°F. Cooler temperatures definitely contribute a perception of balance to sweeter white wines. Red wines are best enjoyed at a cool room temperature of between 60° and 68°F. Again, there are exceptions, as some very light reds, like Beaujolais, can be served at 50–55°F. Review the chart in Table 6–1.

Some restaurants are guilty of keeping their white wines in multipurpose coolers set at 40°F. If this is the case, the wine should be removed a few minutes prior to service to ensure a correct temperature. Likewise, red wines can often be found housed in warm kitchens. Here, a quick chill in an ice bucket can revive a light style red before it is served.

FOOD AND WINE PAIRING

A knowledgeable server will be able to gently guide guests into the right food and wine combination that fits their personal needs. Many guests will only drink one style of wine, either red or white, for example, but may enjoy food which does not pair well with their preference. For example, a guest may want red wine due to its health benefits with fish. Heavy red wines will overpower a delicate fish therefore the server may suggest either a lighter red wine or a meatier fish. There are some basic rules applied to food and wine pairing which are accepted by many and are a good foundation to begin with. The key is to start as simply as possible and build on that foundation. White wines generally are lighter in style and flavor; therefore they match well with lighter style foods, such as many common appetizers, flaky filet of fish, simply prepared chicken and veal.

Sweeter whites pair with rich and highly spiced foods, whereas dry acidic wines, which make your mouth water, pair best with foods such as lemon or tomatoes, which also have acid. It is import to consider the components of a sauce which will be served with a protein before matching the food with a wine. Tannin in red wine can be described as having an astringent or bitter flavor that come from several places, including the skins of the grapes. They generally dry your mouth out. Tannin helps to cut through fat in food. Therefore red wines can be matched to richer foods. There are many websites to help with food and wine pairing—for example: www.foodandwinepairing.org.

ICE BUCKET USAGE

Ice buckets are appropriate on many occasions. They can be used in conjunction with a stand, as shown in Figure 6–2, or set on a dining table as long as they do not overwhelm the china or glassware. It is a good idea to use a bucket with Champagne or sparkling wines. A special occasion deserves an exceptional presentation. White wines probably do not require a bucket unless expressly requested by the guest. Instead a marble wine chiller is an appropriate service companion for a white wine because a wine chiller will simply maintain a wine's temperature. A wine will warm only slightly over the course of a meal, and this may even enhance its flavor. Another consideration for when to use an ice bucket is the number of people sharing the bottle of wine. Three or more will quickly empty the bottle, and thus will usually not require an ice bucket. However, one or two will take longer to consume the wine, making the use of an ice bucket appropriate (Figure 6–2).

Ice buckets should be filled half-full with shaved or cubed ice. If a bottle needs to be chilled quickly, cover it with ice then pour salt on top of the ice and let it stand for about five minutes. Add some water to loosen the ice and speed the chilling. Servers who choose to add water to their buckets should periodically check to make sure that the label is not sliding off the bottle. The server should also be readily available for prompt service to avoid the guest dripping on themselves or on the tablecloth. A server should be prepared with a side towel when using an ice bucket.

Figure 6–2
Ice Bucket. Gerald Lanuzza.

PRESENTATION AND SERVICE

The person who selected the bottle of wine is "the host." After the host is identified the server will proceed. The host will examine the label and then instruct the server to open the bottle; after the bottle is opened "the host" tastes the first 1–2 ounce poured in the glass for approval. This ritual is very important because it insures that the wine is acceptable before more than one glass is poured. If there is a flaw/fault in the wine the server should get another bottle and re-present the second bottle to the guest. It is industry practice to inform your wine sales representative that there was a flaw/fault in the wine. The sales representative will replace the bottle with a new one. There are some common flaws/faults that a server will be exposed to, each having distinct aromas. Flaws/faults can happen naturally and should not be of any great concern.

Figure 6–3
Presenting a Bottle of Wine to a Guest. Gerald Lanuzza.

The server should follow the steps of opening wine carefully. It is a systematic way to serve wine in a proper manner and is easily learned. The server should have a wine key, a napkin, and a small plate to present the cork to be properly prepared to open a bottle of wine. The server should present the bottle on a clean white side towel, held at an angle with the label facing the guest, as shown in Figure 6–3. The server should recite the producer's name, the type of wine, including either grape varietal or place of origin and vintage, in a soft but clear voice, making eye contact with the guest. Once the bottle has been approved, generally with a nod from the host, it can be opened according to the steps in Figure 6–4.

The lead or plastic foil must first be cut below the bulge in the glass to ensure that the wine will not have any contact with the foil during pouring (make sure the knife blade is sharp); see Step 1. A traditional wine opener, as shown in Step 2, is excellent to use because of its versatility. It has a knife at one end for cutting, a thin corkscrew for easy insertion into a cork, and a bottle opener at the opposite end. Wipe the neck of the bottle to remove dust or microorganisms that may have developed under the foil, as shown in Step 3.

The cork should be removed by following the procedure shown in Figure 6–4. Hold the neck of the bottle in one hand, pointing the bottle away from the guest, and with the other hand insert the tip of the corkscrew into the center of the cork, as shown in Step 4 (Note: many prefer to rest the bottle on a side-stand or on the corner of the table). Twist the corkscrew

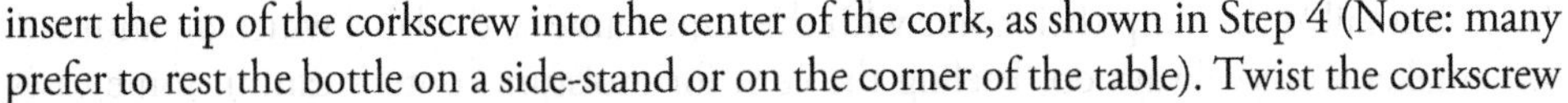

Step 1 Cut and Remove foil

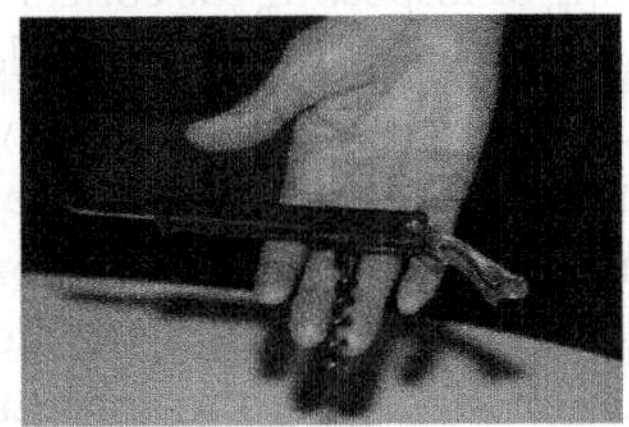

Step 2 A traditional wine opener

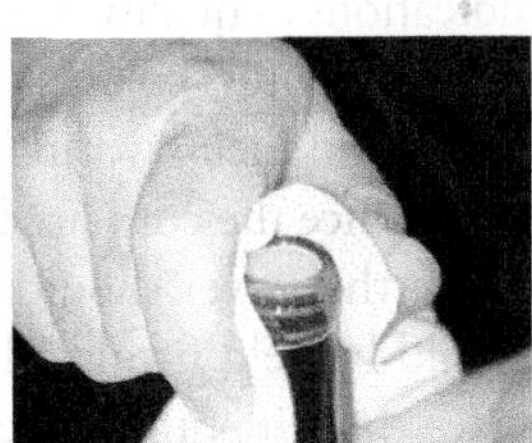

Step 3 Wipe the neck

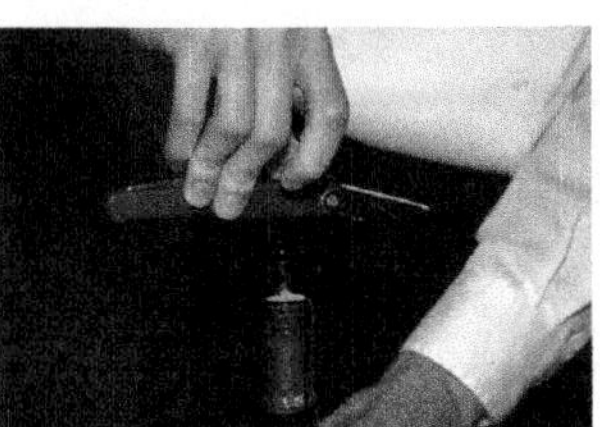

Step 4 Insert the Corkscrew

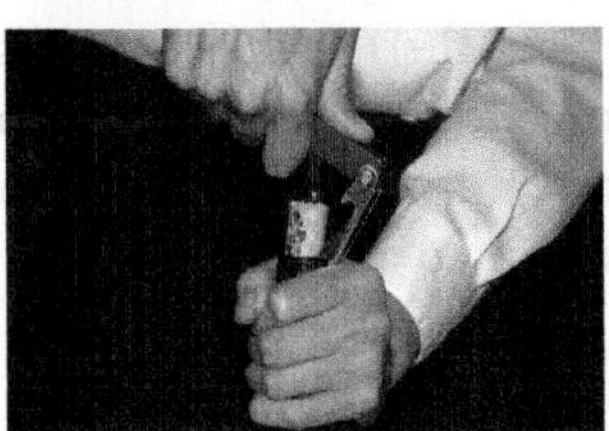

Step 5 Remove the Cork Part 1

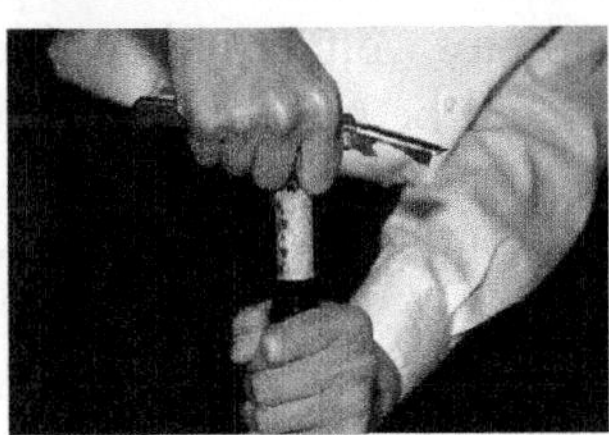

Step 6 Remove the Cork Part 2

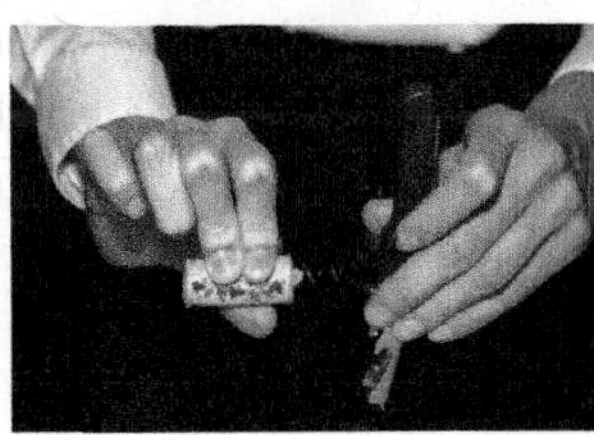

Step 7 Unscrew the Cork from the Corkscrew

Step 8 Place the Cork and Foil on a Bread and Butter Plate Next to the Wine Bottle

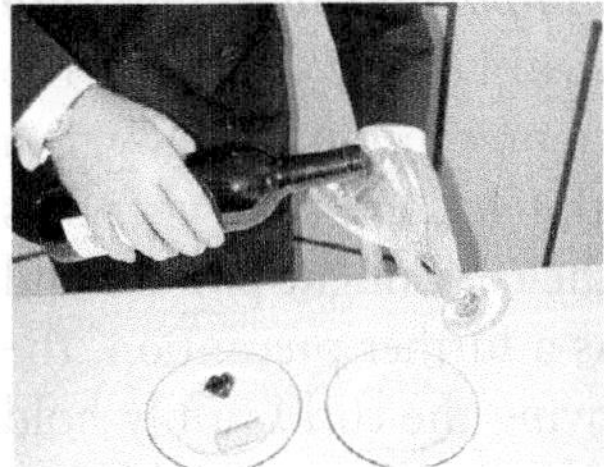

Step 9 Pour the wine

Figure 6–4
Serving Wine. Gerald Lanuzza.

into the cork for a firm grip, hold the corkscrew straight, and twist into the cork without pushing down on the cork; place the edge of the bottle opener on the lip of the bottle, holding it in place with your finger, and with a firm grip slowly pull out the cork, as shown in Steps 5 and 6. Unscrew the cork from the corkscrew as shown in Step 7; wipe off fingerprints or cork dust from the neck of the bottle with the side towel or a clean linen napkin. Practicing wine opening will built confidence in the server and will allow a server to remove even the most difficult corks without a break. Place the cork and the foil next to the bottle preferably on a small plate so the guest can inspect both as shown in Step 8; then pour the wine for the guest to taste and approve (Step 9). Take care not to stain the tablecloth with the cork. Using a napkin as a scarf on the bottle will assist the server with a clean pour and lessen the likelihood of soiling the linen tablecloth.

Occasionally a cork may break. When this occurs the server should do the following: Remove whatever cork is on the corkscrew; reinsert the corkscrew into the center of the cork remaining in the bottle and gently twist all the way through the cork, being careful not to push the cork further into the bottle; slowly remove the cork. Place both pieces of the cork side by side for the guest to inspect. If the cork accidentally falls into the bottle, do not panic—apologize, and offer to bring the guest another bottle of wine. If the guest prefers a new bottle of wine, inform the manager and return the bottle with the cork to the bar for decanting (discussed in the next section)—this wine could later be served as a house wine by the glass.

The practice of smelling and fondling the cork came about due to fraudulent wine practices by a few unscrupulous wine producers many years ago. It was important to check the writing on the cork to insure authenticity of the wine. Some winemakers counterfeited labels but failed to stamp their corks with the same name as the label which an authentic winemaker would always do. Feeling the cork for moisture content can, in some cases, identify if the wine was stored properly, on its side. It is true that we can detect some early indications of quality by smelling or inspecting the cork. The best way to analyze a wine is by looking at its color, smelling its aroma, swirling it to release its bouquet, and best of all tasting and then savoring its unique characteristics and flavor profile.

Once the cork has been removed, and the lip of the bottle wiped with a clean side towel, the server should pour about 1 ounce of wine for tasting purposes. The bottle should be held firmly while pouring. While the host, the guest who ordered the wine, tastes the wine, the server should be holding the bottle at the base with one hand and the neck with the other hand, with the label facing the guest. After the guest has given approval, the server should pour the wine for the other guests at the table, starting with the guest to the right of the taster (or women and/or older guests first), with the taster's glass filled last. The bottle should be twisted with a turn of the wrist as poured to prevent dribbling on the table. Glasses are generally filled one-third to half-full, which permits swirling to experience the full bouquet that the wine has to offer.

OPENING CHAMPAGNE OR SPARKLING WINE

When opening a bottle of champagne or sparkling wine, ***it is important to understand the great pressure the bottle is under and take great care.*** Loosely cover the top of the bottle with a side towel or linen napkin as a safety precaution, as shown in Figure 6–5. Then remove the foil and wire cap (usually with five complete twists plus one half-twist of the wire). If the bottle has been shaken, the cork might pop off and accidentally injure someone if the bottle is not covered. As a further precaution, the server should have a hand on top of the cork. When removing the cork, firmly hold the cork in one hand, with the bottle pointing away from the guest, and slowly twist the bottle as the cork is removed. The cork should be removed with quiet precision,

(a)

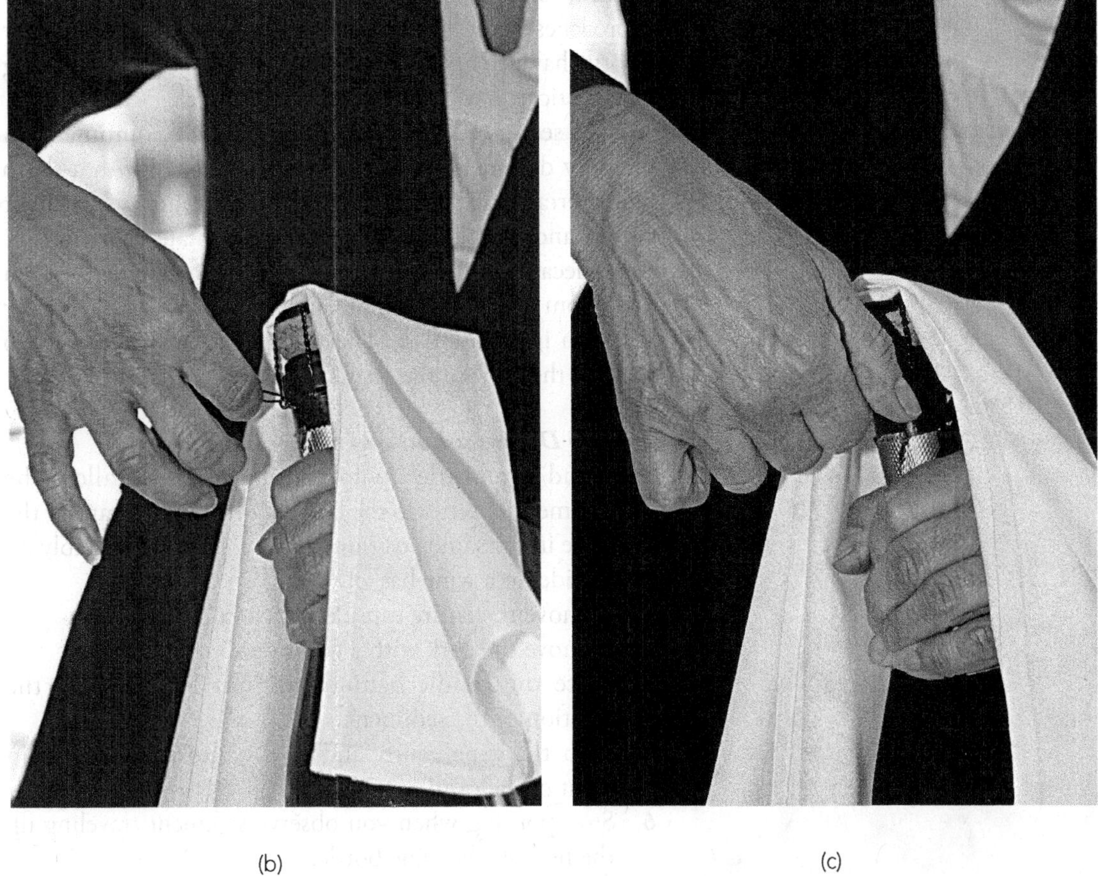

(b) (c)

Figure 6–5
(a) Champagne Bottle in Bucket (b) Opening Champagne Bottle and (c) Pulling Top off of Champagne Bottle. Gerald Lanuzza.

retaining the pressure in the bottle that creates the bubbles. Contrary to popular belief it is not the best practice when opening Champagne or sparkling wine to create a loud POP. Always have one champagne glass close at hand for quick pouring. Occasionally, when the cork is removed, the champagne may quickly overflow as the pressure is removed from the bottle. This is usually controlled after the first glass is poured.

DECANTING WINE

There are two common reasons to decant a wine. Young full-bodied wines typically need time to *breath,* a term meaning to allow oxygen to have contact with the wine, so that the aromas and flavors are released. Decanting speeds up the process of oxidation by pouring the wine from the bottle into a decanter which is typically an elegant crystal vessel. Older wines sometimes have a layer of sediment at the bottom of the bottle, and therefore need to be decanted. The server should be careful not to shake the bottle, to avoid activating and distributing the sediment throughout the wine. Decanting a bottle of wine may present problems to a novice server, but it is not as difficult as it may seem.

Most wine lists offer wine that is ready to serve straight out of the bottle. However, a great, old bottle of French Burgundy or Bordeaux that has thrown a good deal of sediment can be rendered clear by using the process of decanting. Decanting allows an older red wine to react with air, also known as "breathing." A very young red that is considered "closed in" will open up and appear less harsh and tannic once aerated.

Wine is decanted by slowly pouring from a bottle to a decanter without disturbing any sediment. A light source, such as a candle or flashlight, behind the shoulder of the bottle (entire foil should be removed) will be the clue when to stop as the sediment approaches the neck. The same process would be followed for a bottle having cork particles. Another method for removing cork particles is to pour the wine through cheesecloth.

A server will first need the proper equipment to properly decant a bottle of wine: a wine key with a sharp knife (serrated works well), glass decanter, candle for the light source, and a napkin. Be careful not to agitate the sediment. After decanting the wine ask the guest for approval then serve from the glass decanter. An example of a glass decanter is shown in Figure 6–6. The wine bottle should always go back on the table so the guests see what they are drinking.

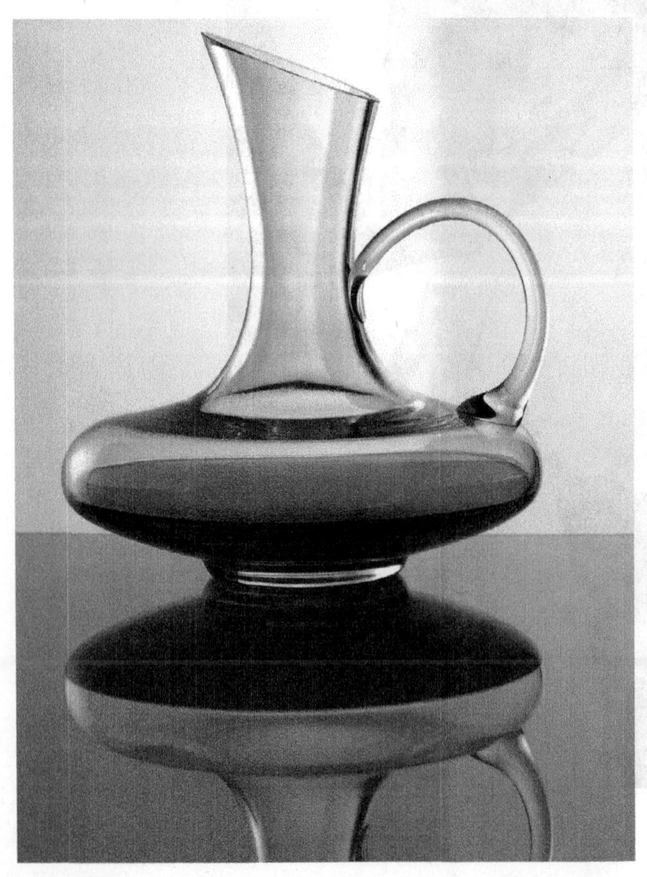

Figure 6–6
Wine Decanter. Courtesy of Stolze.

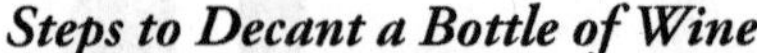

Steps to Decant a Bottle of Wine

1. Stand the bottle up for several hours to allow the sediment to settle to the bottom or carefully transfer the wine in the same position as it was stored, preferably on its side, to a wine basket.
2. Remove the entire capsule with a knife.
3. Remove the cork with a corkscrew.
4. Place the candle behind the bottle to identify the location of the sediment.
5. Pour the wine gently and slowly into the decanter in front of the candle.
6. Stop pouring when you observe sediment traveling up the neck of the wine bottle.
7. Let the wine aerate in the decanter 30 minutes to 1 hour before serving.

WINE GLASSES

Wine glasses should always be clear and made of glass. Etched or colored glasses are not suitable when one is attempting to appreciate the true color of wine. Colored stems may be acceptable if a maître d' is attempting to create ambiance related to a regional or theme dinner.

Wine glasses should always be carefully polished before service begins. There are many styles and shapes of wine glasses; most wine glasses possess long stems for handling and have a wide enough bowl for swirling and smelling, as shown in Figure 6–7. Wine purists prefer a smaller bowl for white wines and a larger one for red wines. Typically the smaller the bowl of the glass, the more aromas are directed toward the nose, thereby being easier to identify. A wider bowl with a smaller opening allows the wine to breathe therefore letting oxygen get to the wine and release aroma and flavors when tasted. The key is never to present the wine in a small glass that does not allow free movement of the wine. An excellent interactive website to explore styles of wine glassware is www.riedel.com (click on wine & glass guide).

Lengthy and multiple-course dinners often command several wine selections. The host will usually dictate which wine is to be poured first. However, a good rule of

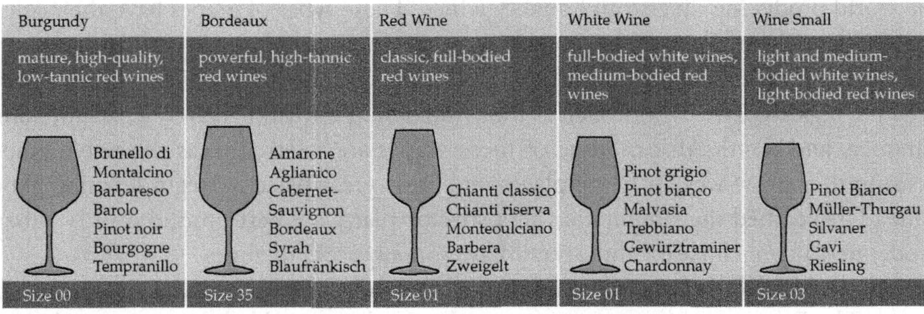

Burgundy
mature, high-quality, low-tannic red wines
Brunello di Montalcino
Barbaresco
Barolo
Pinot noir
Bourgogne
Tempranillo
Size 00
Bordeaux
powerful, high-tannic red wines
Amarone
Aglianico
Cabernet-Sauvignon
Bordeaux
Syrah
Blaufränkisch
Size 35
Red Wine
classic, full-bodied red wines
Chianti classico
Chianti riserva
Monteoulciano
Barbera
Zweigelt
Size 01
White Wine
full-bodied white wines, medium-bodied red wines
Pinot grigio
Pinot bianco
Malvasia
Trebbiano
Gewürztraminer
Chardonnay
Size 01
Wine Small
light and medium-bodied white wines, light-bodied red wines
Pinot Bianco
Müller-Thurgau
Silvaner
Gavi
Riesling
Size 03

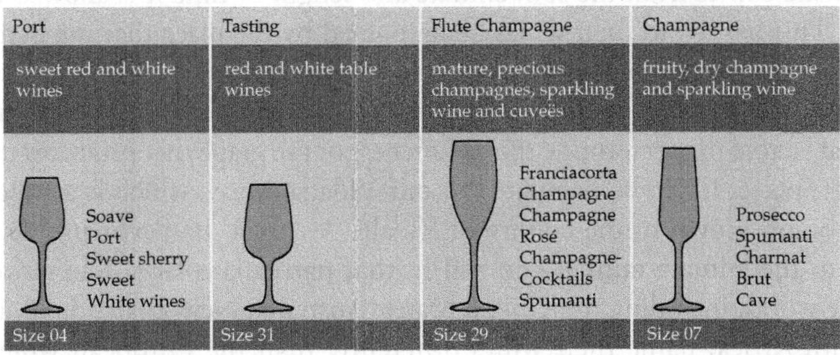

Port
sweet red and white wines
Soave
Port
Sweet sherry
Sweet
White wines
Size 04
Tasting
red and white table wines
Size 31
Flute Champagne
mature, precious champagnes, sparkling wine and cuvées
Franciacorta
Champagne
Champagne
Rosé
Champagne-
Cocktails
Spumanti
Size 29
Champagne
fruity, dry champagne and sparkling wine
Prosecco
Spumanti
Charmat
Brut
Cave
Size 07

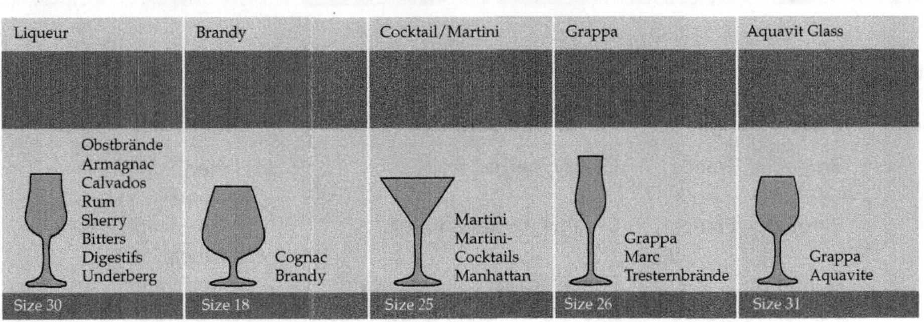

Liqueur
Obstbrände
Armagnac
Calvados
Rum
Sherry
Bitters
Digestifs
Underberg
Size 30
Brandy
Cognac
Brandy
Size 18
Cocktail/Martini
Martini
Martini-
Cocktails
Manhattan
Size 25
Grappa
Grappa
Marc
Tresternbrände
Size 26
Aquavit Glass
Grappa
Aquavite
Size 31

Figure 6–7
Wine Glasses. Courtesy of Stolze.

thumb is not to overwhelm the palate. White wines usually are better enjoyed prior to red wines, younger before older wines, and dry wines before sweet wines.

Basic knowledge goes a long way in any discipline. The often mysterious world of wine is no different. Servers should be trained in the fundamentals and let their personalities do the rest. The server who desires to go beyond the fundamentals should take a special course in wine and alcohol beverages at a community college or culinary school.

WINE VARIETALS

When viewed from a distance, capturing wine knowledge can seem a daunting task. This does not have to be the case, however. Although thousands of grape varietals exist, beginning with six and building slowly could quickly and easily lead to a mastery of perhaps a couple dozen varietals. Some noble grape varietal to begin with are listed in Table 6–2. A server should feel confident of their knowledge and will soon be able to recognize wines from around the world. Wine has been made for centuries and certain grapes have been the backbone of wine making throughout the world. The *Vitis,* or grapevine, produces a number of different rootstocks. Each rootstock gives birth to many grape varietals. The European rootstock *Vinifera* is the family that is considered to produce the finest of the grape varietals. These European grapes are now seen around the world producing diverse and quality wines. These types of grapes have their origin in specific areas of Europe due to specific soil types and climate that allow them to thrive. We now see the Vitis Vinifera thriving in what is considered the newer wine-growing regions of the world, such as the United States, Australia, New Zealand, South America, and South Africa. Some of these grapes are referred to as the noble grapes because they grow well in many places and are a great place to begin learning about wine. They earned their reputation in a specific place, are best produced in Northern moderate-to-cool climates, and overall have some specific qualities.

Wine guidelines have been set up for many of the wine-growing regions of the world. The European wine areas are steeped in tradition and believe, as many do, that a grape's characteristic comes from the soil, climate and length of time it is allowed to ripen on the vine. This has led to their wines being named by the place that the grape is grown, which can be a town, a region, or a specific vineyard.

It has also led to a term called *terrior,* which is not easily translated into English but includes the natural factors that determine the uniqueness of the grape that produces the wine from a specific place. It can be compared to our Vidalia onion, which is a sweet, flat, thin-skinned onion grown in the county of Vidalia, Georgia. Its flavor profile is said to be linked to the climate rainfall and soil in that particular place. The newer wine regions of the world, including the United States, Australia, New Zealand, South America, and South Africa, name their wines differently than the European wines.

TABLE 6–2
SOME NOBLE GRAPE VARIETALS

Grape	Style of Wine	Place of Origin	Flavor Characteristic	Other Places Grown
Sauvignon Blanc	White	Bordeaux, France	Grassy, herbal, fruity	United States, New Zealand
Chardonnay	White	Burgundy, France	Creamy, buttery, fruity	United States, Australia, S. Africa
Riesling	White	Germany	Fruity, acidic, spicy, delicate	United States, Australia
Cabernet Sauvignon	Red	Bordeaux, France	Red & black fruit, spice, vegetal	All new regions
Pinot Noir	Red	Burgundy, France	Cherry, liquorice, plum, spice	All new regions
Merlot	Red	Bordeaux, France	Soft, plum, berry, currant	United States, Australia

In the newer regions the wine is named by the grape varietal which will guarantee at least 75 percent of the grape named on the label will be in the wine. Many people find this way of labeling easier and embrace these wines for their recognizable labels. Regardless of the type of label, most winemakers agree that grape varietals prosper differently in varied climates and are now trying to plant grapes in an environment which will allow them to do their best. There is a true sense of pride among winemakers and vineyards that have a grape varietal that thrives on their land.

In choosing wines for a restaurant's wine list, the owner/manager should take the same care that is taken with the food items that are selected for their menu. A restaurateur could begin by understanding which grapes grow best in which region and which wines will enhance the menu of the restaurant. It is important to match the type of wine with the style, atmosphere, and price point of the restaurant. An example of a restaurant wine list is shown if Figure 6–8.

Carpe Diem Restaurant & Caterers

white wine

Sparkling and Celebratory	***glass***	***bottle***
Segura Viudas Aria Estate Brut Cava, Catalonia, Spain	7.00	35.00
Canella Prosecco di Conegliano, Italy		39.00
Heidsieck Monopole Brut Blue Top, Champagne, France, NV *93pts WE "There's a lush creaminess in the mouth, packed with flavors of candied orange, apricot & pineapple. The wine scores a flavor bulls eye in every possible way..."*		75.00
J Cuvee 20, Russian River, California, NV *91pts WN "Pretty scents of lightly toasted bread, jammy fruit & hints of charred oak. Foamy on the palate with peach juice & a tart backing of white grapefruit..."*		48.00
Bruno Paillard Premiere Cuvee, Reims, France, NV *91pts WA "...gorgeous, understated Champagne laced with subtle, perfumed fruit & a silky, textured palate. This is an exceptionally elegant Champagne that impresses for its overall harmony & finesse..."*		75.00
Domaine Carneros Brut, California, 2005		55.00
Besserat de Bellefon Brut Rose, Champagne, Moines, France		90.00
Fun, Funky, and Delicious Whites	***glass***	***bottle***
J Cuvee, Pinot Gris, California, 2009	9.00	36.00
Civello(pinot grigio/chard/verdelho/gewurztraminer), California, 2007	7.50	30.00
Burgans Albarino, Rias Baixas, Spain, 2008	7.50	30.00
J Lohr Riesling, Monterey, California, 2009	7.00	28.00
Domaine Houchart Rose, Cotes De Provence, France, 2009		28.00
Pierre Sparr Reserve Gewurztraminer, Alsace, France, 2006		34.00
Joh Jos Prum Riesling Kabinett Mosel-Saar-Ruwer, Germany 2007, 91pts WS		58.00
Hyatt Vineyards Pinot Gris, Rattlesnake Hills, Washington, 2008, 90 pts WE		30.00
Sauvignon Blanc and blends	***glass***	***bottle***
Nobilo Icon Sauvignon Blanc, Marlborough, New Zealand, 2009	8.50	34.00
Pellegrini Leveroni Vineyard Sauvignon Blanc, Lake County, California, 2007	7.50	30.00

Figure 6–8
Wine List. Courtesy of Carpe Dien Restaurant and Caterers.

	glass	bottle
Thomas Labaille l'Authentique Sancerre, Loire, France, 2008		36.00
Evolucion Sauvignon Blanc Reserve, Maule Valley, Chile, 2008		28.00
Cloudy Bay Sauvignon Blanc, Marlborough, New Zealand, 2008		49.00
Chardonnay	***glass***	***bottle***
Selby, Russian River Valley, California, 2008	11.00	44.00
Darby and Joan, South Australia, 2008	7.00	28.00
Jean Manciat Macon Charnay Franclieu, Burgundy, France, 2007		35.00
Novelty Hill Stillwater Creek Vineyard, Columbia Va., Washington, 2007 *91pts WA "attractive aromas of slate/mineral, apple, pear, & white peach. Crisp & restrained on the palate"*		39.00
St. Innocent Anden Vineyard, Willamette, Oregon, 2006		51.00
Novy Rosella's , Santa Lucia Highlands, California, 2008		46.00
Robert Young, Alexander Valley, California, 2006		60.00
Frank Family, Napa, California, 2008		52.00
Pinot Noir	***glass***	***bottle***
Oyster Bay, Marlborough, New Zealand, 2008 *91pts WS "light, polished, & highly perfumed, with lavender & spice overtones to the currant & cherry flavors, lingering easily"*	8.00	32.00
Stephen Ross, Central Coast, California, 2008	10.00	40.00
Arbor Brook Block 777 , Chehalem Mountains, Yamhill, Oregon, 2007 *velvety-textured wine with a solid core of sweet fruit with all components nicely integrated*		65.00
Lemelson Vineyards Thea's Selection, Willamette, Oregon, 2007		53.00
Sineann, Oregon, 2008 90pts WE "Tightly woven scents of sweet herb, tobacco, clove, forest floor fungus & spicy red fruits provide an introduction to a wine that can only be called svelte. It's as smooth as silk in the mouth, loaded with flavor & polished to a warm glow."		55.00
Domaine Serene Yamhill Cuvee, Willamette Valley, Oregon, 2007		65.00
Elk Cove Mount Richmond, Willamette Valley, Oregon, 2008		80.00
Ken Wright Cellars Savoya Vineyard, Yamhill-Carlton District, Oregon, 2008		85.00
Jermann Red Angel, Friuli, Italy, 2006 *90pts RP " a gorgeous bouquet & lovely notes of red cherries, earthiness & licorice, The wine offers outstanding length & silky tannins that dry out ever so slightly on the long finish."*		57.00
Row Eleven, Santa Maria Valley, California, 2006, Half Bottle		32.00
Acacia Lone Tree Vineyard, Carneros, California, 2006		60.00
Orogeny, Green Valley, Sonoma, California, 2007		65.00
Truchard, Carneros, California, 2006		50.00
Migration by Duckhorn, Anderson Valley, California, 2007		58.00
Spanish and South American Varietals	***glass***	***bottle***
Clos de los Siete Malbec Blend, Mendoza, Argentina, 2007	8.50	34.00
Celler Can Blau Can Blau(mazuelo/syrah/garnacha), Monstant, Spain, 2008		38.00
Alonso Del Yerro Ribera del Duero(tempranillo), Spain, 2006		48.00
Numanthia Numanthia(tempranillo), Toro, Castilla Leon, Spain, 2006 *93pts WS" Firm tannins frame black cherry, mineral, licorice and herbal notes in this chewy red. Well-proportioned, with lively acidity and a lovely floral finish"*		75.00
Artadi Vinas de Gain Rioja(tempranillo), Spain, 2006 *92pts RP "...alluring perfume of truffle, pencil lead, vanilla, blackberry, & black cherry jam. Full bodied, the wine is opulent yet elegant."*		50.00
Alvaro Palacios Les Terrasses(cariñena/garnacha,/cabernet), Priorat, Spain, 2006		60.00

Figure 6–8 (continued)

Pardevalles Prieto Picudo Gamonal Vineyard, Tierra De Leon, Spain, 2006		45.00
Alto Moncayo Veraton(100% garnacha), Campo de Borja, Spain, 2007, 92pts WA		49.00
Mendel Malbec Oak, Mendoza, Argentina, 2007 *92pts RP ..."medium-bodied wine in which notes of cola, coffee, and caramel emerge on the palate. Elegantly styled, with racy flavors, good balance, and a pure finish..."*		48.00
Vall Llach Vall Llach(Carinena/Merlot/Cabernet) Priorat, Spain, 2003 *94pts WS "Cocoa, licorice, blueberry, mineral & floral notes mingle in this powerful & complex red. It has plenty of tannins, wood & alcohol, but all in balance "*		90.00
Rhone and New World Rhone Varietals		
Ferraton Crozes-Hermitage(100% syrah), Rhone, France, 2008	8.50	34.00
Vieux Telegramme Chateauneuf-du-Pape, Rhone, France, 2007		60.00
Delas Freres Cote Rotie Seigneur de Maugiron, Northern Rhone, France, 2005 *94pts RP "The gorgeous, dense ruby/purple-hued Cote Rotie offers abundant aromas of bacon fat, tapenade, black cherries, & black currants. Medium to full-bodied with good acidity, high tannin, & beautifully layered sweet fruit..."*		130.00
Owen Roe Syrah Ex Umbris, Columbia Valley, Washington, 2007 *92 pts WS ..."Smooth & velvety, offering a plush mouthful of spicy cherry & red berry flavors, playing against plush tannins & hints of milk chocolate on the long, vivid finish.*		46.00
Clayhouse Petite Sirah, Pao Robles, California, 2006		45.00
Lolonis Orpheus Petite Sirah, Redwood Valley, California, 2005		49.00
BR Cohn Syrah-Cabernet, Sonoma, Calfornia, 2006		57.00
Edwards Sellers Grenache, Paso Robles, California, 2005		59.00
Chateau Chateau Skulls Red(grenache/mataro), South Australia, 2007 *90 pts RP "...blend of 60% Grenache & 40% Mataro raised in stainless steel. Dark ruby -colored, it offers up an expressive bouquet of garrigue, forest floor, spice box, & herry."*		38.00
R Wines Strong Arms Shiraz, South Australia, 2007		28.00
Hare's Chase Shiraz, Barossa, Australia, 2003		50.00
Torbreck The Struie Shiraz, Barossa, Australia, 2006		78.00
Italian and New World Italian Varietals	***glass***	***bottle***
Salvestrin Retaggio, Super Tuscan Style Blend, Napa Valley, California, 2007 *90pts WA "...dark ruby/plum/garnet color is followed by aromas & flavors of strawberries, black cherries, spicy unsmoked cigar tobacco, earth, & cedar. This is a sexy, open-knit, lush, medium to full-bodied wine..."*	12.00	48.00
Enamore(cabernet/cab franc/syrah/malbec/bonardo), Mendoza, Argentina, 2007 *WS 91pts Made with grapes dried on the vine and vinified in the Italian Amarone style. "Shows a sweet, dried fruit style, with raisin & date hints that stay fresh, thanks to layers of crushed currant and black cherry"*		47.00
Avignonesi Vino Nobile di Montepulciano(sangiovese), Italy, 2007		48.00
Dei Vino Nobile di Montepulciano(sangiovese), Italy, 2006		49.00
Terrabianco Campaccio, Super Tuscan, Tuscany, Italy, 2005		50.00
Zinfandel	***glass***	***bottle***
Ottimino Zinfandel, Sonoma, California, 2006	9.00	36.00
Davis Family Old Vine Zinfandel, Russian River Valley, California, 2006		52.00
Easton Zinfandel, Amador County, California, 2003		42.00
XY 50 Year Old Vine, Russian River, California, 2007		48.00
Hendry Block 7 & 22 Zinfandel, Napa, California, 2006		54.00

Figure 6–8 (continued)

Cabernet Sauvignon, Cabernet Blends, Cabernet Franc and Merlot	***glass***	***bottle***
Uppercut Cabernet, Napa, California, 2007	10.00	40.00
Barnard Griffin Merlot, Columbia Valley, Washington, 2007	10.00	40.00
Flora Springs Merlot, Napa, California, 2007		45.00
Novelty Hill, Columbia Valley, Washington, 2007, 92pts WS		48.00
Bookwalter Foreshadow Cabernet, Columbia Valley, Washington, 2007, 94pts WE		66.00
Arrowood Cabernet, Sonoma, California, 2005 *88pts RP "It is a delicious, modestly-priced Cabernet offering plenty of tobacco leaf, black currant, licorice, & spice box characteristics, loads of fruit, & subtle notes of white chocolate as well as wood."*		55.00
Bennett Lane Maximus(cabernet/merlot/syrah), Napa, California, 2006		59.00
Hess Mt. Veeder 19 Block Cuvee(cabernet/malbec/syrah), Napa, California, 2006		54.00
Bernard Baudry Chinon Le Clos Guillot(cabernet franc), Loire, France, 2007 *92pts WS "...kirsch & linzer that courses along vibrant acidity. Well-imbedded with iron minerality & a long, pure, stone-tinged finish"*		52.00
Anderson's Conn Valley Reserve Cabernet, Napa, California, 2006 *RP 96pts "Classic Pauillac-like nose of creme de cassis, cedar wood, a hint of tobacco leaf, & very subtle smoke, the wine displays charcoal and roasted herbs, full-bodied power,* *wonderfully sweet tannins, & a long, long finish.*		98.00
Justin Isosceles(Cabernet/Cab Franc/Merlot), Paso Robles, California, 2007		85.00
Lewis Alec's Blend(Syrah/Cab/Merlot), Napa, California, 2007 *Combines richness with delicacy, offering a firm, subtle mix of plum, red currant, cedar & spice. Gains depth & finesse, with hints of mocha, sage & dried berry. syrah, cabernet & merlot.*		95.00
Kamen Cabernet Sauvignon, Sonoma, California, 2005 *RP 95pts "...this wine displays plenty of power & loads of meat, dry, serious tannins, hints of graphite, and admirable creme de cassis*		98.00

Vintages are subject to change without notice

cocktails

House cocktails are 1/3 off on Tuesday nights

Bulldozer Martini — 8.50
Vodka blended with fresh ginger syrup and orange juice with a splash of St. Germain Elderflower Alsatian liquor. Great with cava too!

Mojito — 8.00
Bacardi rum muddled with fresh mint, lime juice, and sugar over ice

Caipiroska — 8.50
Luksusowa vodka with fresh lime juice and sugar, shaken and served over ice with a splash of soda water

Southen Julip — 8.00
South Carolina Firefly sweet tea vodka on ice with fresh mint infused lemonade

French Martini — 8.50
Vodka with a splash of chambord raspberry liquor, pineapple juice, shaken and served up with a twist of lemon

beer

Miller Light, Milwaukee	2.50
Sam Adams Light, Massachusetts	4.00
Stone Brewery Arrogant Bastard Oaked Ale, California	6.50

Figure 6–8 (continued)

Rogue Hazelnut Brown Nector, Oregon, 22oz 2007 World Beer Champion	11.00
Anderson Valley Boont Amber Ale, California	4.50
Paulaner Hefweissen, Germany	4.50
Lagunitas India Pale Ale, Sonoma, California	4.50
La Fin Du Monde Ale on Lees Blonde Ale 9% alcohol) Canada	7.00
Lemon curd, coriander, cinnamon, & candied apricot...Superbly powerful & spicy 96pts BTI	
The Duck-Rabbit Craft Brewery Stout, North Carolina	4.50
Stella Artois, Belgium	4.50
Ayinger Celebrator Doppelbock, Germany	7.50
Deep brown color with rich ground nut, espresso, suede & woody bark aromas...balance finishes with a long honeyed fruit, cocoa, and spice fade. Superb. 97pts BTI	
Pilsner Urquell, Czech Republic	4.50
Rich aromas of fresh baguette, caramelized nuts, citrus marmalade & earthy hops. Tangy, dry-yet-fruity full body of honeyed nut toast & tart grapefruity citrus flavors. 93pts BTI	
Kaliber non-alcoholic, Ireland	4.00

beverages

Counter Culture Coffee, Durham, NC(*available in retail 1lb bags for 14.50*)	2.00
Iced tea, hot red zinger, chamomile, & Earl Grey teas	2.00
Espresso, regular & decaffeinated	2.50
Cappuccino, regular and decaffeinated	3.00
House Cappuccino with Baileys and Frangelico	7.00
Coke, Diet Coke, Sprite, Ginger Ale	2.00
Lemonade or Limeade	2.00
Hot Chocolate	2.00
Panna Natural Spring Water 3.00 San Pelligrino Sparkling Water	SM 3.00/LG $6.00

Figure 6–8 (continued)

Notable Wine Varietals

Red

Cabernet Franc (cab-er-nay frahnk): Mostly used in Cabernet blending but recently has stood alone.

+**Cabernet Sauvignon** (cab-er-nay so-vin-yon): Perhaps the grandest of the "reds." Big, bold, complex. Violet aromas, black currant flavors. Sometimes blended with Merlot (and other varietals) to "soften" the wine. Aged in oak. Has the ability to age well.

Gamay (gam-ay): One of the lighter and fruitier red varietals. Best enjoyed young.

Grenache (gre-nash): Found in the Rhone Valley and Spain. Soft tannins and acids.

+**Merlot** (mur-lo): Softer and rounder than Cabernet. Aged in oak. Gaining in popularity due to its ability to be consumed young.

Nebbiolo (neb-ee-oh-lo): Perhaps the greatest red grape of Italy. Deep, firm, and rich.

+**Pinot Noir** (pee-no-nwar): Fine, full flavored, full body with an "earthy" nose. Velvety and long lasting.

Sangiovese (sang-joe-vay-zay): Rich garnet hue, deep when young, warm red-brick when mature. Slightly earthy and tannic. (Used in Chianti and other Italian wines).Has found its way to the United States.

Syrah (sir-ra): Full, heavy, long-lived wines of great color, scent, and body.

Zinfandel (zin-fun-del): Unique to California. Depending on winemaking techniques it can be made in bigger or lighter style. Berry overtones.

White

+**Chardonnay** (shar-dun-nay): Most classic variety. Pale to yellow color (aged in oak). Vanilla and oak flavors. Dry, rich, and fresh. Nutty and full bodied.

Chenin Blanc (shen-n-blahnk): Fruity with residual sugar (Honeyed richness). Found in Loire Valley and California.

Gewürztraminer (geh-verts-trah-mee-ner): From the German "gewurtz" or spice. Great food wine with increasing popularity. Strong and positive taste.

Muller Thurgau (mule-yer-tour-gow): At various times thought to be a cross grape of Riesling and Sylvaner. Now generally considered a Riesling hybrid. Mass-produced in Germany. Light, inexpensive, and floral.

Muscat (muss-kat): Often made into sweet dessert wine. Pungent taste.

Pinot Blanc (pee-no blahnk): Light, good sipping wine, accessible to all. Fresh fruit.

Pinot Gris (pee-no-gree): (Gree, for gray color). Unrelated to Pinot Noir. Full bodied and great with salmon.

+**Riesling** (rees-ling): Fruity, yet elegant, wine distinguished in Germany, Alsace, and Pacific Northwest. Generally medium-dry. Crisp acidity.

+**Sauvignon Blanc** (so-vin-yon blahnk): Produced in Bordeaux and California. Can produce big, dry wines. Occasionally found in dessert wines. Refreshing acidity. Aromatic.

Semillon (sem-ih-yon): Best utilized in Sauternes district of Bordeaux. Often blended with Sauvignon Blanc to make world-class dessert wines. Sweetness of freshly ripened fruit.

Sylvaner (seel-vaa-ner): Found in Germany, Italy, and Austria. Pleasant but unsophisticated.

Trebianno (tre-bee-ah-no): Light white wine from Italy. Often blended with other less-than-noble varieties.

+indicates inclusion in Figure 6–7 Noble Grape

Styles of Wine

Whites are usually made from white grapes, but in some cases you can make white wine from red grapes by eliminating contact with skin. There are some popular specialty wines made in this way.

Rosés or Blushes are made by fermenting red grapes, skins, seeds, and juice, but only for a short time. This produces a light pink or salmon color and can yield a fruity, light wine.

Sparkling Wines are made throughout the world by creating a second fermentation, in the bottle, in a tank, or by injecting bubbles into a wine that is already made. The best sparkling wines are made when the second fermentation takes place in the bottle because it produces the smallest and most numerable bubbles. Champagne is a place in France; therefore a wine with bubbles can only be called Champagne when it originates from the Champagne region of France. It has it own unique flavor which comes from the "terrior" of that region. It has been described as tasting creamy, yeasty, and nutty. The following terms describe the style and flavor of Champagne from the driest to the sweetest: Brut, Extra Dry, Sec, and Demi-Sec.

Fortified Wines were originally made in the seaports of Spain, Portugal, Madeira, and Sicily. Seafarers strengthened wines with distilled brandies so that they could travel for months aboard ships in both hot and cold cargo bays without spoilage. Fortified wines have many applications, including using them in culinary for basic sauces, in baking for poaching or in dough, serving them as after-dinner drinks, and even as aperitifs before the meal to stimulate the appetite. The most popular fortified wines are Sherry, Port, Madeira, and Marsala.

Knowing the characteristics of a wine can help guide the server in offering suggestions to the guest who may request the server's opinion and/or recommendation for a wine selection. As a general rule, white wine is served with seafood and chicken and red wine with meat. Although there are no firm rules, ideally, the wine should complement the menu item, not dominate it. Consequently, dry wines are normally served directly with the entrée and sweeter wines with the dessert. Contemporary menus offer creative combinations of foods and sauces known as fusion foods, where a seafood item, for example, may be accented with a sauce that would traditionally go with a meat item. The same is seen with wines, such as a red wine being paired with a chicken entrée. Therefore, the server should be familiar with the preparation ingredients and accompanying sauces of menu items. Also, the time of the day can certainly dictate one's choice. A light, fruity, or even blush wine is an excellent choice for lunch. Ultimately, if the server can describe the wine's qualities, the guest will appreciate both the server's expertise and the wine selection. The characteristics of common wine styles that a server should know are listed in Table 6–3.

Table 6–3
Common Wine Styles

Style of Wine	Common Characteristics	Country of Production
White	Pale to golden in color, darken as they age, fermented without skins, flavor from dry to sweet. Serve with poultry and fish.	Europe, United States, Australia, New Zealand, South America, South Africa
Rose/blushes	Pink to salmon in color, fermented with skins for a short period of time, flavor from dry to sweet. Serve with light meats, poultry, and fish.	Europe, United States, Australia, New Zealand, South America, South Africa
Red	Ruby to purple in color, fermented with skins to extract color and flavor, mostly dry, serve with red meats and game.	Europe, United States, Australia, New Zealand, South America, South Africa
Sparkling	Can be white, no skin contact or rose, short skin contact, will have effervescence, flavor from dry to sweet, serve before dinner as aperitif through dessert.	Europe, United States, Australia, New Zealand, South America, South Africa
Fortified	Ruby to tawny in color, alcohol is added to increase percentage, flavor from dry to sweet, serve dry as aperitif, serve sweet with cheese and dessert.	Port, Portugal; Sherry, Spain; Madiera-island of Madiera; Marsala, Italy

Appendix B, Wine Terminology, identifies general descriptive wine terms, along with terms that describe wine by sight, smell, and taste.

DISTILLED SPIRITS AND COCKTAILS

A distilled spirit contains ethanol and must go through the distillation process. The distillation process essentially turns a fermented beverage with relativity low alcohol into a beverage with higher alcohol. The use of fruit, grains, or vegetables is common when making a distilled spirit. Each spirit has a distinct flavor and color which can be consumed by themselves or mixed with other ingredients. Regardless of the time period, human beings have consumed distilled sprits throughout the world. Many distilled spirits have a specific origin throughout the world as well as unique uses, recipes, or processes. Many spirits were first used for medicinal reasons. Spirits have a strong flavor due to their alcohol content; therefore it became common to mix them to create cocktails. The craft of making cocktails became sophisticated and mysterious. Bartenders and their establishments were known for their recipes and soon had a following. There are famous bars with signature cocktail throughout the world; many have lasted for generations. In addition to the traditional signature cocktails new innovative bartenders continue to explore the endless recipes for new and exciting drinks. Martini bars and specific signature martinis using various spirits and exotic ingredients entice consumers all across America.

Common styles of spirits and popular cocktails are shown in Table 6–4.

Vodka

Vodka is a popular white spirit with a neutral flavor, made primarily with grains, sugar beets, or potatoes. It is easily mixed with other ingredients or chilled and consumed by itself. Vodka was first distilled in Poland and Russia; it is a Slavic word meaning

TABLE 6–4
COMMON STYLES OF SPIRITS

Style of Spirit	Color	Fermented From	Origin	Popular Cocktails
Vodka	Clear	Grain, Potatoes, Sugar Beets	Russia, Poland, Scandinavia	Martini, Cosmopolitan, Screwdriver, Moscow Mule, Bloody Mary, vodka Tonic
Gin	Clear	Grain compounded with juniper berries	Holland, Great Britain	Martini, Dry Martini, Gibson, Gin and Tonic, Tom Collins, Gin Rickey
Rum	Clear to Brown	Sugarcane	The Caribbean	Rum and Coke, Daiquiris, Rocks, Mixers (Tonic and 7-up), Rum Martini
Tequila	Clear to Gold	Blue Agave Plant	Mexico	Margarita, straight with lemon and salt, with Sangria (a citrus juice)
Scotch Whiskey	Caramel Amber	Malted barley, grains	Scotland	On the rocks, with soda or water, Rob Roy, Godfather
Irish Whiskey	Caramel Amber	Malted barley, grains	Ireland	On the rocks, with soda or water, Rusty nail, coffee
Bourbon American Whiskey	Caramel Amber	Malted barley, grains	USA	On the rocks, with soda, ginger ale or water, Manhattan, Mint Julep, old fashion
Brandy	Caramel	Grapes	Anywhere	In a snifter, Brandy Alexander
Cognac	Caramel	Grapes	France	In a snifter, sidecar
Armanagac	Caramel	Grapes	France	In a snifter

"little water." As the distillation process improved, vodka production became very popular and widespread in Scandinavia. After World War II, vodka became a favorite of American service men. They added lime and ginger beer to the clear liquid and the "Moscow Mule" was born.

Vodka did not become mainstream in the United States until the 1950s with the Smirnoff brand. Established in Russia as a family business then sold several times to U.S. businessmen until it was made successfully in the United States, Smirnoff brand remains one of the leading vodka makers in America. The U.S. palate was looking for a lighter spirit than whiskey during this time period and vodka was the perfect alternative. Today many brands of vodka from various countries are sold in the United States. Flavored vodkas are very appealing and therefore very popular; they are the perfect ingredient when making specialty martinis or signature cocktails. There are vodkas that are flavored with all different types of fruits and spices. In addition, there are other vodkas that are distilled numerous times to ensure smoothness and to eliminate impurities. These multiple distilled vodkas command a premium price which consumers are happy to pay for. There are many popular traditional vodka drinks as well as new innovative ones created by talented young bartenders.

Scotch, Bourbon, and Other Whiskeys

Whiskey differs considerably from vodka. Whiskeys are brown or caramel in color and have many distinct aromas and flavors. Whiskey has a more complicated distillation process than vodka; added steps need to be taken to make whiskey. Whiskey is made all over the world but had its origins in Scotland or Ireland.

Grains such as, barley corn or rye are the base for whiskey making. Whiskeys are typically aged in oak barrels which add the color, aroma, and flavor to the spirit. The main differences between the leading producing countries of the United States, Canada, Scotland, and Ireland are in the type of grain used, the method of production, the method of aging, and the blending techniques.

Scotch is made in Scotland and its claim to fame is in the malted barley that gives a distinctive aftertaste. Malting is a process that converts the starch in the barley into sugar. This conversion process is important because it aids the fermentation process which converts the sugar into alcohol. ***Single malt Scotchs*** are produced from malted barley and exclusively come from a single cask or barrel. The most popular Scotch is Blended Scotch which is made by combining single malts with unmalted grain whiskeys. Another unique flavor of Scotch comes from the distinctive soft water that is rich in minerals. The use of Peat to dry the malted barley adds a smoky flavor to Scotch which appeals to some Scotch enthusiasts. The peat is cut from nearby bogs and used to stoke the fires during the drying process.

There are specific aging requirements for Scotch. Barrel aging helps to smooth the flavor of the Scotch. It is aged in oak for at least 3 years. Malt whiskeys require up to 12–15 years of aging. Grain whiskeys are best when aged for 6–8 years.

Like Scotch, ***Irish*** whiskey is made from a mash based on barley with the addition of corn and rye. The difference is that in Ireland the malted barley is dried in coal-fired ovens—in Scotland the barley is dried over peat. Irish whiskey lacks the smoky flavor common in Scotch. The Irish use a column still while a pot still is used in Scotland.

Whiskey is also made in the United States. The most popular American whiskey is Bourbon. The name ***bourbon*** comes from a county in Kentucky where the classic drink was first made. For a whiskey to carry the name *bourbon* it must meet several criteria: The whiskey must be made in Bourbon county, Kentucky; made from 51 percent corn; distilled to 80 percent alcohol; and aged in a new charred oak barrel. The use of the charred oak barrel smoothes out the flavor of the bourbon and gives it a mellow flavor.

Straight bourbons must be aged for at least 4 years and other bourbons are aged for shorter periods of time which is indicated on the bottle. ***Single barrel bourbons*** are very popular. They are a premium style of bourbon which command a higher price than other bourbons. They are bottled from a specific single barrel. These bourbons are not blended with any other bourbon. They are numbered, have an individually unique flavor, and come in fancy packages appealing to a premium market. ***Small batch bourbons*** are similar to single barrel but may have additional years of aging, making them even more exclusive.

Tennessee Whiskey is essentially straight bourbon, made in Tennessee from a mash that contains at least 51 percent corn. It is mellower than other whiskeys because it is filtered through charcoal made from Tennessee maple.

Blended whiskeys are a blend of straight whiskey and other batches of whiskey and are probably best known as coming from Canada. The lighter styles come from Canadian Club, Crown Royal, and Seagram's V.O. (Note that America and Ireland use the "e" when spelling whiskey, while Scotland and Canada spell whisky without the "e.")

Brandy

Brandy is simply wine that has been distilled. Grapes are fermented into wine. The resulting mixture is placed in a pot still and distilled to further refine the mixture and increase the alcohol.

The two most prestigious brandies come from the Cognac and Armagnac regions of France. They have a long tradition of brandy making. In these two regions the unique soil types, the use of varied distillation methods, and aging in specific oak barrel give the brandy distinctive flavors, aromas, and color. They are generally sipped straight from a snifter. More common varieties are mixed with other ingredients to make cocktails.

Gin

Gin is a white spirit with a unique flavor which is the result of compounding a white grain spirit with juniper berries. The Dutch originally created a tonic using juniper berries to cure various diseases. Gin became wildly popular in England which led to production of a low-quality spirit with no regulation. When the Coffey Still was introduced Gin became a better product and there were large brands that dominated the market. Soon after the introduction of the Coffey Still, gin was then exported into the United States. Gin was the precursor to vodka and was used widely in cocktails before, during, and after prohibition. Martinis were, and still are, an extremely popular drink. Originally made with gin and vermouth, they are garnished with an olive and served in a stemmed glass. The martini has transformed into hundreds of drinks today with a multitude of ingredients. The original ingredient in martinis gin saw a decline in the American market during the 1960s as vodka took over.

London dry gin is generally the drink of choice, while Holland's gin has a stronger taste and full body, due to its lower distillation proof, malt aroma, and flavor.

Rum

Rum is generally made from sugarcane or molasses. Because of this it is best produced in the tropical ports of Puerto Rico and Jamaica. Early Spanish settlers in the West Indies saw that the residual molasses from their sugar factories fermented easily. Soon the rum industry was more lucrative than sugar. Each of the rum-producing countries in the Caribbean has their own style of rum which can satisfy a vast clientele. Rums can be either light (or white) or dark. Light rums are made in column stills that distill away much of the flavor and color. Dark rums are made in pot stills to retain basic ingredients and aged in oak.

Tequila

"Pulque" is considered to be the first fermented beverage produced in North America. The Aztecs drank the wine-like liquid made from the blue agave plant called "pulque." If this is true, tequila is a close descendant of this beverage.

Just as with "pulque," the blue agave plant is the source of fine tequila. Grown near the town of Tequila in Mexico, the agave is steamed, fermented until a coarse wine is produced, then distilled to make tequila. Most Americans prefer the distilled, more refined, tequila.

Aged tequilas are called "anejo" and are more expensive. The oak aging also produces tequilas referred to as "gold" due to their rich color. Premium tequila has become extremely popular and what was once a spirit mixed with other ingredients, such as in the popular margarita, is sipped and savored on the rocks.

Liqueurs (Cordials)

Liqueurs, also called cordials, were originally produced as medicinal remedies for all ailments known to man. One can argue that the original distillers were not too far off their target. After all, various roots, herbs, seeds, and flowers do contain properties used today in various drugs.

When the practice of medicine took a separate path from spirits we were left with wonderful liqueurs (or cordials). These are generally sweet after-dinner drinks. Their essential oils make them a natural aid for digestion. These begin as neutral flavored spirits and are flavored by mixing or distilling in various fruits, herbs, seeds, spices, and flowers. They are then sweetened with sugar to finish.

Liqueurs must contain at least 2½ percent sugar (with many including as much as 35 percent). This makes liqueurs popular cooking and baking liquids as well.

Liqueur Notables

- Benedictine, one of the oldest of liqueurs, developed in 1510. From many herbs and plants with a cognac brandy base.
- Chartreuse, still made by monks in France. Yellow is low proof (80–86); Green is 110 proof. Both are spicy, aromatic, and based on brandy.
- Cointreau is an orange liqueur.
- Drambuie combines malt Scotch whiskey and heather honey.
- Grand Marnier is made from a cognac brandy base with orange peels for flavor.
- Irish Mist is a spicy Irish whiskey with a heather honey-flavoring agent.
- Kahlua is a coffee-flavored liqueur from Mexico.
- Southern Comfort is a blend of Bourbon whiskey, peach liqueur, and fresh peaches.
- Tia Maria, from Jamaica, is a coffee-flavored liqueur based on rum.

Appendix C, Spirit Brands and Related Cocktails, identifies some of the notable spirit brands along with popular cocktails.

TERMS TO KNOW

Aperitif: A drink before the meal to stimulate the appetite. Appetizer wine or spirit.

Bitters: Bitters are usually used to flavor mixed drinks.

Blended: Mixed in a blender until creamy. *Flash Blended:* A flash (quick) mix in a blender.

Brown Goods: A term often used to describe distilled spirits brown in color (whiskey and brandy).
Call Brand: When a guest requests a drink by brand name.
Coke: Any cola soft drink.
Diet: Usually diet cola.
Dirty: A beverage that includes green olive juice.
Dry: Usually refers to martinis, meaning a touch of vermouth. *Extra Dry:* no vermouth
Easy: Smaller portion.
Frappé: Iced. A liqueur served with finely crushed ice.
Garnishes: Products accompanying a cocktail used to enhance or alter the flavor. Also used to provide a decorative presentation. These could include olives, cherries, cocktail onions, pineapple, orange, grapefruit, celery, limes, lemons, and fruits in general.
High: A term indicating the beverage is to be served in a highball glass over ice.
Mary: Bloody Mary cocktail or spirits served with Bloody-Mary mix.
Neat: Not mixed. Liquor never touches ice. Brandy-based spirits are served in a snifter glass and heated on request. Liqueurs are served in a cordial glass. Brown spirits are served in a rocks glass.
Proof: This is the alcohol content in a given spirit. Note that in America alcohol is doubled to equal proof. Therefore, 50 percent alcohol is 100 proof. This is how a 151 proof rum consists of 75.5 percent alcohol.
Rocks: Served over cubed ice.
7-up: Seven-up, or lemon-lime soft drink.
Shot: Can range from 7/8 ounce to 1½ ounces depending upon the policy of the house.
Shaken: Shaken by hand, usually in a bar mixing tin.
Smokey: A beverage that includes a splash of Scotch.
Soda: Club soda.
Tall: Tall glass.
Tonic: Tonic water.
Twist: A slice or sliver of lemon or lime rind.
Up: Usually refers to martinis and served in the classic martini glass. Spirits are chilled and strained.
Virgin: No alcohol.
Well Brands: Brands that the house has identified as a standard.
White Goods: A term often used to describe clear spirits (vodka, gin, rum, and tequila).

BEERS, LAGERS, AND ALES

Ice-cold beer! If you are thinking that beer is not always served "ice cold," you are right. *In fact, beer should never be served ice cold because excessive cold deadens the flavor of beer and gives a weak, watery taste.* That being said, can you imagine a better way to introduce a section on one of our favorite drinks, the beer?

The impact of beer on humanity has been significant. Beer making has been dated to 5000 B.C. *One of the oldest recipes know to man was found in the pyramids and is a recipe for a type of beer.* The religious priesthood and monasteries were central to its progression *and still produce some of the most sought-after beers in the world, the Trappist Monasteries in Europe.* However, neighborhood bakers also led the charge by combining barley and yeast to ferment and then finish beer. *Beer is a product we have been making in civilizations around the world for centuries.*

Beer, as defined by the Rheinheitsgebot, also known as the Purity Law of 1516, is made with malt, water, hops, and yeast. Yeast was not in the original Law but was added decades later after its discovery. Beer may also be made with the addition of other cereal grains, in addition to malt, including corn grits, brewers rice, unmalted barley, unmalted wheat, and oatmeal to name five. Beer should not be confused with another type of malt beverages known as Malternatives, which are beverages made from malt, but do not contain hops, are clear (unless colored by the addition of natural or artificial coloring agents), and are usually flavored (most commonly by fruit extracts or flavorings) and carbonated. What many people refer to as beer is most commonly divided into two designations: lager and ale. However, a third, and rarer, product is a class of beers know as spontaneously fermented.

The primary difference between lagers, ales, and spontaneously fermented beers is the yeast added by the brewer. In lagers, the yeast settles to the bottom of the fermentation tank, while in ales, the yeast floats. Spontaneously fermented beers do not have any yeast added by the brewer. Instead, after the wort (unfermented beer which has been boiled in the brew kettle) is cooled, it is then transferred into a large, shallow, open top tank, where it is exposed to the air. Any wild yeast floating in the air will settle on the wort and begin fermenting, spontaneously. This is a very old and seldom-used practice, but is one of the original ways in which fermentation took place before we knew about yeast and how to grow and control it. The most recognized group of spontaneously fermented beers come from Belgium, are known as Lambic's, and can be fruit flavored, like Kriek (cherry) and Peche' (peach), or unflavored (Gueze). Lambics typically age 2–4 years before final blending and secondary fermentation.

During fermentation, lagers are fermented at cooler temperatures for longer times than ales, using yeast that settles to the bottom of the fermentation tank. Lagers take longer to make, are clear, and have a clean taste that is less complex than ales. Ales are fermented at higher temperatures than lagers, for shorter time, take much less time to make, and have more complex flavors than lagers. These differences in production result in different carbonation levels and different handling and serving practices, which will be covered later in this section.

The brewing process is quite simple but requires stringent sanitation practices to avoid problems. The following steps are used in brewing:

Malting: Allowing barley (or wheat) to begin to germinate (sprout).

Kilning: Cooking the malt by steaming (for pale malt), stewing (for caramel malt), and roasting (for dark or chocolate malt)

Mashing: Steeping the malt in hot water to extract the sugars from the malt.

Lautering/Sparging: Separating the sweet liquid from the malt.

Brewing/Boil: Boiling the sweet liquid (now called wort) in a brew kettle and adding hops at prescribed intervals for a specific flavor.

Cooling: The hops are separated from the wort, the wort is cooled through a heat exchanger, and transferred to a fermentation tank.

Fermentation: Yeast is added to the wort to begin fermentation. This is where the wort becomes an ale or lager.

Filtering/Conditioning/Maturation: After fermentation, the beer is filtered and transferred to a conditioning tank and aged. For ales, this is a short process taking days up to about two weeks; for lagers, it can be many weeks or longer.

Packaging: The beer is bottled, canned, or kegged.

Hops provide the bitterness and floral qualities in beer as well as help preserve the beer. There are many types of hops grown and each provides a different bitterness and aroma profile. A few examples of hops include Cascade, Hallertau, and Fuggle. Hops are added to the brew kettle while the wort is boiling. Hops are volatile and the flavor and aroma will cook out. The brewer controls the amount of hop flavor and aroma in beer by (a) selecting and blending different hops and (b) by adding hops at different stages of the boil in the brew kettle. The earlier the hops are added in the brew kettle, the less floral and bitter the beer will be and the more malty and sweeter the beer will be. As hops are added later in the boil, the beer will become more bitter and floral. The bitterness in beer is measured by its IBU (International Bittering Unit) number. The range generally runs from about 3 to 75, but some craft brewers have created beers with IBUs in excess of 115. The higher the number, the more bitter the beer, the lower the number, the more malty the beer.

Clarity in beer is measured by its SRM (Standard Reference Method). The higher the number, the more cloudy the beer. Some beers are naturally cloudy, like hefeweizen, made from wheat malt, while other beers should never be cloudy, like pilsner. Knowing the characteristics of a beer can tell you if it is a good beer or has a fault.

Some basic definitions and terms

Beer is brewed and fermented using malted barley *or wheat, sometimes include cereal* grains, and *always use* hops. *The fermenting can be bottom, top, or spontaneous with reference to the yeast. Bottom fermentation is when the yeast falls to the bottom of tanks during fermentation.*

Bock beer is *a lager that is generally* heavier, darker, and sweeter than regular beer.

Pilsner is *the most common style brewed in the United States. It is golden to pale in color and can be made in traditional and* **light** styles. O*riginal pilsners* come from the town of Pilsen, Czechoslovakia. The pilsner (or pilsener) name *now describes the style of golden* colored and bright lagers.

Lagers represent *the largest classification of* beers made in the United States. Lager is *the general classification of bottom-fermented beers. This classification covers a wide variety (style) of beer from Pilsners at the light end to Ambers in the middle range of color to Double (doppel) Bocks at the dark end of the color scale. Lagers have a higher amount of carbonation than ales, are clear, and are clean tasting.*

Malt liquor is brewed like beer *but uses a higher percentage of grain in the mash* and generally has higher alcohol content.

***Ale** is more complex in flavor than lager, is served warmer than lager, and can cover a flavor range from hoppy and bitter like an IPA (Inda pale ale) to sweet and malty like Scotch ale. This classification of beer is* top-fermented *at warmer temperatures and can be produced in less time than lagers. Colors of ales can range from golden (pale ale) to black (Scotch ale and Imperial Stout).*

Stout is very dark ale flavored and colored by the addition to the brew of dark roasted barley malt *(chocolate malt). Stout is a top-fermented beer.*

Porter is somewhat like stout but may be lower in alcohol and with a *malty* taste. *Porter is a top-fermented beer.*

Nonalcohol beer can be brewed by two different methods: traditional brewing and then removing the alcohol (an expensive process, but it maintains the taste of the beer), or brewing without alcohol, which often results in a grainy taste.

Saké is a specialized form of beer produced in Japan. It is made from rice and because of its high alcohol content many people refer to it as "rice wine."

Beer can be served with meals or by itself. The hops in beer stimulate appetites. Beer is used in various food preparations from soups to stews. It can be served with cheese and is used instead of yeast in some pancakes and fritters. The tangy quality of beer makes it popular with highly flavored or spicy dishes such as corned beef, Irish stew, sausage, cold cuts, pork dishes, fried dishes, or curry.

In judging the quality of beer one should *compare the beer with accepted standards and guidelines for the specific type or style of beer. A full list of beer styles is available at http://www.bjcp.org/2008styles/catdex.php or other beer-judging sites on the Internet or in beer-judging books. Other quality-control measures are handled at the brewery which include the quality of the grain, hops, chemical analysis and makeup of the brewing water, brewery sanitation, to name a few.*

The American craft beer industry is small but growing at a faster rate than large brewers in both sales and volume. In 2009, when major brewers saw declines, the craft beer industry increased its volume by 7 percent and sales by 10 percent. According to the Brewers Association, a craft brewer is small (produces less than 2 million barrels of beer per year), independent (less than 25 percent of the brewery is owned or controlled by an industry member who is not a craft brewer), and traditional (produces at least 50 percent of its volume from in either all malt beers or beers which use adjuncts to enhance, not lighten flavor).

Due to the small size of craft brewers they often find their niche by creating interesting, nonmainstream beers with unique character that attracts a small, but dedicated, following. Large brewers can't or won't produce these unique beers due to economics (the beers are too expensive to produce for their market), or the market is too small (there are not enough consumers for the unique flavor, so it is not cost-effective to produce the beer). In the United States many craft brewers create extreme beers that can be excessively hopped; aged in unique, small batch containers (like bourbon barrels); are high in alcohol (high gravity beers); or some other interesting or unique style or flavor profile. Craft beer is a good choice for those who are interested in protecting the environment. If you select a craft beer which is brewed close to home it cuts down on the travel time and expense of large beer companies. There is less use of fossil fuels in the transportation which helps the environment. Also less preservatives are required for these beers which makes them a better choice. To learn more about craft beer, go to *http://www.hopsaficionado.com/*

Let's return to our first phrase, "Ice Cold Beer." One cause of "flat beer" is serving it too cold. The perfect temperature for most beers and lagers is 45–47°F. Ales are served a bit warmer at about 50–52°F. Dark beers should be served at a cool room temperature (but that of most European rooms, 58–68°F).

Glassware varies from pilsners, pub glasses, mugs, goblets, and specialty glasses (for those operations desiring an out-of-the-ordinary type of glass). Figure 6–9 shows different types of beer glasses.

A clean glass is a must for the perfect head as well as the ultimate taste. Glasses should be free of oils, soaps, and fingerprints. *The term* beer clean *is a description for a clean, no-residue glass that will not impart any off flavors in the beer, nor break down*

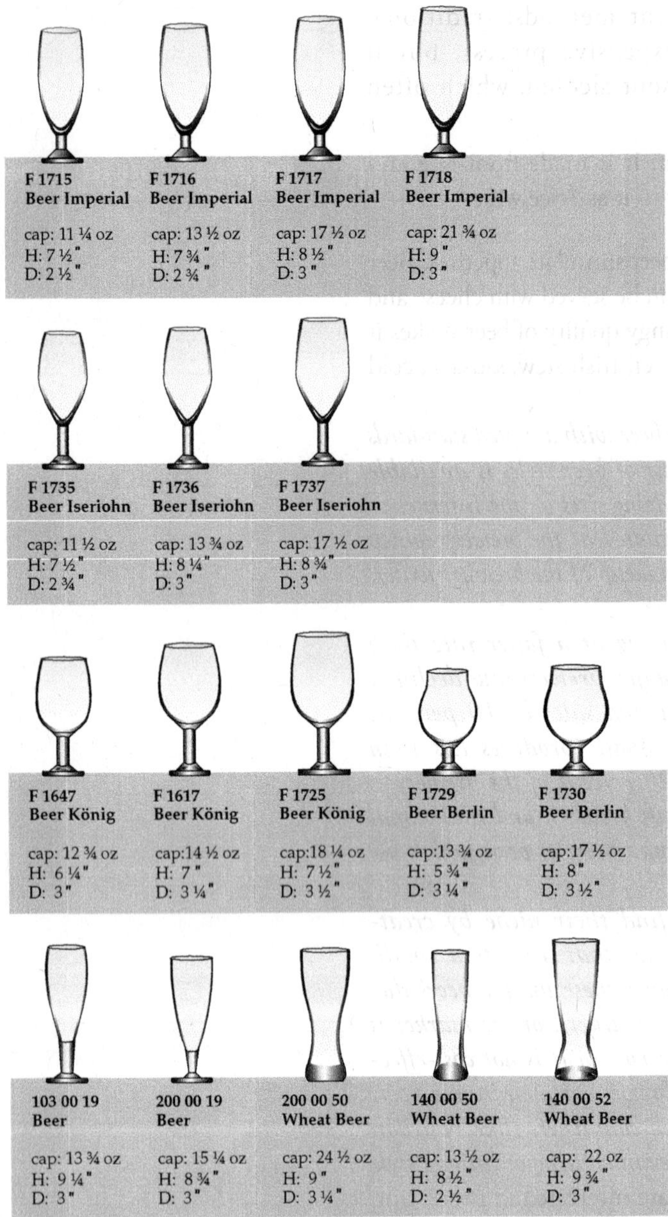

Figure 6–9
Beer Glasses. Courtesy of Stolze.

the head of the beer. A detergent and rinse agent specifically designed for bar glasses should always be used for the cleaning and sanitizing of beer, wine, and bar glassware.

Many bartenders pour beer by tilting the glass at an angle to prevent an overwhelming head of foam. This style has its supporters. However, the traditional serving style is to let the glass remain standing on a flat surface. The beer is poured directly into the bottom of the glass. The foam should be *between ¾ and 1½* inches high *depending on the type and style of beer,* as shown in Figure 6–10. They do this to release *excess* carbon dioxide. *Many American* beers in particular contain more carbon dioxide than European beers, *primarily because lagers are the dominant beer in America while ales dominate Europe.* Beer drawn from tap should be promptly served to the guest.

Premium or imported beer is often served in the bottle to the guest. When the server is pouring beer at the table, the glass should be placed to the right of the guest. If the guest prefers to do the pouring he or she will inform the server. Most often the server pours the beer. The server should carefully pour the beer directly into the center of the glass, allowing about 1½ inches of foam to appear and come to the rim of the glass, followed by a quick twist of the bottle to prevent dripping. The bottle is then placed above and to the right of the glass.

In terms of storage, remember that beer is extremely perishable. Odors, bacteria, air, and even artificial or natural light can destroy a beer before it reaches our palates. Beer should be stored at around 40°F. Bottled beer should be stored in a dark, cool place. Beer in cans is not affected by light, but still needs to be stored in a cool place.

Appendix D—Ales, Lagers, and Nonalcohol Beer—identifies ale and lager types along with common brands of ale, lager, and nonalcohol beer.

BOTTLED WATERS

Many guests enjoy bottled water as part of their everyday lives as well as with their meals. Certain guests have a preference for the mineral content or taste of a particular brand of nonsparkling water. Other guests prefer a naturally sparkling mineral water from a particular natural spring because of their traditional health benefits. Because bottled waters have become so popular many fine restaurants have a water list that will give their guests a selection of bottled waters to choose from. Some guest may even compare bottled water to wine because of its unique flavor characteristics due to the area in which it is bottled.

Bottled waters are typically opened, brought to the table, and poured by the server. The restaurant will determine the size and shape of glass to be used for bottled-water service. The server places the glass with ice on the table to the right of the guest and pours the water to about three-fourths full. Occasionally, a guest may prefer not to have ice with the water to get the full unique taste of the bottled water. The bottle is then placed above and to the right of the glass. The guest may request or the server may offer (depending upon the policy of the restaurant) a lemon or lime twist. The glass may also be served on a paper coaster.

Figure 6–10
Beer Glass with foam. Courtesy of Stolze.

COFFEE

Ethiopia is considered to be the birthplace of coffee. Legend has it that goats or sheep ate the small red berries that contained the coffee bean seeds. They became agitated and excited. The indigenous peoples decided to partake of the same plant. Their energy and alertness were also raised. The plant was passed on to monks who created various drinks, including the current form of coffee.

Coffee quickly spread from Arabia to Syria to Constantinople. For centuries, coffee production was carefully guarded by the Arab world. The cartel was not broken until Dutch traders secured precious seeds to take to the west.

By the early 1600s coffee was enjoyed by the French. They soon introduced the style of serving coffee after dinner. Their method of preparation (the "French Press") is still used today and has seen a comeback in recent years, particularly in fine dining restaurants. The superb quality of the coffee produced with a French Press and upscale presentation have added to its resurgence in popularity. Near boiling water is poured onto ground coffee, typically a courser ground than coffee for an automatic machine. This allows for more surface area to come in contact with the grinds for better extraction of flavors. The coffee is held together by disks that act as filters, as shown in Figure 6–11. A French Press can also create coffee for the drink that is unique. Prepared tableside, this visual display is tremendous, especially with the addition of a spirit cart. The press makes coffee for one or more guests (3-cup, 8-cup, or 12-cup French Press) and can be brought into any space without wires or plugs.

Over the centuries, cultivation spread from Africa to South America and then to the West Indies. Two types of coffee bushes supply most beans to the consumer. Arabica is considered the highest quality, while Robusta contains more caffeine and yields a somewhat nutty taste.

Coffee beans are roasted to bring out various flavor characteristics. Beans roasted at lower temperatures are lighter and smoother than their darker-roasted cousins. Higher temperatures during the roast produce dark, reddish-brown beans with "fiery" taste. Grinding is also a critical element in coffee making. While coffee can be ground weeks before it is brewed, the premium tastes and aromas are produced from beans that are ground directly prior to extraction, allowing time to stabilize. There is an increasing popularity in organic and fair-trade coffees. The coffee plantations are governed by organizations that control the way they are farmed. Fair-trade means that the farmer gives a portion of the money that he receives from the sale of his crop back to the community to stimulate such projects as health care and education.

Figure 6–11
French Press. Gerald Lanuzza.

Types of roasts commonly seen are:

1. Cinnamon Roast—seen in most commercial uses. Beans are roasted for 5–6 minutes and usually still have a sour taste.
2. City Roast—beans are light brown and still high in acid. Light bodied coffees are made from these beans.
3. Full City Roast—medium-to-chestnut brown beans. Sugars begin to develop and add a balance to flavor.
4. Espresso Roast—deep brown with caramel and spice notes. Roast lasts at least 12 minutes.
5. Italian Roast—beans are a dark brown and oils start to be released. A sweet flavor develops with smokey notes.
6. French Roast—beans are close to black in color, sweetness starts to become less, and smokey notes become predominant.

Darker-roasted coffees are not necessarily stronger than those that are lightly roasted. The longer the bean is roasted different flavors develop, giving unique taste characteristics.

Decaffeinated coffee starts when the beans are still green and unroasted. After roasting they can often look darker than that of caffeinated coffee but could be the same roast. A good way to tell the difference between the two is decaffeinated coffee beans will look darker and dry while regular beans are oily in appearance.

There are two processes to decaffeinate coffee: (1) The Swiss Water Method where the beans are passed through a high-pressure filter and soaked in water for up to 12 hours and (2) Direct Contact Method where a food-grade solvent is used to remove the caffeine during a soaking process.

Coffee service can be somewhat unique depending upon where it is served. In the United States, we now serve coffee in almost every possible way and at all times of the day. We have coffee drinks of all kinds served in paper cups "to go," so that we can keep up with our busy schedules.

Baristas and Barista Training

Professionals preparing and serving coffee drinks are called baristas. The term *barista* is of Italian origin which means bartender or a person who would typically work behind a counter, serving coffee drinks, nonalcohol beverages, and alcohol beverages. Baristas in the United States are individuals who have acquired expertise in the art of coffee making. A barista will have comprehensive knowledge of coffee origin, coffee blends, coffee varieties, type of roasts, the use of coffee-making equipment, and equipment sanitation. There are many barista schools and barista competitions worldwide where individuals learn, practice, and compete with each other to demonstrate their great coffee service and making skills needed to be a coffee professional. There are some basic guidelines for coffee served by a qualified barista. The coffee should always be of the best quality and the freshest it can be. Beans ground to order are the ultimate in freshness and will produce the best tasting coffee. Once coffee is brewed it should be held for no more than 2 hours in an insulated coffee pot with limited exposure to oxygen. If the coffee is sitting on a burner it should stay there for no more than 30 minutes due to evaporation and cooking as it sits. There should be a brand standard set for the coffee made in an establishment. Specific guidelines should be set forth then the employees should be trained then tested on the guidelines. Coffee equipment must be cleaned thoroughly and well maintained. If any part of a coffee or espresso machine is not working, it should be immediately reported to the management. An example of an espresso machine is shown in Figure 6–12. Barista service should be quick and friendly. Even when there is a line each guest should be acknowledged within no more than 2 minutes by a friendly greeting.

Figure 6–12
Espresso Machine. Gerald Lanuzza.

One of the most important parts of a baristas job is steaming milk properly. This can be the difference between a good and great coffee experience. Always start with the freshest cold milk and a clean pitcher. Pour only what you need for the particular drink that you are making. Milk steamed more than twice can get a bitter and burnt taste. Always make sure that you are working with a calibrated thermometer; temperature is very important. Milk scorches at 160 degrees and then you must begin again. You can never recover burnt milk.

Bleed your steam wand into a towel to remove condensation. Insert it into the milk and turn on to full. Never bring the wand completely out of the milk but hold it just below the surface allowing the milk to aerate; this is what creates the foam. If you hear a high-pitched screaming, this is a sign of milk burning; check your temperature or you are not aerating the milk enough. Once the milk reaches about 100 degrees fully submerge the wand to heat all the milk evenly. Remove the pitcher from the steam when the temperature reaches 140–150°F. Nonfat milk is easier to get fluffy foam because of the low fat content; soy milk can be steamed as an alternative but it is only recommended to be heated to 130°F before the taste gets bitter.

Types of Coffee Drinks

Espresso is an Italian style of coffee. It involves a process in which a specialty blended and roasted coffee, finely ground, is brewed rapidly (20–25 seconds) under pressure, through a fine mesh screen filter. Espresso is traditionally served in a demitasse (small) cup. There should be golden foam on the top of a quality espresso which is called the "crema."

Americano is a shot of freshly brewed espresso added to hot water, similar to a fresh cup of coffee. Originated in Europe during World War II when the Americans who where stationed in Italy found espresso to be too strong and added hot water to it.

Macchiato is a shot of espresso with foam on top.

Caffé lattes are approximately 10 percent espresso, 80 percent steamed milk, and 10 percent milk foam, depending upon the size of the cup.

Cappuccinos are approximately 1/3 espresso, 1/3 steamed milk, and 1/3 foam. The resultant brown concoction is reminiscent of the color of robes of the Capuchin monks—hence the name.

Mochas are approximately 10 percent espresso, 10 percent chocolate syrup, and 80 percent steamed milk. Mocha is a term used to describe the combination of chocolate and coffee.

A wide variety of flavored drinks can be created by adding syrup flavorings to caffé lattes, cappuccinos, or mochas.

Table 6–5 provides a comparative reference to types of coffee drinks by name, ingredients, appearance, flavor, and how served.

Decaffeinated coffee

- A minimum of 97 percent of the caffeine is removed from coffee in this process. Unroasted beans are steamed to release caffeine from the bean. A decaffeinating agent (solvent or water) is then used to remove the caffeine. Many people feel that this process, while quite sophisticated, leaves coffee a shadow of its former self.

TABLE 6–5
TYPE OF COFFEE DRINKS

Name	Ingredients	Appearance	Flavor	Served In
Espresso	Finely ground coffee pushed through a basket with great force	Dark in color with a golden froth on top called "crema"	Bitter and dark	Small demitasse cup ½ full and saucer with a twist of lemon
Americano	A shot of espresso combined with two parts hot water	Looks like a regular cup of black coffee	The water lessens the strength of the espresso	Coffee cup ¾ full and saucer
Macchiato	A shot of espresso with steamed milk on top	Dark in color with milk on top	Slightly creamy	Coffee cup ½ full and saucer
Caffé lattes	A shot of espresso, with hot milk added and froth milk on top	Carmel in color due to the high percentage of milk and froth	Creamy and smooth	Coffee cup with ¼ espresso, ½ steamed milk, and ¼ froth
Cappuccino	A shot of espresso, steamed milk, and froth	Similar to the robes of monks, brown	Rich but less bitter due to the milk	Coffee cup and saucer with equal amounts of espresso, steamed milk, and froth
Mochas	A shot of espresso, chocolate syrup, and steamed milk	Light brown in color	Smooth coffee flavor with a hint of chocolate	Coffee cup and saucer with 1/8 espresso, 1/8 chocolate syrup, and ¾ steamed milk
Café au Lait	Half drip coffee and half steamed milk	Light brown in color	Creamy and smooth	Coffee cup and saucer with ½ coffee and ½ steamed milk
Flavored Café au Lait	Half drip coffee and half steamed milk flavored with 1 ounce of Italian syrup such as, almond, raspberry, chocolate, vanilla	Light brown in color	Creamy and smooth with a sweet flavor	Coffee cup and saucer with ½ coffee and ½ steamed milk with 1 ounce of syrup
Café Coretta	Espresso with liquor, usually brandy added	Dark brown	Bitter and rich with the flavor of the alcohol	Coffee cup and saucer with a shot of espresso and liquor

Tips for correct brewing

- Always start with a clean coffee maker.
- Use only cold, fresh, pure water for brewing. Heavily chlorinated water should be filtered, or you should use bottled water.
- Temperature for brewing should be nearly boiling.
- Grind must be right for the type of brewing equipment.
- Follow a ratio of 14–20 ounces of water to 1 ounce of coffee, adjusting to taste.
- Always use superb-quality coffee.
- Store coffee in a cool, dry place to preserve optimal freshness.

"A cup of coffee with a twist"

For centuries, people have enjoyed wine with their meals, but what about after dinner—the twilight hours of the day?

Some say the art of spiking coffee with alcohol began even before shepherds matched wine with food. Ghengis Khan was said to provide his invading soldiers with a hot drink made from pillaged wine and coffee before making forays into new lands.

Many who prefer wine as a complement to food still enjoy a properly mixed after-dinner drink utilizing coffee. It is often the perfect crowning touch to an evening. Some popular spirited coffee drinks are as follows: Spanish Coffee flambéed tableside consists of a blend of Kahlua, coffee, 151 rum, and triple sec and matched only by their showmanship and artistry. Café Diablo is prepared by flaming an orange peel into a silver chalice filled with coffee, brandy bitters, and vermouth.

Some other favorites include Café Royale (with bourbon or brandy) and Mexican Coffee (with tequila and sweetened with Kahlua); Café Pucci is an outstanding drink made with Trinidad rum and Amaretto; Kioki (or Keoke) Coffee tastes wonderful with brandy; and Royal Street Coffee is exceptional with Amaretto, Kahlua, and nutmeg, served dry (no sugar).

TEA

People around the world have enjoyed tea for over 5,000 years. Next to water, tea is the most commonly consumed beverage in the world, with an estimated 1 billion cups consumed daily worldwide. Tea leaves come from the *Camellia sinensis* plant which grows throughout the world, including the United States. There are four categories of tea that come from the *Camellia sinensis* plant: white, green, oolong, and black. The type of tea is directly linked to when the leaves are picked and then how the leaves are processed. White and green teas are popular due to their high antioxidants, which are linked to health benefits. There are also numerous varieties of tea found throughout the world. Some teas are named after their places of origin, such as Ceylon from Sri Lanka (formerly Ceylon) and Darjeeling from the Himalayas. Each tea has its own unique flavor, color, and aroma. Often different teas are blended to create a new flavor. Earl Grey, English breakfast, and orange spice are examples of teas that are blends of different varieties. Decaffeinated teas are available, and herbal teas are 100 percent caffeine free. The herbal teas are made from dried leaves and flowers that are steeped in boiling water. Tea service has become increasingly popular therefore the professional server should understand the basics of teas and tea service to better serve their guests.

Tea can be served with a cup of hot (near-boiling) water and a tea bag placed next to the cup, with a teapot of hot water and the tea bag placed next to the teapot when served, or with a tea press that retains the leaves when pouring into teacups. The teapot should be placed to the right of the cup with the handle turned at 4 o'clock. This allows the guest to open the package containing the fresh tea bag and place it in the hot water to steep to the desired strength. The tea press should also be placed to the right of the cup. The tea press is used in fine dining restaurants that offer premium loose-leaf teas for guest selection. If the guest desires a lemon wedge and/or milk (or cream), it should be placed on a small plate lined with a doily. The plate is placed above and to the right of the cup.

Iced tea is served in a large glass with ice, a lemon wedge, and a long-drink spoon. The glass is typically placed on top of a small plate with a paper doily or coaster. Sugar and/or artificial sweetener are also brought to the table. When served, the iced tea is placed to the right of the guest. Iced teas flavored with syrup have become popular.

SUMMARY

Wine service begins with the knowledge of serving temperatures and the correct use of an ice bucket during the service of wine. The importance of properly presenting a bottle of wine or Champagne to a guest along with being able to open and serve it is a measure of a server's professionalism.

Occasionally, wine will need to be decanted. The server should be able to recognize when this occurs and what the procedure is to decant a bottle of wine. Servers should be trained in the fundamentals of wine varieties and other alcohol beverages such as vodka, Scotch, bourbon, blended whiskeys, brandy, gin, rum, tequila, and liqueurs (cordials). Also, the server should know what to look for in recommending beer along with the best serving temperatures of beers, and to be able to explain the differences between beers, lagers, ales, bock beer, pilsner, malt liquor, stout, porter, and saké. Ultimately, if the server can describe the qualities of the various alcohol beverages, the guests will appreciate the server's expertise and the selection.

Servers should always be conscious of taking good care of their guests and should protect them from the effects of misusing alcohol. Along with being a legal obligation, it constitutes good business, and is the "morally correct" thing to do. Many states have a mandatory server education program for owners and employees of licensed businesses that serve alcohol. These states require alcohol servers to have a service permit, which is obtained by taking a class in responsible alcohol service.

The server should know how to serve coffee, as well as espresso and espresso drinks, such as caffé lattes, cappuccinos, and mochas. In addition, he or she should understand the different types of teas and tea service.

DISCUSSION QUESTIONS AND EXERCISES

1. What is the server's legal responsibility when serving an alcohol beverage, and when should an Incident Report be used?
2. What is the recommended temperature for serving each of the following wines: white wine, red wine, and dessert wine?
3. Explain how to prepare an ice bucket for use and when salt should be added.
4. What is the correct way to present a bottle of wine to a guest?
5. Explain the procedure for removing a cork from a bottle of wine.
6. When a bottle of wine is opened, what should be done with the cork?
7. What is the true test of a bottle of wine?
8. Explain the procedure for pouring wine once the cork has been removed.
9. How full should wine glasses be filled?
10. Explain the procedure for opening a bottle of champagne.
11. Explain the process of decanting wine.
12. When red wine reacts with air, what is this called?
13. How does climate affect the grapes that produce wines?
14. When would fortified wines be served and how else could they be used?
15. List three examples of fortified wines.
16. Explain how vodka is made and name five popular vodka drinks.
17. Explain the origin and production process of both Scotch and bourbon.
18. What distinguishes Tennessee whiskey from other whiskeys?
19. Name two popular brands of Canadian blended whiskeys.
20. What is the difference between Irish whiskey and Scotch?
21. What is brandy?
22. What are two popular drinks made from gin?
23. What is rum generally made from?
24. Name three popular drinks that are made from rum.
25. Explain the process of producing tequila and name two popular tequila drinks.
26. What are liqueurs?
27. Identify seven different liqueurs and explain the characteristics of each one.
28. Define the following terms: aperitif, frappé, neat, and proof.
29. Describe bock beer.
30. What are light style beers generally known as?
31. What is brewed like beer but has higher alcohol content?
32. Explain the difference between beer and ale.

33. Describe the difference between stout and porter ale.
34. What is saké and how is it made?
35. How is beer judged?
36. What is one of the main causes of flat beer?
37. What is the recommended temperature for beers, lagers, ales, and dark beers?
38. Name and describe five types of coffee roasts.
39. How is a French Press used to make coffee?
40. Explain the process of making espresso.
41. Name the ingredients and their approximate percentage in the following espresso drinks: caffé lattes, cappuccinos, and mochas.
42. Discuss several coffee and alcohol combinations.
43. How are herbal teas made?
44. Explain two ways of serving hot tea.
45. How is iced tea served?

7

Guest Communication

learning objectives

After reading this chapter and completing the discussion questions and exercises, you should be able to:

1. Describe how to make a personal connection with guests.
2. Demonstrate server introductory greetings to guests.
3. Understand how to develop server enthusiasm.
4. Measure the effects of server enthusiasm.
5. Identify and describe several different types of guests.
6. Anticipate the guest's needs.
7. Recognize nonverbal cues and prompts that can assist in anticipating the guest's needs.
8. Explain and demonstrate suggestive selling.
9. List the five different types of suggestive selling.
10. Describe the benefits of suggestive selling.
11. Explain the three basic guidelines for suggestive selling.
12. Give examples of when dining room showmanship suggestively sells.
13. Understand and explain the procedure to follow when taking a guest's order.

Exceptional customer service can be summed up as "exceeding guest expectations in a professional, friendly, competent, and timely manner." The job of a server requires the use of psychology in making an emotional connection with guests, the techniques of a salesperson to be able to successfully suggest food and beverage items, and a professional attitude accompanied with charm and grace. Guests often want to feel pampered and special which requires the server to be able to effectively meet and exceed the personal expectations of every guest.

Each guest brings a personal opinion on service to each and every restaurant experience. Their expectations may change depending on the style of the restaurant. As the dining level, and concurrently the price of the meal, increases a guest's expectations will also increase. Some guests like to eat quickly and appreciate and expect the server to respond in a prompt, efficient manner that keeps pace with the speed of their eating habits. They may simply be very hungry and want their food as fast as possible: The server must FEED THE NEED. Other guests may want to relax over a leisurely meal and savor the dining-out experience. Dining out has become a social event that many people look forward to as they enjoy a fabulous meal in a special setting accompanied by excellent service. The server must READ THE NEED. The server in the second example must read all the cues that the guests send. The guests who are dining leisurely want more than just to eat because they are not only hungry, they also want the experience of dining and the pleasure of enjoying the atmosphere and server's interaction.

Servers are the individuals that become the "personality" of a restaurant. They are familiar faces to regular guests and new acquaintances to first-time customers. The servers are the salespeople and providers, selling food and beverages, and providing service. The server's job consists of the following:

1. Serve guests to their complete satisfaction by positively managing the guest experience.
2. Represent the restaurant and the management in a positive way.
3. Perform within the restaurant's established standards of quality and service or protocol.
4. Earn the privilege of receiving maximum tips.

Many people seem to believe that there is a mysterious "secret" to being a successful server. The fact is that there are no hidden secrets; instead the techniques required can be easily learned. The learning process begins with the self-discipline and commitment needed to acquire new skills, accompanied by the dedication to providing the best in customer service, which is rewarded with a feeling of personal satisfaction as well as, financially, by earning good tips.

GETTING TO KNOW YOUR GUESTS

14. Identify several procedures that can help a server to conserve steps and improve service timing during rush periods.
15. Explain what the server should do in an emergency situation or when a guest becomes ill.

A server's task is more than taking an order. If a server is only interested in order taking he or she does not live up to their full potential as a professional server. The server must have the desire to become knowledgeable about all of the food and beverage menu offerings, have the ability to recognize and greet repeat customers by their name, and be able to help guests with menu selections with a sense of enthusiasm. This begins with the server's ability to initially gain the guest's confidence, followed by an implied trust that generates the expectation of service that will provide the best dining experience possible. This personal connection can be initiated in several ways and, surprisingly, under the most common circumstances.

First and foremost is the server's perceived attitude about service. At times the server's enthusiasm is more important than the technicalities of service itself. Every restaurant has rules and protocol necessary for smooth, consistent operations. However, in the personal exchange between the server and guest it is important that the server show his or her personality in a manner that will have a positive effect upon guests. The result is a smooth and enjoyable dining experience.

Acknowledging guests within the first few seconds after they are seated displays an important sense of urgency on the server's part. The first impression can be lasting and often sets the tone for the remainder of the meal. A positive first encounter can be accomplished with a smile and a nod of the head, a small wave of the hand, or even eye contact, including raising the eyebrows while still serving another table.

Typically, the server greets guests by introducing himself or herself. Often, a server wears a nametag that is clearly visible to guests. If the server learns the guest's name through a reservation or was introduced to the guest by the host, it is then appropriate to address the guest by name—for example, Mr., Miss, or Ms. Jones.

The server's introductory greeting must be genuine and original to each guest and table. Other guests seated at nearby tables will certainly hear the server's greeting for each arriving guest or group. The greeting should be different for each table; otherwise, the server may appear to be robotic, using the same script over and over. It is important to remember to find a personal greeting you are comfortable with that reflects your unique personality. Table 7–1 offers some appropriate greetings.

Remembering names, what the guests ordered at their last visit, their preferred beverage, and the memorable event of their last dining experience with the server are several factors that enhance the personal connection between server and guests. It is important

TABLE 7–1
APPROPRIATE GREETING

Good	Better
"Hello"	"Good evening, my name is Martin"
"Welcome to (restaurant's name)"	"Welcome to the (name of the restaurant) My name is Martin, how may I accommodate your needs this evening?"
"Hello, is this your first visit to our restaurant?"	"Good evening, are you new to the area? I will be happy to help you with the menu and bring you a beverage while you are deciding."
"Welcome to (restaurant's name), would you care for some water?"	"Good evening, welcome to (restaurant's name), I will bring some water while you decide on one of our famous specialty drinks."
"Good evening , Mr. Allison"	"Good evening, Mr. Allison, it's good to see you again. Would you like me to bring you your usual or maybe something new?"

to repeat guests that you are able to remember their name and it reflects positively on the restaurant. The guest will have a personal connection to you and will request your service in the future. The food may be equally as good in a competitor's restaurant but the server's connection to their guest ultimately may be the deciding factor when they choose where to dine. Customer service studies have revealed that among the many things that a restaurant can do to make a guest feel welcomed is to welcome the guest by name.

When guests trust the server, they are inclined to respond favorably to appetizer, entrée, dessert, and beverage suggestions. This will affect sales and tips, and it provides the spark that encourages guests to return again and again.

CONNECTING TO THE GUEST TO CREATE GUEST LOYALTY

John L. Avella, Ed.D., has 45 years of human resource development and operations experience in the hospitality industry. He has been vice president of human resources for Marriott Corporation, The Rainbow Room, and Windows on the World. As a consultant some of his clients included: Marriott Corporation, Restaurant Associates, Hilton Hotels, Culinary Institute of America, Holiday Inns, American Red Cross, Compass Group, Coca Cola, and Port Authority of New York and New Jersey. In 2001–2002 Dr. Avella was the Human Resource Director at the Winter Olympics in Salt Lake City for the food services facilities, serving 125,000 meals per day. He has also managed several large projects, including the opening of the new Cleveland Brown's stadium (1999) and the US Tennis Open (2002). He is currently President of EQ International Perspectives (EQinternationalperspectives.com). As a distinguished speaker/trainer/consultant, Dr. Avella offers the following:

Connecting emotionally to the guest is the most critical part of a successful guest interaction. A good definition of guest service is: "creating a unique emotional experience for the guest." When you think of it, it is a relatively simple process—connect emotionally to the guest—develop a relationship—create loyal guests.

Positive service is all about the interaction with the guest; as a matter of fact research tells us that servers who connect emotionally to the guest make 127 percent more in tips than servers who don't connect. When you think about it the server's section is his or her own little business, and he or she has to treat it like they own it. He or she benefits from the sales from that section, the higher the sales the bigger the tips. His or her percentage is higher than the restaurant owner. The server makes 14–20 percent of sales, whereas the owner makes 2–4 percent on sales. An important thing to remember is that when building sales, guests buy from people they trust and like—there is that emotional influence again. To piggyback on the emotional influence the Gallup organization, based on their research (2003), "Regardless of how high a company's satisfaction levels may appear to be, satisfying guests without creating an emotional connection with them has no real value."

It would seem obvious that we would want loyal guests, but there are economic benefits from creating guest loyalty. Frederick F. Reichheld, author of *The Loyalty Effect*, lists some of these benefits:

- Raising guest retention rates by 5 percent could increase the value of an average guest by 25–100 percent
- Loyal guests always return and become a dependable lifetime sales stream
- Loyal guests brag about your organization and create the most effective advertising strategy—word of mouth and it's free of cost
- It costs five times more to acquire a new guest than to keep an existing one
- Referred guests tend to be of higher quality—that is, their business is more profitable and they stay with the business longer, creating more revenue and profits
- Loyal guests are willing to pay more for your product or service
- Loyal guests are more forgiving when you make a mistake

So what does this mean? More sales and profit for the organization and more business and tips for the server.

Let's talk about a recent experience where you were the customer or guest. What was memorable about it? Was it positive or negative? What made it such? How did you feel about it? What emotions were involved? How important were the emotions in this experience? Are emotions important in the guest experience? Think about the answers to these questions: Would you rather deal with a restaurant you like or dislike? How many purchasing decisions are based on emotion, instead of need? Would you rather deal with a restaurant that was highly recommended by someone you know or a restaurant you saw in an advertisement? The answer seems obvious but do we think in these terms?

Emotions matter in the guest experience because guests and staff are always emotional. In the service industry, the emotions of the guest and staff can be more intense. So let's look at what emotions tell us about guests. The more concerned a guest is about an experience, the stronger the emotional response. Many times the intensity of a guest's emotion has nothing to do with the present situation; those guest emotions can be influenced by memories, life circumstances, and the guests' and staff's emotional state at the time.

So as a guest service provider how do I know what emotions the guest is feeling? Well, there are many verbal and nonverbal cues that the guest displays if you are watching for those cues. Properly reading those cues could turn a negative guest experience into a positive one. By reading the cues you can control the interaction. Again your job is to manage the guest experience and make sure it turns out to be a positive one. Reading the guest starts with observing the guest as he or she enters the dining room. How fast is he or she walking, head down what is the expression on their face? Based on that observation you can determine how you will approach that table. For example, if the guest seems to be in a hurry, make sure you take that into account when you recommend drink and food. Don't suggest a 5-course tasting menu. If the guests are involved in a conversation wait for an opportunity to speak, always leaning forward toward the guest and at the same time trying to make eye contact with one of the guests. Don't interrupt by saying, "excuse me"; you need to work on their agenda, not yours.

If a guest leans toward you as if looking for help or reassurance, lean toward them using a reassuring tone of voice. If the guest's facial expression seems sad or depressed, be ready to help in a sympathetic way. If the guests seem joyful and celebratory, that's easy. Keep the positive emotions rolling, but don't get too familiar. Remember the occasion is about them, not you. If guests seem embarrassed or reluctant, perhaps with heads slightly bowed and not making eye contact, be positive and reassure them you are there to help and make the experience a great one. If there is anger or tension, guests are likely to have arms crossed, be leaning back, and have a scowl. Be just the opposite with your best "happy to see you" expression and positive body language. Show interest, listen carefully, pick up on cues that might change the mood. You can have a dramatic influence on each interaction by setting a positive tone. Use your smile and body language to create the right atmosphere for a great guest experience. If their emotions are negative, your positive emotions can change them to positive or neutral. If Guests are in a positive mood, you can reinforce and enhance their pleasure. Remember a healthy way to view emotions is not as a problem to be solved BUT as the basis for forming relationships—this is how you create loyalty. An even bigger opportunity to form a relationship with the guest is if they have a problem that you solve.

To create a positive relationship with the guest you need to start with you. Remember, you can't change the guest but you can change yourself. Research tells us that if you don't know yourself physically and emotionally, your system reverts to "hostility" in stressful situations. Remember, self-awareness is the emotional foundation of service. So we start by taking a look at your body language. There is an old expression that states, "I can't hear you because your body language is drowning out your spoken word." What nonverbal messages are you sending to the guest? Have a friend look at your body language and give you some feedback. What is your posture, eyes and expression saying?

- Welcome, I value you
- Talk fast, I have other guests
- Don't ask such dumb questions
- I want to help you have a great dining experience

With every guest you should be conscious of:

- Your facial expressions and attitudes as you approach the guest; be sure you are focusing on those guests and no one else
- Make eye contact; avoid slouching or leaning on the table or counter
- Be welcoming, warm, and engaging
- Avoid behavior that suggests you are preoccupied or hurried
- Communicate delight at having the opportunity to serve them

The last thing to discuss is developing trust. Why? Because people naturally gravitate toward those they trust. When you have established trust, the guest will be interested in your suggestions and make a point of seeking to be helped by you. The keys to trust are:

- Be yourself
- Give the guest your full attention
- Put the guests' interests ahead of yours
- Be knowledgeable and honest about quality and costs
- How would you serve this person if he or she were a family member or friend?

Since your job is 80 percent emotional and 20 percent technical make sure you focus on that 80 percent. The bottom line in a successful guest experience is to connect emotionally to that guest, and create a relationship which will create guest loyalty—the ultimate guest outcome.

restaurant reality: It happens every day all across america

There is a small restaurant in an average-size city named "The Corner Place" where Mr. Smith has lunch three times a week. The food is consistently good but it is not what has kept him coming to the restaurant for the past 15 years. It is not what makes him recommend the restaurant with a smile as he often does. The reason that Mr. Smith comes to the restaurant is a server named Barbara.

Barbara has worked part-time for the past 18 years at "The Corner Place," beginning when her two children started school. Barbara enjoys meeting and serving people and likes the flexibility of her server's schedule. Mr. Smith met Barbara 15 years ago when he decided to have lunch at "The Corner Place." His office is in walking distance to several good restaurants and he tried them all, but his favorite quickly became "The Corner Place."

Upon their first meeting, Barbara welcomed Mr. Smith to "The Corner Place," and through a casual conversation learned that his office was nearby and that it was his first visit to the restaurant. She promptly accommodated his request to have no ice in his water or soft drink. Then Barbara offered some menu suggestions that helped him to quickly become acquainted with the menu. As he finished his lunch she informed him that it was the policy of the restaurant to offer special first-time guests a complimentary dessert. Mr. Smith not only enjoyed his lunch and dessert, but also never forgot how Barbara made him feel welcome and appreciated as a guest at "The Corner Place."

Although at different times Mr. Smith would try other restaurants for lunch, he always returned to "The Corner Place" to be served by his friend Barbara, who always has a bright smile and a warm greeting and remembers how he likes having no ice in his drinks. She appreciates the friendship and the nice tip that is always left by Mr. Smith.

SERVER ENTHUSIASM

The server with enthusiasm demonstrates the following attributes:

- Smiles often.
- Always well groomed.
- Walks quickly and has good posture.
- Alert and attentive to guests.
- Friendly, tactful, and tolerant.
- Poised and composed.
- Speaks clearly and distinctly—voice carries conviction with proper inflections.
- Knows what he or she is doing and why.

Enthusiasm comes naturally to some people, but for most, it takes a concentrated effort to develop the traits that evolve into an enthusiastic personality. It begins with identifying where you are now and where you want to go. You have to visualize what you want to accomplish. This begins with asking, "How will enthusiastic behavior help me in becoming more professional as a server?" The answer of course lies within the fact that servers work for tips. A good server truly is a good salesperson who truly believes in the product they are selling. It is easy to be motivated by an increase in salary each and every night. Most other professions rely on a boss who controls their yearly increase in salary. There is a direct link to the amount of enthusiasm a server has for their job, the products they sell, and an increase in their tips. Guests can see this excitement and undoubtedly they are more generous when it comes time to tip.

The act of smiling is the first step toward developing enthusiasm. What a difference it makes in your appearance! A smile communicates to the guest, "I am glad to see you." It is essential to start guests off right when they come to dine, so smile and greet them enthusiastically with your own personalized greeting. Many servers may not be aware that they are smiling, because they usually do it as a natural reflex. If necessary, the server should become conscious of when he or she is smiling and work at enhancing those smiles.

The server who develops vitality and a few internal creative forces will be able to generate an enthusiastic atmosphere for guests. When a server is sincerely enthusiastic, the server's face lights up, eyes shine, and the voice is vibrant. The server compels the guests' attention, and every word carries conviction. Enthusiasm is the key that unlocks the minds of your guests, causing them to like you. It is also important to remember that it does not overshadow poor service and/or poor quality food. Remember, to be enthusiastic, you must act enthusiastic!

A server should always approach guests with the feeling that they are nice people who will be enjoyable to serve. This positive expectation can translate into a self-fulfilling prophecy. People tend to act as they are expected to act. If you expect your guests to be nice people and you treat them that way, the odds are in your favor that they will be nice people. To be able to realize this full potential, a server needs to display an ability to generate sincere enthusiasm. If enthusiasm is not sincere, it may be seen as patronizing, which can generate negative feelings from guests. Genuine enthusiasm is contagious and a server who displays it in personal performance will achieve positive results. However, there are guests who are unpleasant no matter how positive and enthusiastic a server may be. Then it becomes a real opportunity for the server to turn a difficult guest into a happy, satisfied one.

DIFFERENT TYPES OF GUESTS

The server needs to be prepared to serve all types of guests. Some are young, others are old; some are pleasant, and some are unpleasant. The server has to take them as they are and do the very best for each of them. They are the guests.

There are certain situations that require a great deal of patience and tact on the part of the server, especially when a guest is difficult. However, the guest is there and the server has to take care of that guest, and not allow him or her to disturb other guests. The following are some examples and approaches to handling different types of guests.

The Procrastinator This is a guest who just cannot make up his or her mind. This is where you have the opportunity to practice suggestive selling skills. The procrastinator would probably appreciate you helping in the decision-making process. You can do this very skillfully by suggesting two or three menu items. If that does not work, allow the guest to have a little more time, mentioning that you will check back in a few minutes. Then check back every few minutes to see if the guest is ready to order.

The Skeptic This type of guest may be doubtful about the quality of food or the way it is prepared. The guest is often very fussy and wants it exactly a certain way. In this situation, your knowledge of menu item ingredients, cooking times, preparation, and serving methods will help you to solve the problem. Furthermore, you need to be very positive with a guest like this, speaking with assuredness and in a professional manner.

The Sender Backer The guest who will send items back is a person who knows exactly what he or she wants. Therefore, it is important that you thoroughly understand the guest's complaint. Also, you must give this guest exactly what he or she wants; demonstrate that you genuinely desire to please in every detail. The guest will appreciate it and you will have succeeded in turning around a difficult situation. If the guest proves to be a heckler or a person who is just trying to show off, if it is impossible to meet his or her request, sincerely apologize, and report the situation to the manager. Most restaurants have a policy of allowing the guest to order something else. If something else is ordered, be very specific and ask the necessary questions to ensure that the guest's order is cooked and prepared exactly as desired.

The Older Guest A little extra care goes into serving an older guest. Occasionally, help may be needed in seating the guest, reading the menu, or speaking a little louder. Some restaurants have a senior menu that offers smaller portions. Your knowledge of menu item ingredients, cooking times, preparation, serving methods, and the nutritional information will be very helpful. The older guest will appreciate patience and not being rushed.

The Child Always ask the parents whether they want a booster seat or high chair for the child, being careful not to offend the child who may think that he or she is old enough not to need one. If the restaurant has bibs for children, special place mats, or games of any type, promptly bring them to the table. If appropriate, ask the parents if they would like you to bring some crackers for a small child or baby. This would help pacify the child until the meal is served. Furthermore, look to the parents for the lead in ordering for the child. If the restaurant has a special child's menu, make sure that it is available. If a child orders an expensive menu item, always check with a parent for final approval, and be prepared to suggest another item or two from which the child can choose. Be patient with children, be alert for spills, and be prepared to provide extra napkins if needed.

The Wise Guy This type of person seeks attention and as a result can be somewhat irritating. The person may pass a degrading remark, tell a crude joke, or ask the server for a date. The server should be polite but firm in ignoring the comments. If the person continues, respond by stating that you will have to inform the manager. Give the person the same type of professional service you would give any other guest, remaining polite but firm.

The Talker The guest who wants to visit and impress you with his or her knowledge can be frustrating. This type of guest would like to dominate your time and receive all of your attention. Answer questions with short answers, have a pleasant smile, and keep busy.

The Silent Type This type of guest is a shy and soft-spoken individual, so listen with care. Smile and do everything you can to make this guest feel as comfortable as possible; it will be appreciated.

The Dieter The guest who has diet restrictions will expect the server to be knowledgeable in answering questions and in making appropriate menu suggestions. The server should be competent in answering specific questions regarding menu item ingredients, cooking times, portion sizes, preparation and serving methods, sugar or salt substitutes, etc. Also, most restaurants will try to accommodate a guest's special dietary request. If it is impossible to fulfill the request, the server should be quick to explain that fact and in turn suggest something else for the guest's consideration.

The Coffee Drinker The guest who only orders coffee, reads a newspaper or book, or visits with a friend and sits at a table for an hour or more is using productive space without spending much money. This type of guest has to be carefully handled. The server should be tactful in not offending the guest, but needs to control the situation. The server may suggest a piece of pie or dessert to accompany the coffee. If the guest declines, after the second refill, the guest could be charged for a second cup of coffee, depending upon the policy of the restaurant. If the dining room is busy and other guests are waiting to be seated, then the server, using good judgment, may need to inform the guest politely that the table is needed for lunch or dinner guests.

The Budgeter Many times the price of the menu item is a serious consideration for guests. An experienced server will quickly recognize when price is a factor, and will suggest medium and lower priced entrées. The important thing is that the guests do not feel ill at ease and that they enjoy dinner and feel that they got more than their money's worth.

The Bad Tipper When a guest who frequents a restaurant is recognized as someone who does not leave a tip or tips only a small amount, that guest should be served in the same professional manner as any other guest. Not every guest will leave the traditional 15–20 percent or higher tip. A guest may honestly not understand how to tip correctly. Also, there are some guests who do not tip for any reason, even when they receive excellent service. It is important for the server to remember that not receiving a tip should not affect his or her actions and service to other guests. The best way to react is to double the efforts in providing the best of service.

GUESTS WITH SPECIAL NEEDS

It is very important for a server to understand how to serve a guest with special needs. The ADA (American Disabilities Act) requires reasonable accommodations for people with disability such as, hearing, seeing, and physical restrictions. These reasonable accommodations are easily applied when a server and service establishment are aware of them.

The Hearing Impaired A guest who is hearing impaired may require a server to incorporate several techniques into their service. The first thing a server should be aware of is that this type of guest may have a service dog to assist them in their daily life. The service dog will have identification that clearly states the dog's training and purpose. The dog is allowed in the restaurant. In addition the server should look directly at the guest when speaking; the guest may read lips. If not, extra care can be taken to complete the guest's order. A pen and paper is helpful or a guest may want to point to the desired items on the menu. A server must be attentive to the order-taking process to correctly execute the order.

The Blind Guest A blind guest may or may not be accompanied by a sighted person; the server should not hesitate to offer services if needed, such as helping the person to be seated at a table or booth. This type of guest may also have a service dog to assist them; just as stated earlier, the dog is allowed in the restaurant. Service animals generally lay under the table near the guest. A server should refrain from petting or feeding the animal. Many restaurants have a menu available in Braille. When this is the case, it should be offered to the guest. The guest may prefer the server to read several menu items along with the prices. The server should do everything in a normal way, the only difference being that when something is set on a table, the server should say the name of the item, such as, "Your salad, Sir/Ma'am." If the guest needs assistance in any way, the server should be available to promptly accommodate the guest. When the guest check is brought to the table, the server should offer to read the menu item and price, the sales tax amount (if applicable), and the check total. In addition, the server should inquire if the guest would like to have the check and payment taken to the cashier.

The Physically Challenged Guest Be helpful with a physically challenged guest, and if possible, seat the guest away from the traffic flow if in a wheelchair. If the guest has a hand or arm injury that would make it difficult to eat, offer three menu suggestions. Suggest two easy-to-handle entrées and one that you could offer to cut up, if this seems appropriate. Be prompt and willing to help the guest in any way needed. Also, the physically challenged guest may appreciate the server offering to take the guest check and payment to the cashier for them.

ANTICIPATING THE GUEST'S NEEDS

A professional server will always anticipate the needs of guests by keeping an alert eye on guests and by promptly attending to their needs before they occur. Anticipating guest needs is a combination of close observation and being able to interpret nonverbal communication from the guest. This is also referred to as "reading the need," which involves determining the guest's priorities. For example, during lunch a guest may have time restraints that necessitate fast service. The nonverbal message from the guest might be frequently looking at his or her watch. By reading the nonverbal cue, the server may present the check right after delivering the entrée, at the same time suggesting dessert and coffee. Another example is when guests have business papers spread on the table and are engaged in conversation. The server should avoid interrupting the guests and wait for the proper moment (the same as if guests were engaged in social conversation) to become available to serve guests. Bringing glasses of water to the table and presenting menus could accomplish this.

The server must develop an expertise for "reading (observing and listening to) the guest" in order to build a comfortable personal connection. Servers with an anticipatory understanding of guest needs are perceived as providing exceptional service. "Reading the needs of guests" correctly allows the server to be proactive with responses that not only meet but also exceed guest expectations. When service surpasses the guest's expectations, the guest may feel that the server has gone "beyond the call of duty," which is rewarded by a generous tip and the desire to return often. The reality is that often this perception is achieved via the simplest levels of "reading the need" correctly. Some helpful suggestions are as follows:

- Always remove extra place settings as soon as the guests have been seated, to allow extra room on the table.
- If guests are seated in an area that may be drafty, or if the sun is shining in their eyes, the server should offer to seat the guests at another table or adjust the blinds.
- Salt, pepper, and sugar should be moved within easy reach of guests, particularly when guests are seated at counters.
- Never break into a guest's conversation, and time questions so that the guest will not have to try to answer with a mouth full of food.
- Check each food plate from the kitchen to ensure completeness and for the best plate presentation prior to serving.
- Be alert and notice when a napkin or piece of flatware has been dropped on the floor; pick it up, and immediately replace it with a clean item.
- Recognize when guests are not in any special hurry, such as after a movie, date, or ball game, allowing for additional suggestive selling opportunities.

NONVERBAL CUES AND PROMPTS

Nonverbal cues and prompts from the guest can assist the server in anticipating the guest's needs. They appear in common body language displays and facial expressions that are used every day in normal communications. There are also some behaviors unique to the dining experience, such as the following:

Menus: Guests do things with menus that communicate when they are ready to order and their level of urgency. They will close the menus, and as the urgency increases they will stack them, or move them to the edge of the table, or even push the stack out over the edge of the table to get the server's attention.

Napkins: Guests will unfold napkins and place them on their laps when ready to order. As the meal is completed they may lay the napkin back on the table or place the napkin on top of their empty plate. They may also push the plate to the side or center of the table when they are finished eating.

Looking Around: When a guest is looking around it generally means something may be wrong or the guest may need something else.

SUGGESTIVE SELLING

When a server uses suggestive selling, he or she is helping guests discover what is on the menu, and furthermore preparing the way for their desire to return again, along with increasing sales for the restaurant. Suggestive selling helps the server to engage in conversation with the guest instead of just taking an order. Guests generally appreciate it when a server takes a personal interest in helping them get better acquainted with the menu choices, and to further enjoy their meal by having items suggested that would complement their selection. This is a specific responsibility of the server and the more skillful the server becomes, the greater the opportunity to earn increased tips. The server's skill begins to develop with increased self-confidence, believing that the guest will have a more enjoyable dining experience, and the enthusiasm reflects in the server's voice and facial expressions.

To be successful at suggestive selling it is absolutely essential to know the menu, as presented in Chapter 5, Service Readiness. The server should be prepared to answer any questions the guest may have about any menu item; for example, the quality and ingredients used, the method of cooking, the portion size, the way it is served, the flavor and taste, and the cooking time. Guest satisfaction should always be the first consideration.

There are several types of suggestive selling, and each is geared toward helping the guest enjoy the meal more, and having a better dining experience. The different types of suggestive selling are as follows:

Upselling

This type of suggestive selling entices the guest to spend more money and is a real service. Many times the guest is not aware that he or she can get more value and enjoy the meal more by spending a little more money—for example, by ordering the complete dinner instead of à la carte, or by ordering an appetizer, Caesar salad, or a bottle of wine with dinner. Also, larger drink sizes are typically a better value than the regular drink size.

Suggesting "Related" Menu Items

Related menu items refer to items that "naturally" seem to go with other items, such as soup or salad with sandwiches, cheese on a sandwich, French fries along with a hamburger, or a scoop of vanilla ice cream with apple pie.

Suggesting New Menu Items or the "Chef's Specialties"

Most guests appreciate it when the server tells them about new menu items or "specialties" for which the restaurant may be famous for.

Suggesting Items for Special Occasions

On birthdays or anniversaries, and during holidays such as Mother's Day, Father's Day, Valentine's Day, and St. Patrick's Day. During the Christmas and New Year's season, people are interested in creating a memorable occasion along with a fine meal. Most restaurants offer special menu items that can add to the festivities. Therefore, the server needs to suggest those menu items along with any other special items such as cakes for birthdays and anniversaries, if the restaurant offers them.

Suggesting "Take Home" Items

Many restaurants have items available for "take home," such as pies, cakes, cinnamon rolls, and salad dressings. The server should always take the opportunity to mention those items to guests. If the guest does not have a dessert with the meal, the server may suggest taking a dessert home.

Some guests welcome suggestions and others resent them. The experienced server will recognize the signs when suggestions are appreciated. It is also important for the server to recognize the importance of professionalism that supports suggestive selling versus high-pressure selling that annoys guests. Successful suggestive selling depends on the interest and enthusiasm of the server who has a thorough knowledge of the menu, as well as knowledge of the different types of guests.

A server can quickly qualify guests by inquiring if they have eaten in the restaurant previously. If they are return guests they already have a feel for the menu items and staff, and may not require the full menu introduction given to first-time guests. But if it is their first visit, the server should be prepared to provide all the information necessary to make their dining experience complete.

Many menus have an "à la carte" section. On an à la carte menu, each item is individually selected by the guest, and is charged according to the selections. Therefore, the à la carte menu offers a greater opportunity to the server for suggestive selling.

salads

House 6.75
mixed greens, grape tomatoes, pumpernickel croutons, shredded carrots, beets, and fennel. Choose from Dijon-balsamic vinaigrette, creamy blue cheese, carrot-bacon dressing, or extra virgin olive oil and aged balsamic vinegar

Grilled Grape Salad 9.00
arugula and romaine tossed with Great Hill blue cheese vinaigrette, grilled grapes, Bermuda onions, roasted pistachios and drizzled with a white balsamic vinegar reduction

Grilled Romaine Salad 9.50
grilled romaine heart with Bermuda onions, bell peppers, Kalamata olives, roma tomatoes, banana peppers, and Cackleberry Farms Feta topped with a green olive feta vinaigrette

Warm Goat Cheese 9.00
hazelnut crusted goat cheese served over mixed greens with wine poached red onions and apricot jalapeño vinaigrette

Add grilled shrimp to a salad 4.50

Add grilled chicken to a salad 3.50

Salads are also available in entrée sizes

appetizers

Cremini Mushroom Tart
crisp tart with cremini mushrooms, goat cheese, and caramelized red onions. 11.00
Served with a timbale of roasted beets in a walnut vinaigrette

Indian Lentil Dip and Kabob Plate 10.50
grilled chicken kabobs, lentil dip, peppadew peppers, and Indian spiced grilled pita bread

Cheese Plate 10.50
Eiffel Tower triple cream and a daily cheese served with pears, grapes, dried fruit, crackers, cornichons, and a caramelized onion-garlic compote

Calamari 9.50
lightly fried and served with a roasted garlic-grain mustard aioli

Thai Beef Carpaccio 10.00
seared beef tenderloin sliced with capers, minced chili peppers, micro basil, fresh ginger matchsticks, miso garlic infused olive oil, grilled ciabatta bread

Pizzetta 10.00
grilled herb flatbread with garlic shallot confit, asparagus tips, portabella mushrooms, spinach, mozzarella and crumbled goat cheese. Drizzled with a smoked tomato coulis

PEI Mussels 10.00
steamed in a lemongrass green curry coconut broth served with toasted baguette slices and a drizzle of basil cilantro oil

Carpe Diem Caterers is available for off - premise full service catering for up to 250 guests

Our private room can be booked any evening for up to 37 guests
The entire restaurant is also available for private daytime events

Figure 7–1
Dinner Menu. Courtesy of Carpe Diem Restauran and Carterers.

We feature daily appetizer and entrée specials

entrees

Spinach Ravioli 16.00
spinach raviolis tossed with artichoke hearts, olives, tomatoes, and spinach in a garlic white wine sauce

Szechuan Tuna 16.00
4 ounces of seared rare chilled yellowfin tuna, wasabi creme, cucumber relish, roasted shitake mushrooms, cilantro micro greens, Szechuan pepper dusted won ton crackers. Served with Szechuan noodle salad

Eggplant Roulade 16.00
eggplant stuffed with zucchini, arugula, and Chapel Hill Çreamery fresh mozzarella served in a smoked tomato marinara with fresh grated Parmesan

Shrimp or Vegetarian Cous Cous
Israeli cous cous with sauteed shrimp or cremini mushrooms, tomatoes, black eyed peas, vidalia onions, chiffonade of Swiss chard, white wine, and olive oil

with sauteed cremini mushrooms 16.50
with sauteed shrimp 21.00

Brick Chicken 22.00
marinated Ashley Farms all natural chicken breast, brick seared and served over black pepper gnocchi tossed with roasted chicken jus, herbs, and Parmesan. Served with green beans in whole grain mustard vinaigrette

Duck Breast 24.00
pan seared coriander and orange rubbed duck breast with an Earl Grey honey orange butter sauce over brown rice and sautéed spinach. Garnished with pickled red onions

Filet of Beef 30.00
grilled 8 ounce filet topped with Great Hill blue cheese compound butter and artichoke fritters. Served with roasted Yukon gold potatoes and haricots verts tossed in whole grain mustard vinaigrette

Pork Tenderloin 22.00
porcini crusted grilled pork tenderloin served over creamy Parmesan polenta with caramelized onions, seared cherry tomatoes, and grilled okra. Finished with a vermouth vinaigrette

NC Trout 24.00
grilled local sustainable Rainbow trout drizzled with a lemon tahini emulsion. Served with a roasted red bliss potato, haricot verts, roasted red pepper, olive & herb salad

Chicken 19.00
buttermilk fried chicken breast over spinach with a shallot black pepper gravy. Served with Yukon gold mashed potatoes

Scallops 24.00
seared sea scallops, crusted with garlic and herbs, served with fresh farmers market corn and bean succotash, sun dried tomato butter drizzle

Side of spinach sautéed in olive oil 3.50
Entrée split charge – includes extra sides 5.00

Our local organic farm partners include New Town Farms, Poplar Ridge Farms, Tega Hills Greenhouses, Cackleberry Farms, Fisher Farms, Anson Mills, and Grateful Growers
Please notify us of any dietary restrictions or allergies even if the ingredient is not listed
20% pre-tax gratuity will be added for parties of six or more
No separate checks on parties of 12 or more.

Figure 7–1 (continued)

The menu itself is the best way to guide guests through the restaurant offerings. The server can guide the guest through the menu by highlighting categories and suggesting personal favorites or top sellers. The dinner menu in Figure 7–1 is listed in categories: salads, appetizers, and entrées. This is one of the most popular ways to design a menu. Tasting menus have become very popular and offer guests the opportunity to have smaller portions of signature items offered by the chef. The server should suggest the tasting menu, when available, to offer the guest a pleasurable dining experience as discussed in Chapter 5. There is a tasting menu available on the second page of the bi-fold menu and it is listed on the top right in a prominent place so it gets noticed by the guest.

All menu items should have descriptions that promote, entice, and feature attractive preparation and ingredients. The server should always include those descriptions to help develop a mental image when describing menu items. Words such as *fresh, tasty, mouthwatering,* and *scrumptious* generate interest and build enthusiasm for the item.

The following example situation is given to demonstrate the importance of "reading the need" prior to any suggestive selling.

After having quickly looked at the menu, the guest asks the server, "What do you recommend?" The server eagerly describes, in delicious detail, "Our house favorite is fresh salmon filet with blackened spices pan seared, then baked and served with a tequila-lime-sour cream sauce." With furrowed brow and pursed lips the customer replies, "I hate fish!"

The server made a mistake by not asking about the guest's interests before launching into a recommendation. The server has been placed in an awkward position, and possibly annoyed the guest.

The server should have responded with the following inquiry: "Do you have a preference this evening? Are you looking for beef, chicken, seafood, or pasta?"

When narrowing the guest's interests the server can then make the appropriate suggestions from the menu. By asking the right question(s), listening to the answers, and being alert to nonverbal cues, the server can guide the guest to the appropriate choices. This illustrates the importance of first "reading the need" and effectively anticipating guest needs and expectations.

The effect of suggestive selling is to let the guest know what is available and to suggest items that "go with" the ordered menu item, because they fit into and create the guest's "needs." If the guest does not "need" the suggested item, he or she will reject the suggestion. The server's experience will help develop an intuitive understanding of what the guest's needs are, then guide the guest into making decisions through suggestive selling. The server should typically suggest two of the possible choices within each food and beverage category, so that the guest's choice will be made easier, as compared to five or six choices. Following are a number of examples showing how suggestive selling works.

Beverages

The server should always suggest one alcohol and one nonalcohol beverage choice. Furthermore, the server should note whether the guest's eyes are scanning the beer or wine list, or looking at table tents. These are nonverbal cues to what may interest a guest. If it is beer, ask the guest if he or she prefers light or dark beer, imported or domestic. If it is wine, ask the guest if he or she prefers red or white wine, dry or sweet. These are excellent opportunities to suggest regional wines or local micro-brews. When a guest asks, "What do you recommend?" the server should respond with questions like, "What do you drink at home?" "What is your favorite type of beer or wine?" The answers will indicate the guest's flavor and taste preferences.

Many wine menus have suggested pairings of wine and food. Some restaurants offer samplings of wine as well. This affords the more sophisticated guest the opportunity to have a small taste of various wines so that they can choose which wine matches their entrée best. Once a selection is made the wine is served immediately. Restaurants that are promoting certain house brands may even offer sample tasting to guests.

For spirits, again inquire what type the guest may like. Then suggest common brand names that are easily recognizable. For example, if the guest likes scotch, suggest Chivas Regal, JB, or Cutty Sark. These three scotch brands are internationally recognized and offer three levels of quality and price. If the guest says, "I'll just have water," ask if he or she prefers bottled or tap. If the guest wants coffee, suggest the choices that may be available, such as espresso, latte, cappuccino, mocha, and decaffeinated, along with any specialty blends that the restaurant may have (see Chapter 6).

Appetizers

Appetizers should be suggested in pairs. The dinner menu in Figure 7–1 has a variety of appetizers and salads; the server could suggest two of them as follows: "We pride ourselves on our Warm Goat cheese salad, and among our most popular appetizers is the Calamari." On the salad there are additional items to be added. The suggestion of an addition of shrimp or chicken is very important. This will increase the total of the check and enhance the guest's experience. The server must also be prepared to promptly provide additional information, when asked, about any of the menu items. What is an Aiolo (a garlic mayonnaise), or the portion size of the additional shrimp? When guests want to split an appetizer, the server should know what the additional charge would be, if there is one.

Entrées

Suggesting entrée selections should begin with finding out the guest's preferences. Many dinner menus have a variety of meats, chicken, pasta, seafood, and shellfish selections, along with a vegetarian choice. Ask what the guest enjoys from those categories, and then offer two suggestions, being ready to follow up with additional information in response to questions regarding cooking methods, sauces, portion sizes, accompaniments, etc. For example, if the guest orders a Signature Steak Dinner, which includes the cooking technique of char-broiled, deglazed with Madeira and served with béarnaise sauce. The following questions could arise: "What is charbroiled?" (quick cooking by open flame and/or direct heat); "What is Madeira?" (A rich brandy-based wine from Spain); "What is in a bernaise sauce?" (Eggs, butter, shallots, tarragon, and lemon).

Desserts

Desserts can be suggested with a menu, as discussed in Chapter 5, or by a presentation tray or cart, as discussed in Chapter 3. In either case the words used to offer the suggestions are important; for example, saying something like, "Our home chocolate molten cake with fresh sliced strawberries topped with fresh whipped cream is sensational, can I bring you one?" While presenting a dessert tray, the server could say, "The crème brulee is my favorite." Another approach if a dessert menu is used is to place the menu on the table for the guest to pick up and review. This can prepare and entice the guest. The server can then follow up with some great suggestions. Desserts can always be sold to take home as a treat for later.

After-dinner Drinks

These include coffee, espresso drinks, teas, alcohol beverages, spirited coffees, and house specialty drinks. Again the key is to suggest two items every time, such as, "May I bring you an Irish or Spanish coffee?"

Guidelines for Suggestive Selling

The basic guidelines for suggestive selling are as follows:

- When taking the guest's order, always suggest.
- When reading back the order for accuracy, always suggest.
- Before finalizing the guest check, suggest if appropriate.

Always suggest during the following situations:

- If an à la carte item is ordered, suggest "Would you like the dinner special?" Then explain that the dinner is a better value.
- If no beverage is ordered, suggest, "And what would you like to drink?" Then suggest the large size, if appropriate for the guest.
- When an order has been placed à la carte, read back the order and suggest items that will "go with" the item ordered, suggest "Would you like soup or salad?" "May I recommend either French fries or onion rings?"
- When a salad is ordered, suggest an "add-on" by asking, "Would you like it topped with shrimp or crab?" If there is a large size, suggest, "We have a special chef's bowl which is a complete meal."
- If the guest check appears to be complete, always ask, "Will there be anything else?" Never say, "Is that all?"

The server should know what to suggest and understand the relationships between food items. The server should be specific in naming food and beverage items, not categories. Say, "Would you like a piece of our popular hot cherry or apple pie for dessert?" and not "Do you care for dessert?" Say, "Would you like a root beer or coke?" and not "Do you want a beverage?" Dessert and beverage are not descriptive words. They do not taste like anything to the guest. When you suggest and describe specific items, a picture develops in the guest's mind, which may make it difficult for the guest to refuse. Furthermore, while the server is creating this mental picture, if he or she smiles and approvingly nods "yes," the guest quite often will be inclined to smile and nod "yes" back, agreeing that the server's suggestion is a good one.

Offering Servers Incentives

Most often servers know the relationship between suggestive selling and an increase in their tips. Management, however, could encourage the servers to sell as much as they can to their guests by using incentives. Incentives are an excellent way to reward the servers who sell on a regular basis and to motivate servers who need to hone their selling skills. A good incentive should be well defined and easy for management to track. It is popular to pick one particular item for the server to sell. Define a specific length of time the incentive program will run and offer a desirable prize. A good example of an incentive program could be selling a specific wine by the bottle. The wine would be presented to servers for tasting followed by a discussion about the characteristics of the wine and menu items that could be paired with the wine. The time the incentive program is running should be identified; for example, one month. The server who sells the most bottles of that wine would be awarded a prize which is determined by

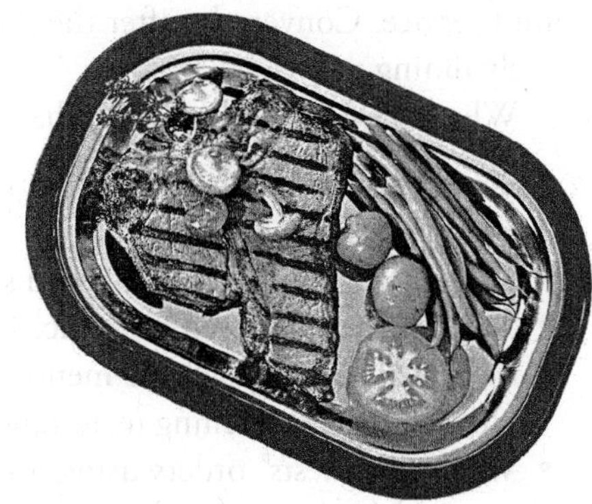

Figure 7–2
Thermo *Plate Platters.* Courtesy of Service Ideas, Inc.

the manager. It could be a cash prize or even a bottle of the wine that is featured in the incentive. This can create excitement, friendly competition, as well as an increase in the restaurants wine sales.

Showmanship Sells Suggestively

Certain food items can be served with flair, excitement, and showmanship by displaying a special technique or method of presentation. When these items are served, they have a visible presence in the dining room that attracts guests' attention, and creates interest and curiosity. The result is that other guests will be tempted to order the same items. Also, the server has the opportunity to point these items out, as they are being served and/or enjoyed by other guests, while suggestively selling. For example, the server could say, "Our sizzling T-bone steak is outstanding, and it has just been served on a hot platter to the guest seated at the nearby table."

Foods that can be fun and exciting for guests are flamed dishes and sizzling platters, as shown in Figure 7–2. Examples of flaming dishes include flaming salads, shish-kabobs, desserts, and the famous crepes Suzettes. Certain techniques are used to light the different foods, to display them, and to skillfully put them out at serving time. Cognac, fruit liqueurs, and rum are generally used in flaming desserts. Flaming requires time and special equipment and is suitable only for certain dishes. Flaming does not actually cook the food but does add to the flavor. Restaurants that offer flamed dishes typically have one or two people trained to provide the service competently, such as the maître d' or dining room manager.

TAKING THE GUEST'S ORDER

Knowing when to approach guests to take their order can be a challenge to the server, because guests vary in their likes and dislikes in terms of service. However, the best practice is to approach the table with a welcoming smile as soon as guests are seated. First impressions are important; the server should be prompt, organized, and professional. Courtesy is essential in every detail, beginning with "please" and followed by "thank you" as part of the conversation while taking guests' orders. The server could ask the guests if they would like to dine leisurely or if they prefer a faster service. Many people want to have a casual dining experience, have one or more cocktails, and enjoy the process. On the other hand, other guests may have a limited amount of time and expect to be served quickly. This could be the situation if the restaurant were located near a theater where guests would be dining before theater time and would need prompt service. Conversely, after the theater they would perhaps enjoy the pleasure of leisurely dining.

When taking a guest's order, the following procedure should be followed:

- Stand straight, at the left of the table if possible, and close enough to hear the guest's voice.
- Listen carefully and lean forward slightly to hear if necessary.
- Some guests may need assistance in reading the menu.
- Be prepared to explain the menu and answer the guests' questions.
- Utilize suggestive selling techniques.
- Write the guests' orders using a guest check (as shown in Figure 7–4) or POS terminal (according to the restaurant's procedure).
- Read the order back to the guests in order to prevent any possible misunderstanding.
- Thank the guests for their order.
- Immediately place the order with the bar and/or with the kitchen if using handwritten guest checks.
- Begin the service at the table as soon as possible.
- While all of this is happening, be enthusiastic, smiling, courteous, and efficient.

When taking guests' orders a system needs to be followed; most restaurants have such a system. The purpose of the system is to help the server remember who is served what dish, so when the meal is served it is done in a fast, efficient manner. A tool to assist servers in accurate order taking is WaitRpad® as shown in Figure 7–3.

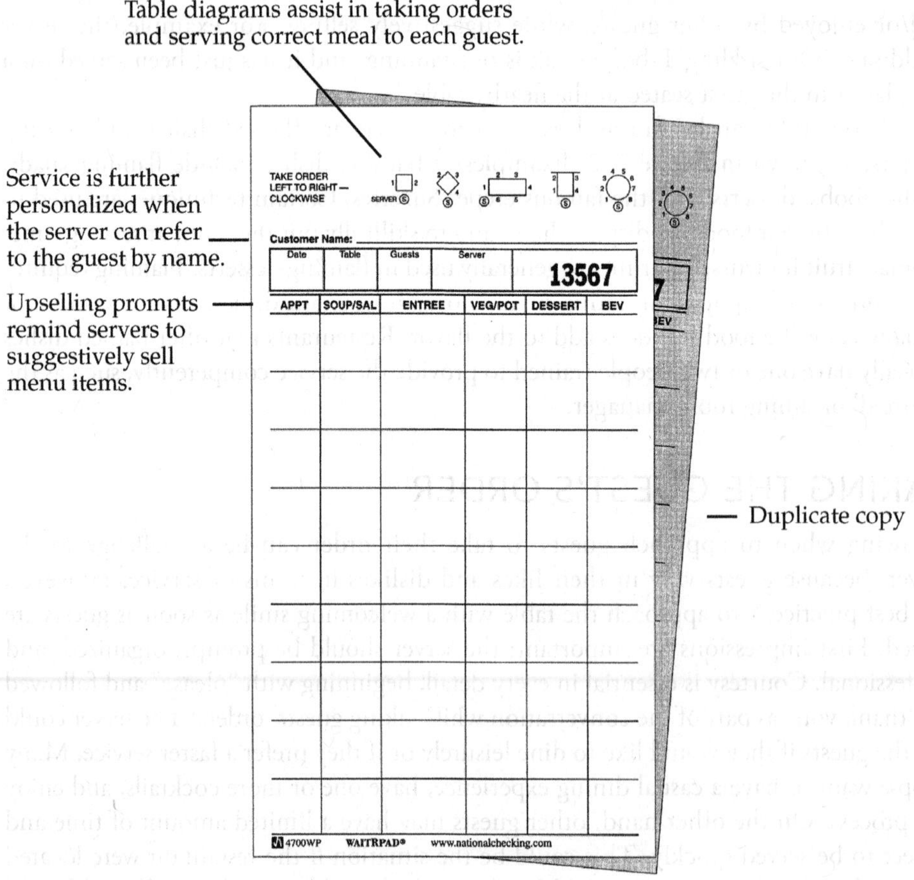
Table diagrams assist in taking orders and serving correct meal to each guest.
Service is further personalized when the server can refer to the guest by name.
Upselling prompts remind servers to suggestively sell menu items.
Duplicate copy
TAKE ORDER LEFT TO RIGHT — CLOCKWISE
SERVER
Customer Name:
Date
Table
Guests
Server
13567
APPT
SOUP/SAL
ENTREE
VEG/POT
DESSERT
BEV
4700WP
WAITRPAD®
www.nationalchecking.com

Figure 7–3
WaitRpad®. Courtesy of National Checking.

This pad helps the server to remember what each guest orders and even prompt them to suggestively sell. This system of writing things down can also help when the restaurant is busy. The server can take the order and then input it into a POS (point-of-sale) or deliver the order to the kitchen. Chapter 4 discusses a pivot point service system with a designated starting position with all orders served clockwise from that point. Chapter 8 explains how server banking functions when a restaurant requires its servers to handle payment transactions directly for the guest without going through a cashier.

SERVICE TIMING

During a normal shift an adequate amount of time can be allotted to serve each guest. However, during a Friday night dinner rush, the server's speed and efficiency are critical to giving proper attention to all the tables without seeming to "rush" the guests. During these rush times, the server may constantly have to change speed and direction. Therefore, reading each table and anticipating its needs is critical in controlling the service timing for all tables in the server's station. The server must observe them carefully and plan steps in advance of guest requests. This will save the server time and stress, and ensure good tips because the guests did not have to wait or ask for service.

The following procedures can help to consolidate steps:

- When two or three tables are seated at the same time, the server should take the orders from each table, one right after the other, using good judgment and considering how many people are seated. Then submit the orders to the kitchen and/or bar at the same time.
- If one person orders a second beverage, invite the other guests at the table to have a second beverage.
- When returning to the station, take several seconds to size up each table. What is each table going to need next? That is, beverage refills, pre-bussing, desserts, entrée orders, guest check, initial greeting, appetizer plates, etc. It is critical to always stay focused.
- When leaving the station follow the same procedure. Look to see what needs to be brought back out to the tables when returning to the station. Never leave or go to the dining room empty-handed.

EMERGENCY SITUATIONS

There has been an increase in the incidences of food allergy reactions within the restaurant industry. A food allergy can be mild or, on the contrast, fatal. Therefore, a server must be attentive to guests who are communicating their food allergies to them. The server must double-check that the allergy issue from the guest is communicated properly to the kitchen. If not, an emergency situation can occur. If a guest becomes ill during the meal, or is choking, notify the manager immediately so that action can be taken. The server should try to remain with the guest as much as possible to attend to any needs, such as bringing a drink of water or a cold towel. If a guest has fallen, do not try to move the guest. Also, do not attempt to administer first-aid, except to ensure the guest's comfort. The manager or a designated person on the staff should be certified in first-aid training and qualified to provide immediate care. Ask the guest or those accompanying him or her if you should call 911 for emergency help. The restaurant should have standard guidelines for all employees to follow during any type of emergency situation.

SUMMARY

A server's task is more than just taking an order; it begins with the server's ability to gain the guest's confidence, and provides the best in food and beverage service. A server who generates an enthusiastic atmosphere for guests, coupled with personal enthusiasm, can produce a positive dining experience that will result in repeat business for the restaurant and increased tips for the server.

The server needs to be prepared to serve all types of guests, particularly those who may need special attention, such as the following: The *procrastinator* needs suggestions to help with a decision; the *skeptic* needs reassurance; the *"sender backer"* knows what he or she wants and the server must understand those needs; the *older guest* may need some special consideration and help; the *child* may need patience and understanding and a parent's approval for menu selection; the *wise guy* needs to be handled with tact, but very firmly; the *talker* needs to be given short answers and quick service; the *silent type* appreciates understanding; the *dieter* wants knowledgeable answers regarding ingredients and cooking methods; the *coffee drinker* should be handled according to house policy; the *budgeter* will need to know the less expensive items on the menu; and the *bad tipper* should be treated with the same attention and service as everyone else. In addition the server must apply the necessary skills to accommodate guests with special needs, such as the hearing impaired, blind, and physically challenged.

A professional server will always anticipate the needs of guests by keeping an alert eye on guests and promptly attending to their needs. The server should also be aware of nonverbal cues and prompts from the guests, such as menu and napkin positioning, body language displays, and physical expressions.

Suggestive selling needs to be done with tact. It requires the server to have self-confidence and a positive attitude. It takes complete knowledge of the menu and of the combinations that go well with the item selected by the guest. Suggestions should be made with enthusiasm and by using the menu descriptions to create an appetizing image. The server who successfully uses suggestive selling will increase guest check averages and tips. The larger the guest check, the larger the tip. Also, suggestive selling provides a definite service to the guest with the opportunity to have a better meal and a better value. The different types of suggestive selling include "upselling," suggesting "related" menu items, suggesting new menu items or the "chef's specialties," suggesting items for special occasions, and suggesting "take home" items. Also, showmanship in the dining room with specially served food items can effectively enhance sales to other guests.

The proper procedure for taking the guest's order needs to follow a system, and most restaurants will have a designated system for servers to follow. Finally, all emergency situations should be handled according to the policy set forth by the restaurant.

DISCUSSION QUESTIONS AND EXERCISES

1. What is involved when a server makes a personal connection with a guest?
2. Give three examples of a server introductory greeting to guests.
3. How can a server measure the effects of his or her service enthusiasm?
4. What is the first step in developing server enthusiasm?
5. List and describe the characteristics of 10 different types of guests.
6. How should a server react if a rude guest looks at the server and loudly says, "Hey shorty, I need more bread"?
7. When anticipating guest needs, what does "reading the need" mean?
8. Give five examples of when a server can be proactive in anticipating guest needs.
9. List and describe two nonverbal cues and prompts from guests that can assist the server in anticipating guests' needs.
10. What is suggestive selling?
11. Explain the five different types of suggestive selling.
12. Which offers a greater opportunity for suggestive selling, a dinner or an à la carte menu? Explain your answer.
13. Why should the server always include menu descriptions when describing menu items to guests?
14. What is the effect of suggestive selling?
15. When practicing suggestive selling, how many choices within each food and beverage category should the server suggest to the guest?

16. List the three basic guidelines to follow for suggestive selling.
17. Give an example of when dining room showmanship suggestively sells.
18. Describe the procedure to follow when taking a guest's order.
19. Since timing can be critical during rush periods, identify three procedures that could help a server conserve steps.
20. What should a server do in an emergency situation when a guest becomes ill?

8

The Technology of Service

Electronic cash register and POS (point-of-sale) systems have surprisingly only been around since the 1970s. These systems which are used both for retail operations and in the hospitality industry helped to create more competitive and efficient businesses. They increased the speed and efficiency of businesses which greatly improved customer service and satisfaction. The first POS systems were large and cumbersome and it was difficult to customize them to fit the needs of a retail business or restaurant. They were quickly replaced with systems that were computer based with diverse software that could easily be customized to a business's needs. Many terminals throughout a restaurant or hotel are interconnected, which speeds up every aspect of the business. POS systems track sales in real time, assists a host with seating in a restaurant, unites the servers to the kitchen, and, in addition, simplifies all types of accounting within the hospitality industry. Some of the innovations that have been very effective are the handheld touch-screen systems that are widely used today.

Web-based and wireless technologies have simplified the efforts in efficiency and speed with the end results being improved customer satisfaction. Web-based POS systems are widely available and benefits both restaurants and consumers worldwide.

Every restaurant operation relies on technology in one form or another and in varying degrees, from the small deli that uses a limited function POS terminal to the massive computer system with over 400 terminals and thousands of employees for food, beverage, and merchandise sales in large high-profile events, such as the Olympics. Technology is used to increase productivity and to satisfy busy customers whose time is very valuable. It is fortunate that many forms of technology have become mainstream and that many employees feel comfortable with that technology; they can easily apply what they know to the restaurant environment. The employees, managers, and owners of restaurants must become technologically literate in order to succeed and remain competitive. Broadband Internet reliability and security are critical to today's restaurant environment. Additionally, as customers become more wireless, this enables the restaurant to facilitate integration with the guest's devices and data. This integration has raised significant security considerations for the restaurateurs. This chapter will discuss current applications of technology as it pertains, primarily, to the server and to restaurants in general.

learning objectives

After reading this chapter and completing the discussion questions and exercises, you should be able to:

1. Define the terms that are most commonly used when discussing the operation of a POS (point-of-sale) system.
2. Understand and explain the areas of improved guest service when technology is properly implemented.
3. Describe how a table service management system functions.
4. Explain the advantages of a guest paging system.
5. Discuss the advantages of product management software.
6. Know when the use of handheld touch-screen terminals would have the best application.
7. Explain how a server paging system functions.
8. Describe the purpose of a kitchen display system and explain how it works.
9. Know how a handheld pay-at-the-table device functions.
10. Understand customer relationship management software and how storage and query of guests visit history, order history, and preferences can be used to enhance the guest experience.
11. Understand and describe the functions of various POS system software applications and their benefits.

BASIC POS AND TECHNOLOGY TERMS

The following is a list of terms that are most commonly used when discussing the operation of a POS system.

- ***Back Office.*** Interface between POS and "back office," generating management reports that can include accounting, inventory, and payroll.
- ***Banked Server.*** A server who handles transactions directly for the guest without going through a cashier. The server will typically start

with a personal bank of $40.00 (his or her own money) in change, consisting of four $5 bills, 15 or 18 $1 bills, and the balance in coins. It is the responsibility of the server to have the change amounts before the shift starts. The server settles with the house at the end of the shift.

- ***Electronic Draft Capture.*** A cashier or server swipes the guest's credit card at the POS terminal. Then, automatic processing of credit card authorization through a processing network takes place, followed by consolidation of daily transactions for single batch transmission to the bank for fund settlement.
- ***PCI-CISP Compliant.*** Certification issued by the payment card industry for hardware devices, software applications, and security of networks used in the capture and handling of electronic payments and cardholder data.
- ***Frequent Diner Program.*** Discounts and incentives offered to guests and tracked via the POS. Can also be used to profile buying habits for target marketing and promotions.
- ***CRM (Customer Relationship Management).*** Software application which consists of a database of data points collected about specific customers. Data can be queried to customize marketing messages to guests meeting specific criteria. For example, display the e-mail address of guests who have visited the restaurant five times in the past but have not visited in the last 90 days.
- ***Menu Engineering.*** Using the information gathered from POS and inventory management to compose a mix of menu items for maximum variety, price, and profit.
- ***Modifiers.*** Instructions for food preparation; for example, on the side, medium, or rare.
- ***Outlet.*** A specific area of the restaurant, such as an outdoor patio or bar in which sales are generated independently from the restaurant and represent a separate revenue center.
- ***Requisition Printer.*** The device that prints out the entire order once it has been entered into the POS system.
- ***Remote Printer.*** A printer that is located in a different area of the restaurant, such as in the bar or kitchen. For example, the server rings up a drink order and a ticket is printed in the bar, instructing the bartender to start preparing the drinks.
- ***Terminal.*** Refers to the device the server uses to enter sales. It could be at a fixed location or a handheld remote mobile device.
- ***Upselling Prompts.*** Prompts that are installed into a POS system that serve to encourage the server to suggest additional items, such as appetizers, desserts, and beverages. For example, beverage prompts: When a menu item is ordered, it immediately goes to a beverage screen that is designed to increase beverage sales. This is a forced screen, which means that the server is forced to respond to this screen by suggesting a beverage.
- ***Hosted Solution.*** A software application that resides on a remote server and is accessed via broadband Internet.
- ***Customer Facing.*** A software application which is accessed directly by the guest.
- ***Marketing Client.*** A device on the point-of-sale network whose purpose is to display marketing messages to the guests; digital menu boards are a common example.
- ***Software as a Service (SaaS).*** A software application that is accessed via a subscription by the restaurant. Open Table and Schedulfly are examples of SaaS.
- ***Wireless Hot Spot.*** A public wireless network which can be accessed by guests.

12. Understand various customer facing technologies that are accessed directly by the guest and how to integrate them into the restaurant environment.
13. Know the methods of training available through the advances in technology.
14. Know the variety of online employee scheduling, training, and communication available.
15. Describe software as a service and hosted solution and how they relate to restaurant management applications.

Figure 8–1
Point of Sale System. Courtesy of Micros Systems, Inc.

TECHNOLOGY APPLICATIONS

It is important for a restaurant to define its goals, both short and long term, before purchasing a POS system. The systems of today are innovative and expensive, and they can change quickly so upgrade potential should be considered. POS systems can meet the demands of a wide variety of businesses in the hospitality industry. There are many systems to choose from; therefore, all options should be considered before a system is selected and implemented into a restaurant. Whichever system is installed the main goals are similar. Restaurants are looking for a way to stay competitive in a fast-paced, demanding industry to create excellent guest relations and satisfaction. When technology is properly implemented the results are reflected in employee success and improved guest service. This can begin with efficiently taking reservations, reducing wait-times for seating, and increasing the speed of service. A POS system is fast and easy to use, as shown in Figure 8–1, and is designed to accomplish the following:

- Seat guests more quickly and accommodate any requests.
- Increase the speed of guest service by reducing order turnaround time.
- Increase the accuracy of food and beverage preparation and pricing.
- Accommodate guests who need separate checks, particularly when seated in large parties.
- Eliminate common mathematical errors.
- Provide prompt, accurate guest check presentation when guests are ready to leave.
- Reduce cash-handling problems and/or errors.
- Provide secure and efficient credit card authorization.

ONLINE RESERVATION

Restaurants need to be able to take reservations 24 hours a day. The best way to facilitate this is through an online reservation system. Providers such as Open Table make it easy for guests to reserve tables through the restaurant's own website or through the Open Table website. Guests can reserve a table for a specific time and party size. The availability of time slots and number and sizes of tables are configured by the restaurant. Customers can provide specific information and make specific requests in conjunction with their reservation. For example, the guest might indicate that the reservation is for a birthday dinner, or may request a table on the patio. This information is not only used by the restaurant to meet the guest's needs for the reserved dining experience, but it is also stored in their Open Table CRM database for use in the future. For example, the restaurant might query their Open Table database to show all guests who reserved for a birthday dinner in the past year and then send a personalized e-mail to those guests, inviting them to celebrate their birthday again this year. Hosted solutions such as Open Table also facilitate front-of-the-house restaurant staff having information about the guest from the moment they arrive. For example, if the host greets Mr. Smith by checking in his reservation he or she can see that Mr. Smith has visited the restaurant 10 times in the past, and prefers Sally as a server. The host can then individualize his or her greeting to Mr. Smith upon his arrival at the restaurant. Customer facing technologies, such as Open Tables' Apple I phone app, allow communication and thus service can begin prior to the guest arriving at the restaurant. Using an online reservation system assists the manager and host with planning labor needs and effective seating. Use of these systems also eliminates the need for the restaurant to staff someone to take phone reservations during non-operating hours.

TABLE MANAGEMENT APPLICATIONS

These systems integrate the duties of the host into the restaurant's POS system and facilitate better communication among employees, speed table turns, and manage the waitlist. These systems consist of a graphical table screen for the seating host, a handheld device for the greeting host, a flat screen monitor to communicate information to the guest, and an integrated guest paging system. The graphical table screen Figure 8–2 displays reservations, walk-in parties, server sections, and table status to the seating host. The table management software suggests a table for the host to seat the next guest on the waitlist based on programmed variables such as table size and server availability. The host then "seats" the guests within the application, which pages the guest, opens a check for the appropriate server within the POS system, and assigns the guest's name to the check, allowing the server to greet the guest by name when approaching the table. The graphical table screen will also display *entrées ordered, check printed,* and *check tendered* to the host based on the server's use of the POS system. When the table is cleaned and available to seat, the server or the server's assistant/busser confirms this on any POS terminal and the available status is displayed at the host stand on the graphical table screen. The greeting host uses a handheld device to *check in* reservations as guests arrive at the restaurant and to add walk-in guests to the waitlist. The table management software suggests the waiting time to the greeting host based on the number of parties waiting to be seated, and the historical turn time of the current meal period. The greeting host enters the number of guests into the table management application and presents a pager (Figure 8.3) to the guest. The greeting host also uses the handheld to update the waitlist when guests decide to abandon the wait. Waiting guests can view their position on the waitlist by viewing flat screen monitors located in the lounge, foyer, or other waiting areas. These monitors, referred to as marketing clients, can display the waitlist as a crawl over TV programs, as a list or crawl over in-house content such as promotional videos merchandising menu items, specials, or upcoming events. The use of marketing clients eliminates the inconvenience of guests having to inquire "how much longer" of the seating host.

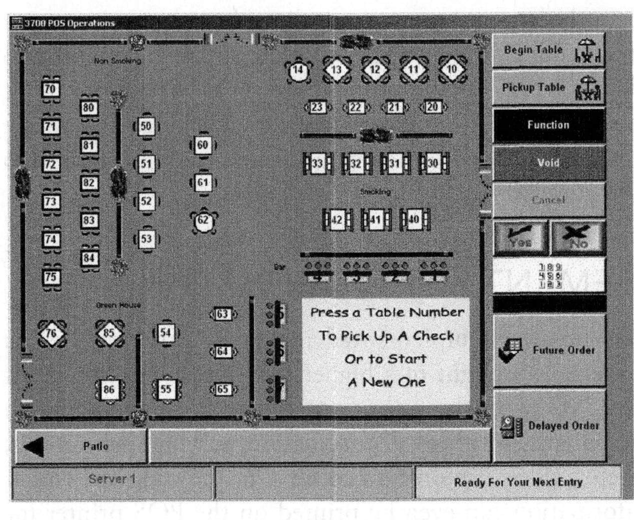

(a)

(b)

Figure 8–2
(a) POS System with Table Numbers and (b) Table Service Management. Courtesy of Micros Systems, Inc.

GUEST PAGING SYSTEM

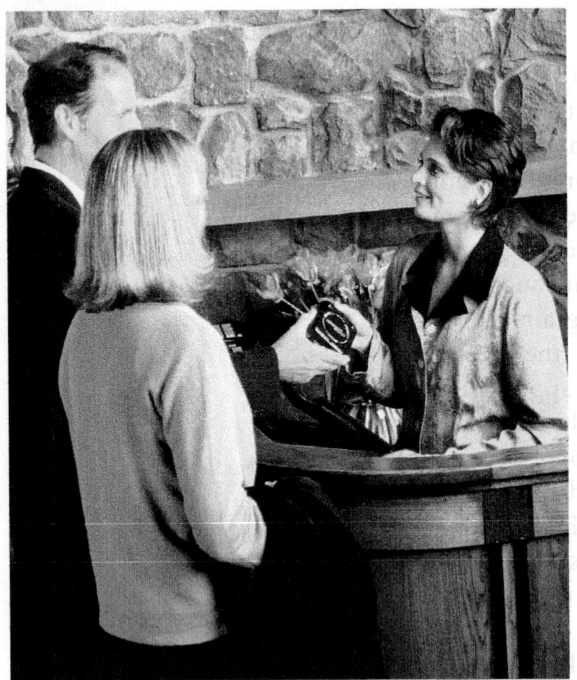

Figure 8–3
GuestAlert®. Courtesy of JTECH Communications, Inc.

The guest anxiety associated with having to wait for an available table has been tremendously reduced with the use of a guest paging system, as shown in Figure 8–3. The number of "no-shows" and walkouts is minimized with the guest-friendly system. These systems can be integrated into a Table Management application or used as a standalone system. The guests can be alerted that their table is ready with the touch of a button, rather than over a noisy public address system. The guest paging system developed by JTECH Communications, Inc., shown in Figure 8–3, vibrates and flashes, and plays an audio message informing the guest that the table is ready. It also alerts guests when they have gone too far from the restaurant.

If the restaurant has a lounge, the guest may prefer to have a drink while waiting for a table. The flashing light and audio message is most effective in alerting the guest. If a restaurant is located in or near a shopping mall, the guest may enjoy visiting the stores. The vibrating function of the pager would be ideal if the pager were in the guest's pocket. The guest pager serves to establish a commitment between the restaurant and the guest by promptly alerting the guest when the table is ready. It further reduces the chaos that sometimes occurs at the host stand during busy times, seats more people, and contributes to a smoother running operation.

Staff-to-Staff/Customer-to-Staff Paging System

The Staff-to-Staff/Customer-to-Staff paging system developed by JTECH Communications, Inc., shown in Figure 8–4, allows for instant communication between staff members or between guests and a staff member which can provide an immediate response to a guest's request. This is a convenient device to have during a banquet, during a catered event, or while in a meeting room during a conference session at a hotel or resort. A guest may need to contact the A/V (audio/visual) service technician for assistance with equipment; food and beverage service for a fresh pot of coffee for the meeting room; convention services to request an additional announcement to be made over the public address system; or the banquet manager to adjust the room temperature. The guest can easily activate the handheld pager by pressing the appropriate button to request a specific service, and can conveniently keep the pager in his or her pocket or place on a table for easy access. The paging system allows the guest to communicate specific needs in a way that accelerates the process in being able to promptly respond to the guest, resulting in improved guest service.

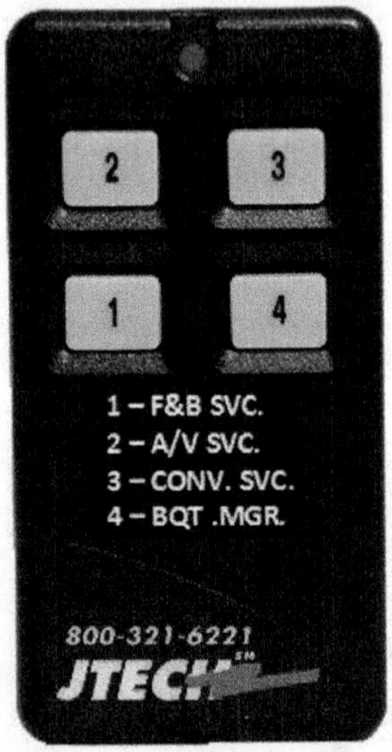

Figure 8–4
StaffComm™. Courtesy of JTECH Communications, Inc.

PRODUCT MANAGEMENT SOFTWARE

When product management software is implemented into a POS system that is designed to handle it, guest service is brought to a higher level by having important information available for servers. At the touch of a button, the server can view a menu item picture, list of recipe ingredients, nutritional information, serving instructions, preparation instructions, or even a video clip on how to serve or prepare the item, as shown in Figure 8–5. The information can even be printed on the POS printer for the server or the guest. This greatly aids in helping a guest avoid any possibility of an allergic reaction to a certain food item or recipe ingredient. Along with menu item descriptions, appropriate wine suggestions and tasting notes may also be included.

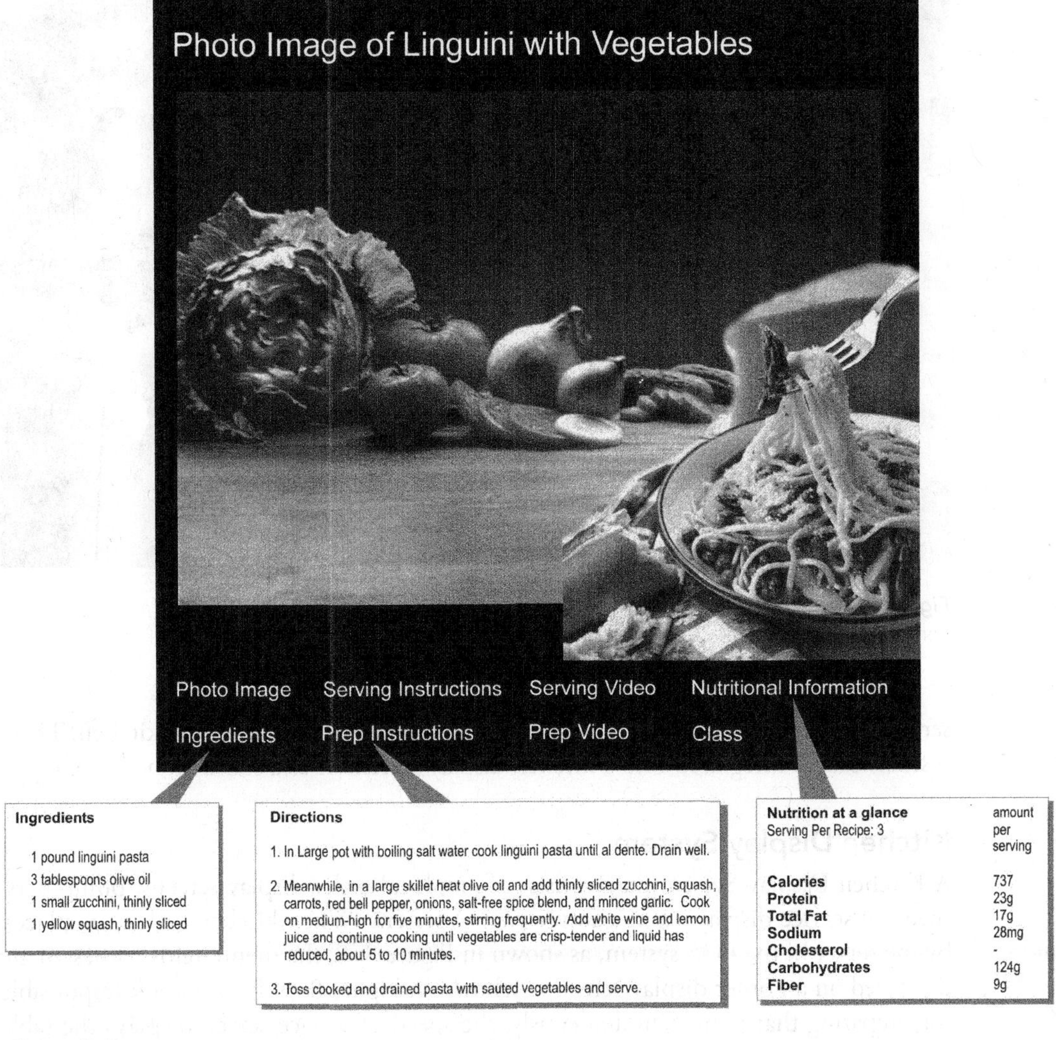

Figure 8–5
Product Management Software. Courtesy of Micros Systems, Inc.

HANDHELD TOUCH-SCREEN TERMINAL

The handheld touch-screen terminal, shown in Figure 8–6, speeds service and allows the server to take orders directly at the table. There are many benefits to the handheld system. This system eliminates frequent unnecessary trips to the kitchen, allowing servers to remain in the dining area to better meet their guests' expectations. It provides flexibility and portability in remote locations like patios and in large facilities such as stadiums, casinos, and resorts where the server must go some distance to serve guests. The handheld terminal provides accurate, up-to-date information if a menu item is out of stock which eliminates guest disappointment before they place an order. Handheld touch-screen terminals are also used as POS terminals, allowing the manager to perform functions which require authorization on the go, such as promotional comps (complimentary food or beverages), adjusting menu item availability, and transferring tables between servers.

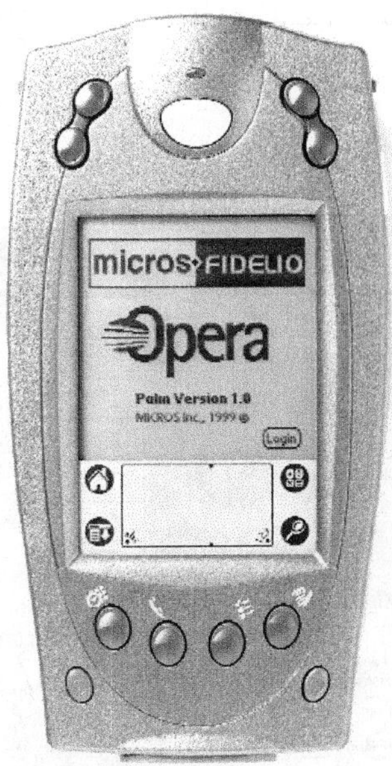

Figure 8–6
Handheld Touch-Screen Terminal. Courtesy of Micros Systems, Inc.

SERVER PAGING SYSTEM

The server paging system, shown in Figure 8–7, clips to the server's belt or pocket and quietly vibrates when activated from the kitchen. This informs the server when food items are ready to be picked up and served to guests. The system allows

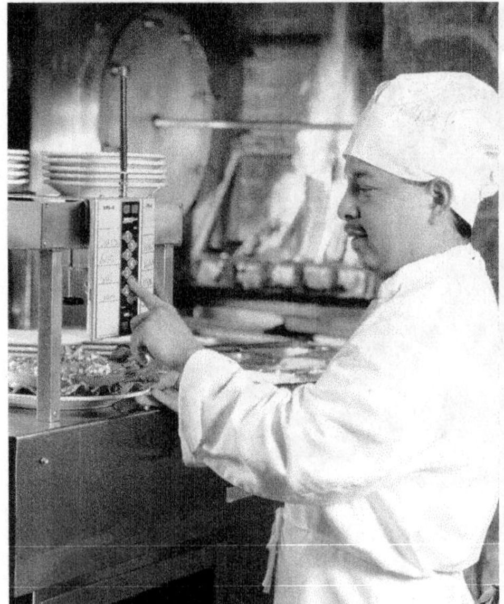

Figure 8–7
ServAlert®. Courtesy of JTECH Communications, Inc.

servers to be more efficient in promptly bringing guest orders from the kitchen. These systems can be integrated into a kitchen display system or as a stand-alone system.

Kitchen Display System

A Kitchen Display System may consist of graphical order display screens, bump bars, speed of service displays, and a server paging system. When kitchen orders are placed by the server in the POS system, as shown in Figure 8–8, the menu items requested are displayed on an order display screen, as shown in Figure 8–9, for the cook responsible for preparing that item. Simultaneously, the speed-of-service screen displays the table that the order is for and initiates a timer which is also displayed. As each cook who is preparing an item for the table completes the item he or she confirms completion by "bumping" the item from his or her order display screen. When all items for the table have been "bumped" the table begins to flash on the speed of service screen. The timer stops, and the server is paged through the server paging system. Additionally, a paper ticket may print at this time, to be used by an expediter or food runner to tray the items and deliver to the table. When the food order leaves the kitchen, the server, expeditor, or food runner bumps the item from the speed of service screen. The system alerts the server and the manager of orders which are taking too long to be prepared so that corrective action can be taken and the guest appropriately communicated with. The speed of service screen displays the number of orders in the kitchen, how long each order has been in the kitchen, and which orders are prepared and awaiting deliveries to the guest.

Figure 8–8
POS Touch Screen. Courtesy of Micros, Inc.

Pay-at-the-Table

Handheld pay-at-the-table devices can be integrated into the restaurants' POS system. These devices can be presented to the guests in addition or as opposed to a paper check, as shown in Figure 8–10. The guest can then review their bill on the

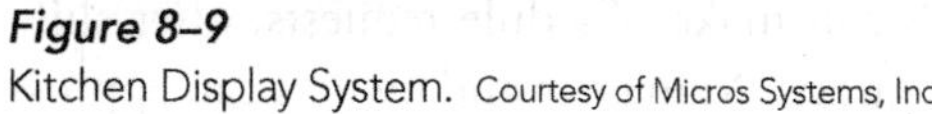

Figure 8–9
Kitchen Display System. Courtesy of Micros Systems, Inc.

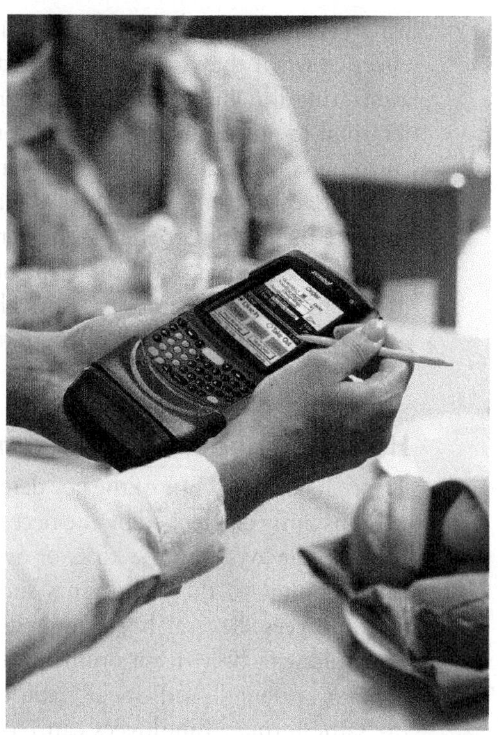

Figure 8–10
Handheld Pay-at-the-Table. Courtesy of Micros Systems, Inc.

handheld screen, pay their bill, and add a gratuity by swiping their credit or debit card on the device. These devices protect the guest from credit card fraud, prevent mistakes when multiple credit cards are used as tenders for a single check, and facilitate PIN (Personal Identification Number) debit transactions as the guests can enter a PIN number on the device. These devices speed the payment process and are also useful for transactions such as curbside to go, or located long distance from a fixed POS terminal, such as poolside and banquet rooms.

Alert Manager

This technology allows for certain POS events to trigger an alert to managers via an RF (radio frequency) pager, text, or e-mail. Certain events concern loss prevention and security such as an extraordinarily large void or discount. Other notifications involve events which may detract from the guest experience such as a long ticket time in the kitchen or a long waiting time to be seated. Alerts can also be configured to notify of events requiring recognition, such as the ordering of a bottle of wine from the reserve list, or a single guest check which exceeds $1,000. This technology facilitates communication among the restaurant staff and insures that guests receive prompt and appropriate attention.

CRM Application

This is a software that is either a hosted solution or integrated into the restaurants POS system which allows the restaurant to collect, store, and query data about each customer. Typically, guest loyalty, frequent diner, VIP cards, and opt in newsletters are examples of CRM programs. The restaurant makes an effort to collect information from guests, such as name, address, phone, e-mail, birthday, and dining preferences, which can then be used to communicate with the guest. These applications are most effective when they can be integrated with the POS system. This is accomplished by associating the guests profile with a magnetic card which can be swiped on the POS terminal to associate with a specific transaction. This allows for the tracking of each customer's purchase history, frequency, and total spend. This information is made available to hosts and servers during a guest's visit and can be used to personalize and enhance the dining experience. Importantly, the information can be stored and queried to customize communication with guests. For example, the restaurant is hosting a wine dinner featuring Italian red wines. The restaurant can query its CRM database to discover the e-mail address of all guests who have purchased any bottle or glass of any red wine during past visits.

Hosted Scheduling and Communication Software

The cost of labor is one of the key determinants of restaurant profitability. Restaurateurs are constantly challenged by the necessity to have enough employees to adequately serve guests while avoiding the costs of overstaffing. The effective scheduling of employees is paramount to the restaurants success, the satisfaction of guests, and the welfare of employees. Several hosted scheduling solutions exist today to meet these needs. Schedules can be written online and then broadcast to individual employees via text message or e-mail. Additionally, critical employee communications can be delivered via the same format. Employees can receive important memos delivered directly to their mobile phone or e-mail account. Employees can make schedule requests, offer shifts for pickup, or trade shifts via these hosted solutions. Managers and owners can approve schedule requests or make schedule changes from anywhere they access the Internet. These applications greatly improve management's effectiveness and productivity and offer employees the utmost in convenience.

Customer Facing Technologies

Restaurant customers are increasingly technology friendly and comfortable using Smart phones and other touch-screen technologies to interact with businesses. Kiosks and Self-checkout are commonplace in the airline and supermarket industries. More and more customer facing technologies are making inroads into the restaurant environment. Examples are I-phone apps which allow customers to connect with online reservation systems and directly place to-go and curbside orders. Lounge environments, and casual entertainment concepts are incorporating POS touch-screen or Microsoft surfaces directly into dining tables, allowing the guests to place their own orders, browse the Internet, or access their applications while dining. These applications will challenge the traditional understanding of restaurant service and place even greater emphasis on service product knowledge and interpersonal skills.

Wi-Fi Hotspots

Today's restaurants offer secure public wireless networks to their guests. These allow guests to connect to the Internet using their Netbook or notebook computers. Properly configured, these networks offer the restaurateur an additional way to gather information about their guests by requiring guests who use the public network to supply name, e-mail address, etc. It also offers another way for the restaurant to market to its guests by displaying information about the restaurant's products and services on the sign-in screen. The wireless environment presents security challenges for the restaurant. The restaurant must protect their customer's machines and data from intrusions and viruses. Additionally, the restaurant must secure its own critical business data from intrusions and hacks that may originate on the restaurant's public network.

POS Functionality

Reputable POS systems have the capacity to strengthen every level of service in a restaurant operation, with the emphasis toward maximizing guest service and optimizing server productivity and selling time. Common POS functionality includes:

- Credit card authorization to eliminate manual charge reconciliations to automate the settlement of funds.
- Speed tendering for a server, cashier, or bartender when taking various denominations of dollar bills; with one step the system can tender and compute exact change due back to the guest.
- Integrated Gift card and Loyalty card program. Allowing for gift card tendering and tracking of guest frequency and purchase history.
- Multiple price levels that allow the restaurant to offer any happy hour or early bird menu pricing that may be needed. Prices can change by time of day and day of the week automatically.
- Separate or split guest check by item, person, group of seats or persons. This feature gives guests any format of guest check presentation they request.
- Gratuities automatically added to group guest checks. Large groups typically expect to pay a gratuity and it becomes easy to add it to the guest check.
- A "send" order allows the server to give appetizers or drinks from the bar a head start during the order process. The send order allows all the items entered at any given point to print immediately at their appropriate requisition printers or display monitors, such as in the kitchen (salad prep area) and in the bar.
- "Hold and Fire" coursing. This facilitates the server taking the guests' entire order but to "Fire" individual courses to the kitchen as the guest's pace of dining dictates. The POS system "Holds" subsequent courses and prompts the server to "hold or fire" each time they access the POS system.
- A training mode (tutorial) for new servers, bartenders, cashiers, etc., that can be turned on or off and will not affect daily reports or print at remote requisition printers, but will walk the new employee through the ordering process.
- Menu item modifiers that prompt the server in the exact way he or she wants to inform the kitchen, salad prep, or bar in specific preparation choices of the guest. If the modifier has not been programmed into the POS, a server can type what he or she wants to type and it will be relayed to the appropriate station. This can eliminate confusion over illegible handwriting and differences in abbreviations or terminology; it reduces the server's trips to kitchen and/or bar.
- Management reports that include the following functions:

    1. Labor management with labor scheduling
    2. Product management with inventory control, ordering, receiving, and supplier bids
    3. Financial management
    4. Employee time and attendance reporting
    5. Transaction analysis of sales activities, employee activities, etc.

BENEFITS OF TECHNOLOGY

A POS system can provide a platform for a complete restaurant management system. The POS system can give the restaurant's operator a solid foundation for all of the restaurant's information requirements and application needs. It begins with eliminating errors between servers and the kitchen. It tracks everything being served and charged to the guest. Guest checks are fully accounted for according to each server. Guest orders instantaneously go directly to the kitchen's printer, with no chance of misplacement. This speeds up production and service, allowing the server to spend more time with guests for personalized service and merchandising. Printers print clean and clear type, reducing errors caused by poor handwriting.

Pre-check features allow the server to look up menu recipes, as shown in Figure 8–11, to correctly advise guests with special requests about ingredients (no salt, diabetics, etc). It can also highlight features and promotions or alert the server of items no longer available. Additionally, the server can see the guests order history and number of visits. The post-check ensures a clean, clear check presentation for the guest. Additionally, some features enhance the speed and accuracy of producing separate checks, transfers between departments (bar tab transferred to the dining room), discounts, coupons, promotions, and adjustments to the bill.

Credit card transactions can be done on multiple terminals or on a pay-at-the-table devices, reducing waiting time. Tips are automatically calculated and tallied, providing tip records for each server and the restaurant owner for tax reporting.

Server productivity, sales analysis, menu tracking (appetizers, wine, desserts, etc.), ticket times, guest waiting times, and labor can be tracked. This is useful for forecasting service and menu focus, performance reviews, scheduling, contests, and seasonal adjustments. Promotions and discounts can be printed on guest checks (happy hour, holiday dinner special, etc.). Some features include the ability for the server to create a personal message on the guest check, such as "Happy 25th Anniversary, Mr. & Mrs. Jones" or any other message with a total of 32 letters.

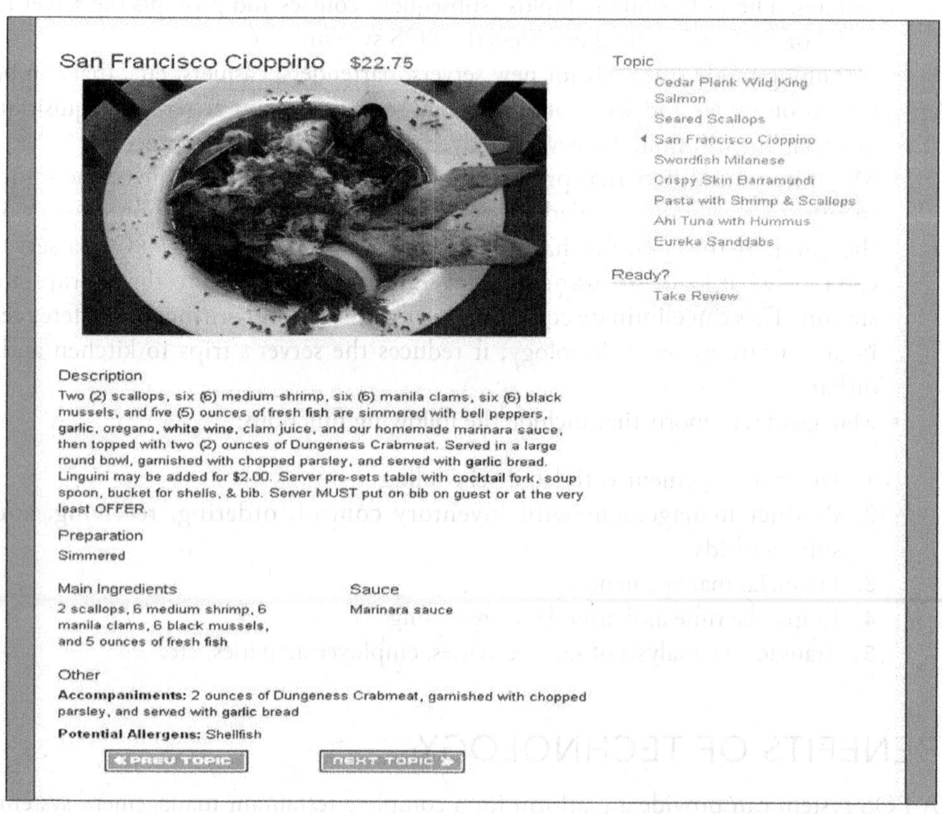

Figure 8–11
Menu Item Screen. Courtesy of Micros Systems, Inc.

Handheld terminals, Pay at the Table devices, and Alert Manager allow the server to provide enhanced tableside service. These are ideal for large properties such as resorts, hotels, convention centers, casinos, stadiums, theme parks, cruise ships, or caterers with multiple remote outlets. The speed of service is increased and the number of server trips is reduced. Guest pagers, which alert the customer when a table is ready, as well as server paging systems, are additional examples of technology that enhances a restaurant's efficiency.

A system can automatically record and report all time and attendance information as employees sign in at the start of a scheduled shift and sign out at the end of the shift, and can also integrate with a payroll service. POS terminals, host displays, and kitchen order displays can access and display printed training materials and videos, allowing new hires to become productive in a short time. There are applications for direct automated purchasing, receiving, and inventory to control waste, theft, and stock levels. These can be programmed for simultaneous access to multiple products and suppliers.

Technology can manage and control all aspects of a restaurant operation if properly used. A POS system can be designed to simplify the difficult task of maintaining tight financial control. It can eliminate costly errors, save time, and be the vehicle that allows the servers to provide the best in customer service by being able to spend more time with guests.

WEB PRESENCE

Many restaurants have created websites to promote their establishment. Websites are a way to communicate vital information, such as menu style, price, location, directions, and hours of operation to potential guests. A restaurant's website is also an important e-commerce opportunity that facilitates the sale of gift cards and branded merchandise. The website also serves as the central portal to the various hosted solutions that the restaurant employs. For example, guests can click through to Open Table or other reservation software, guests can "opt in" to the restaurant's CRM program by providing requested data and agreeing to terms and conditions. Employees can sign in to secure areas of the website to access training videos and materials or click through to the restaurant's hosted scheduling solution such as Schedulefly or HotSchedules. The website can also be used to accept online employment applications. Finally, guests can provide feedback to the restaurant via the website. A restaurant's web presence also includes its website link being placed on other websites. These include various travel and dining sites that potential guests, and leisure and business travelers might visit to decide where to dine. Other sites to consider in establishing Web presence are general information sites which have replaced traditional telephone directory yellow page advertising. Care must be taken to insure that the restaurants website responds favorably to common search terms entered into search engines.

TRAINING WITH TECHNOLOGY

Online content has largely replaced paper training manuals or training CDs. Providers host the restaurant's content on centralized servers and control access via username/password. This insures that content is current, accurate, and also allows for the learner to access the materials anywhere they have Internet access and on any hardware device. Training can be accomplished in the restaurant via the POS terminals, eliminating the need for the owner to invest in additional hardware specifically for training. Employees can access these materials on the job as they perform the job. For example, a bartender can view a drink recipe on the POS terminal, a cook might review the plating of an item by viewing a short video on the kitchen order display, and a host might review how to check in a reservation on his or her handheld by viewing a video on the host graphical table display.

SUMMARY

Restaurant technology continues to grow and expand in fulfilling the requirements and application needs of the rapidly growing restaurant and hospitality industry. Employees, managers, and owners of restaurants must become technology literate in order to succeed and remain competitive.

Some of the most commonly used terms when discussing the operation of a POS system include the following: back office, banked server, electronic draft capture, frequent diner program, menu engineering, modifiers, outlet, requisition printer, terminal, touch-screen, and upselling prompts. A POS system is fast and easy to use, and designed to accomplish the following:

- Seat guests more quickly and accommodate any requests.
- Increase the speed of guest service by reducing order turnaround time.
- Increase the accuracy of food and beverage preparation and pricing.
- Accommodate guests who need separate checks, particularly when seated in large parties.
- Eliminate common mathematical errors.
- Provide prompt, accurate guest check presentation when guests are ready to leave.
- Reduce cash-handling problems and/or errors.
- Provide fast and efficient credit card authorization.

Additional technology applications include table management, CRM applications, guest paging, product management software, handheld touch-screen terminals, server paging, kitchen display system, pay at the table, and hosted Web solutions. Technology can manage and control all aspects of a restaurant operation if properly used. A POS can be designed to simplify the difficult task of maintaining tight financial control, eliminate costly errors, save time, and be the vehicle that allows servers to provide the best customer service.

Restaurant websites have the capability of promoting a restaurant's business, and serving as the central hub of communications between a restaurant and its guests, employees, and business partners.

DISCUSSION QUESTIONS AND EXERCISES

1. Define the following list of terms that are commonly used when discussing the operation of a POS system:
   - Back Office
   - Banked Server
   - Electronic Draft Capture
   - CRM (customer relationship management)
   - Menu Engineering
   - Modifiers
   - Outlet
   - Requisition Printer
   - Terminal
   - PCI-CISP Compliant
   - Upselling Prompts
2. Identify eight areas of improved guest service that result when technology is properly implemented.
3. Explain how a graphical table screen functions.
4. Describe how a guest paging system works and how a restaurant benefits from its use.
5. What are the advantages to servers using product management software?
6. Where would handheld touch-screen terminals ideally be used?
7. Explain how Alert Manager functions.
8. Describe the purpose of a kitchen display system and explain how it works.
9. List three advantages of Pay at the Table technology.
10. Identify and describe the functions of six different POS system software applications.
11. Visit a restaurant website and report your findings in a one-page written report.
12. Search out restaurants in your community that are using a CRM application to communicate with their

customers. Pick one such restaurant and describe your reaction to its e-mail messages.

13. View a training session through an online training service and discuss your judgment of the competence and professionalism of the training presentation.

14. Schedule an appointment with the owner or manager of a restaurant in your community that may be using some or all of the technology presented in this chapter. Inquire how his or her information requirements and application needs are being met. Then write a one-page report describing your findings.

9

The Host

The taste of the roast is often determined by the welcome of the host.

—Ben Franklin

learning objectives

After reading this chapter and completing the discussion questions and exercises, you should be able to:

1. Understand the duties, functions, and responsibilities of a host.
2. Handle table delays when guests may have to wait 15 minutes or more for the next available table.
3. Understand how guests should be seated.
4. Explain how a table service management system functions.
5. Describe the correct way to present menus to guests.
6. List the many other duties that a host will be expected to perform when a restaurant is extremely busy.
7. Understand why the host-cashier would process a guest check payment before seating arriving guests.
8. Understand how the host should handle guest complaints.
9. Describe the procedure that the host should follow when taking a guest's reservations.
10. Describe the procedure that the host should follow when taking a "to go" order.
11. Explain the supervisory functions that a host may have to perform.
12. Identify the items that would be discussed at a menu meeting.

There are different styles of restaurants and restaurant service in the United States and throughout the world. Each of them will require a certain number of employees to serve their guests so that they are able to meet and ultimately exceed the guests' expectations. There are fast-food restaurants where guests serve themselves; there are counter-style restaurants where the guests place an order and a server may deliver the food; there are full-service casual restaurants where a server will take an order, deliver the food, and take payment from guests; and there are full-service fine dining restaurants where the objectives of the restaurant focuses on high-end food and exceeding guests' expectation in service.

There are more positions required to effectively serve a full-service restaurant, either casual or fine dining. The host position is a significant position in this style of restaurants since it is typically the first point of contact for a guest either in person or over the phone. The position of host can function in many different ways, according to the type and size of the restaurant and its organizational structure. Therefore, the responsibilities for the host position will vary and be set forth by the needs of each individual restaurant's operation.

Many guests eat out frequently and are aware of the importance of the whole dining room experience which begins as soon as they walk in the door. It is the first impression that a guest has and it is very important that the guest feels comfortable. This is the beginning of meeting or exceeding the guests' expectations and can ultimately create or lose repeat business. A host must have specific skills to be successful in his or her job. Their success affects everyone in the restaurant, including the servers and the chef in the kitchen.

APPEARANCE

The front-door area and entrance should be immaculately clean, neat, and odor free. There should be clear and appropriate signage informing guests either to seat themselves or to wait for a host to assist them. A host should have a professional appearance and the appropriate uniform. This should include meticulous personal grooming and in most cases a conservative appearance. The host should have no visible tattoos, piercings of any kind, or excessive earrings in their ears. They should have neat hair, minimal makeup for the female host, as well as limited facial hair for the male host. It is also a good restaurant standard for the host to be conscious of the odor caused by smoking and how it may affect guests. Some guests have allergies to smoke and others do not enjoy the strong smell of smoke before they eat. The host as well as any restaurant associate who has contact with guests should be aware of the effects of smoking before their shift begins and thoroughly wash hands and freshen their breath after smoking.

GREETING GUESTS

One of the most effective business practices is to make a good first impression. It is that first impression that a guest will often remember when they are making a future dining decision. The service that guests receive the moment they walk in the door sets the stage for the service that they anticipate receiving once they are seated. Therefore, a host must practice excellent interpersonal skills to make the guest feel welcome; this includes the following: smiling, good posture, open body language, positive attitude, attentiveness, courtesy, and confidence. The essential skills do's and don'ts are listed in Table 9–1.

The host position in most restaurants is one of an official greeter, as this is the person who in some cases actually opens the door and welcomes guests into the restaurant. Therefore, the personality of the host requires the ability to take pressures such as handling a mealtime rush, accommodating various sizes of parties, effectively taking care of guests in a hurry, and assisting families with unruly children. The effective host will never allow this type of pressure to affect his or her performance with guests.

Whenever possible, guests should be greeted as soon as they enter the restaurant. It is a good practice to schedule more than one host during a busy shift. One should remain at the door at all times managing reservations and greeting guests when they enter the restaurant while the other will be responsible for escorting guests to their table.

The things that a guest would expect upon his or her arrival include a smile with eye-to-eye contact, good posture, uncrossed arms, and a positive greeting in a clear voice. Guests expect the host to speak first, and then they will reply. The host who

TABLE 9–1
SKILLS DO'S AND DON'TS

Skills	Do's	Don'ts
Smiling	Genuine smile Eye contact Fresh breath	Insincere or fake smile, No eye contact Unfresh breath
Good Posture	Stand up straight	Leaning on tables, podium, etc.
Body Language	Arms to sides Shoulders back	Crossed arms Slouching
Positive Attitude	Happy to be at work Use time productively Willing to go above and beyond	Unhappy or dreading work Unable to use time wisely Only do what is asked of you
Attentiveness	At the door listening Nodding in agreement Focused on guest	Unavailable at the door Distracted or on the phone Distracted
Courtesy	Use proper language—"please" and "thank you"	Inappropriate and casual language
Confidence	Full understanding of the job Helping wherever needed	Not sure what to do Watching not doing

projects sincerity, maintains eye contact, and conveys a genuine attentiveness for guests will inspire a positive answer to the greeting, "Good evening, how are you tonight?" An appropriate casual conversation between the host and guests helps to eliminate any uncomfortable feelings when a guest enters the restaurant.

Some restaurants take reservations while others do not. If a reservation is expected, ask if they have a reservation when applicable; if not, that is fine as well. A reservation system is an excellent way to get to know guests by name. Therefore, every effort should be made to remember guest's names to add value to their visit. Guests without reservations may be asked their name so the host could then record it and remember it in the future. All guests appreciate when they are recognized from a previous visit, which allows them to feel pampered and special.

After the initial greeting and check-in at the door, the host identifies the number of guests and then selects an appropriate table size and location according to the size of the party. There are different restaurant policies for seating guests; some seat guests as they arrive, while others like to wait until all the guests in a party arrive before seating them. Waiting until all guests arrive allows the server to work more efficiently making fewer trips to the table.

The host should be particularly attentive and courteous to single diners that may be more likely to welcome casual conversation. Whether one guest or a large party of guests, all guests should be made to feel important and treated as individuals. Also, the host should follow the guidelines of the restaurant regarding smoking. The host may have to inform an arriving guest that smoking is not allowed in the restaurant. Many restaurants are now exclusively nonsmoking due to the increase in statewide smoking bans. The most up-to-date smoking information can be easily found on the Internet by doing a search using "smoking bans."

During certain peak periods, there may be a waiting period for guests even if they have a reservation. When this occurs, along with asking the guest's name for a waiting list, the host should communicate the waiting time to the guest in a sincere and courteous manner. If the exact waiting time is uncertain, it is better to slightly overestimate the expected waiting time and be able to seat the guests sooner, rather than underestimating the time and having disappointed guests. Hungry guests can be difficult, so the host must be masterful in communication and keeping guests at ease. If the restaurant has a lounge or bar area, offer to immediately seat the guests in the lounge where they can order drinks and appetizers. Then let the guests know that they will be seated as soon as their table is available. Check on the guests as often as possible to give them confidence in the establishment's operations. When their table is ready, offer to help carry their unfinished drinks to their table, if applicable. Some restaurants may use a guest paging system, as discussed in Chapter 8, where the guest is handed a small message device that is activated with the touch of a button, and alerts the guest by vibrating, flashing, or announcing when his or her table is ready.

TABLE SELECTION

Most restaurants assign servers a section of tables which the host is responsible for seating. The number of tables in a station may vary with the styles of the restaurant. Regardless, proper seating is one of the most important aspects of the host's job. The host must keep track of the number of guests seated in each station so that the servers can carry an equal workload. If the host does not accurately seat the guests it can affect all the positions in the establishment. If the host seats guests in one station repeatedly that server could be overworked and will not provide the best possible service. If overseated, the server may feel rushed and then could make mistakes which may then affect the kitchen staff. To facilitate the speed and accuracy of table selection, some restaurants use table service management systems, as discussed in Chapter 8. These systems help the host seat guests accurately. They typically provide a graphical table display on the POS (point-of-sale) screen that show available tables for immediate guest seating, as well as tables already in use. Controlling the seating flow is essential to maintaining a smooth tempo for the entire restaurant, as guests are alternately seated in servers' stations, allowing for a smooth flow of service which avoids overloading any one station.

It is important to select tables that will provide the maximum comfort for guests. Therefore, guests should never be tightly seated at a table. Guests should always have plenty of "personal space" in order to be able to enjoy their meal. Since all guest's needs are not the same, the host should always personalize table selection. If regular guests request the same table, make it a point of remembering it, and tell them that "their special table" is ready. These are the personal touches that can distinguish a restaurant's service from others in the community.

Strategic seating is an effective tool during slow periods in a restaurant, such as at the beginning of a meal period or in the afternoon when the dining room may be empty. A host should consider the placement of guests during these times. Guests should be seated in the center of the room where they can be seen from the door, near a window, or near other guests, giving the impression that the dining room is somewhat busy. Large parties may tend to be noisy; if possible, they should be seated near the back of the restaurant so they will not disturb other guests. A guest with special needs should be seated in a convenient location away from traffic flow.

PROFESSIONAL COURTESIES

The host should be prepared and ready to help remove guest coats, if appropriate, and if the guest acknowledges wanting the help. When this occurs, the procedure is to stand behind the guest and lift the shoulder of the coat while carefully slipping the coat off the arms. If the restaurant has a coat checkroom this should take place there; otherwise it should take place at the table. Coats then should be taken to a coat rack unless the guest wants to keep it and hang it on the chair. If that is the case, be careful that the coat does not drag on the floor where it could be soiled or tripped over.

When showing guests to a table, the host should always walk a step or two ahead of them at a comfortable pace, perhaps sharing a conversation that will allow them to feel comfortable and at ease. As you arrive at the table, pull out the chairs for guests to be seated. If a woman is being seated, you may want to lightly push the chair back as she sits down, unless her escort advances to do that for her. A high chair for infants or booster seat for small children may need to be furnished. Offer to help seat the child if the guests desire the service.

Open and present a menu directly in front of each guest, suggesting a specific appetizer, chef's specialty, or menu items that have made the restaurant famous. Make sure the guests are comfortable and tell them that their server will be right over. If you know their names, personalize it by saying, "Mr. and Mrs._______, your server Paul will be right with you." If it is extremely busy and the server cannot immediately bring the water to the table, the host should do so, while assuring the guests that any delay in service is only temporary. Also, the host should inform the server of guests' special occasions, such as a birthday, anniversary, and school graduation. Guests will often mention this to the host while making a reservation or while being seated at their table.

The host is usually expected to help whenever possible. When it is extremely busy, he or she may be required to bus tables, pour coffee, fill waters, and help with orders. This means that the host has to be flexible by nature as well as having the capacity to perform multiple tasks in order to help make the operation run smoothly. Therefore, a host should be able to set an effective and efficient pace for the service staff to follow. Then teamwork allows the guest to receive the best possible service.

The host, at times, may also act as the cashier. In this case they should always promptly process guests' payment. The host must juggle seating and payment. This can be difficult. The host should always immediately acknowledge an incoming guest while processing guests' payment. Guests who have finished dining, and wish to leave, should not be inconvenienced by having to wait to pay for their meal. Also, many guests do not put down a tip until after they have paid and acquired change. Therefore, the process should be made quick and easy for the guest.

As guests are leaving the restaurant, the host may have the opportunity to open the door for the guests and bid them good-bye, along with an appreciative thanks and sincere invitation to return again soon.

HANDLING COMPLAINTS

The host may get the bulk of any guest complaints. Guests who have a complaint about their visit to a restaurant sometimes wait until they have paid their check before they complain. The way the host handles a complaint could mean saving or losing this guest's future business. If the complaint is a serious one, the manager should be called immediately to discuss the problem with the guest. It might be a valid complaint that requires the manager's immediate attention. At any rate, the presence of the manager indicates to the guest that management is concerned and wants to correct problems that cause guest dissatisfaction. If the problem does not seem serious enough to call the manager and the guest does not request the manager, the host should write the complaint down on a notepad, in the presence of the guest, and assure him or her that it will receive the manager's attention. Further, ask the guest if he or she would like to leave a name and telephone number for the manager to call. Then thank the guest, sincerely apologize for the problem, and extend a warm invitation to return again soon. The note should be quickly given to the manager with any further explanation, if necessary, at the close of the shift.

TAKING TELEPHONE RESERVATIONS AND "TO GO" ORDERS

The telephone should always be answered according to restaurant policy typically in no more than three rings using the appropriate salutation; for example, "Good evening, (name of the restaurant), May I help you please?"

When recording the reservation, repeat and spell the guest's name: "That is Mr. Wilkinson" (spell the name). Repeat the number in the party: "A party of four"; and the time, "6:00 P.M." Specify the day and date (Friday, month, and day); also note any special occasion, such as a birthday or anniversary. Some restaurants request the guest's telephone number and/or e-mail address along with a credit card number to guarantee the reservation. This is particularly the case during peak times, such as Valentine's Day, Mother's Day, or New Year's Eve. If the guest does not keep the reservation, the restaurant may have a minimum service charge for holding the table that will be charged to the guest's credit card. If this is the policy of the restaurant, guests are informed when the reservation is made, and told what the charge would be.

When taking a reservation for a special occasion, such as a birthday or anniversary, take the opportunity to presell specialty items, such as a small birthday cake or a bottle of champagne. This can also be an opportunity to point out signature items that the restaurant may be known for. When reservations are requested for larger-than-normal parties, they should be referred to the manager, according to the policy of the restaurant. Many times the restaurant will have a limited menu to accommodate large groups.

The host may also be responsible for "to go" orders. The specifics of those orders should be just as detailed as when taking a reservation. The host should know the restaurant menu well and upsell using the appropriate suggestions. Repeat and spell the guest's name; repeat the guest's telephone number, menu order, and the time that the guest will be picking up the order. Then state the cost of the order.

Occasionally, people may call to request directions for getting to the restaurant. This is particularly the case for out-of-town visitors who may be staying in town for a few days or just traveling through. The host should be familiar enough with the community to be able to accurately give directions. Then ask the person to repeat the directions back so that he or she clearly understands them, and say, "We look forward to welcoming you to (name of the restaurant); shall we make a reservation for you?" Often, when paying their guest check, guests will ask for directions to a certain theater, museum, shopping mall, or other place of interest. The host should always be able to provide accurate directions.

People may also call the restaurant to inquire about the menu. The host should use the server skills of suggestive selling as discussed in previous chapters. The key is to ask the right questions and attentively listen to the answers in order to be in a position to intelligently inform the person about the menu offerings and then make appropriate suggestions. Then follow up by asking, "Can I make a reservation for you?"

HOST DUTIES

- Check the work schedules for servers and server's assistants/bussers to ensure proper staffing. Also inquire if anyone on the schedule has called in sick or unable to come to work for any other reason.
- Check the reservation book and compare the number of reservations with the normal amount of open business to verify that there are an adequate number of servers and server's assistants/bussers. If not, the manager should immediately be consulted.
- Assign servers to their stations. Also, assign reservations to stations, if needed. For example, to accommodate a party of 12, three tables may need to be moved together and set.
- Check restrooms to ensure that they are sparkling clean and adequately supplied.
- Check foyer (entrance area) for cleanliness.
- Check menus, remove any that are soiled or damaged.
- If appropriate, check lighting and music.

The host may be responsible for many other front-of-the restaurant details as assigned by the restaurant manager.

MENU MEETINGS

As discussed in previous chapters, a restaurant may have menu meetings just before the shift begins, depending upon the needs of the restaurant operation. The meetings should be short and focused, with specific information to help the service staff, which includes the host, to become better informed. The menu meeting should generate enthusiasm, develop teamwork, and build morale within the restaurant. Items that could be discussed during these meetings include the following:

- New menu items or daily specials. The ingredients could be explained along with the cooking methods and serving procedures. The servers could also be allowed to taste a sample, preparing them to discuss these items when suggesting to guests.
- Recognition and performance praise for accomplishments and good work.
- Be open to feedback from servers and staff.
- Announce upcoming special events or other items pertaining to the restaurant.
- A quick review of restaurant policies, if needed.
- Share valid guest complaints and listen to any service staff complaints.
- Side-work schedules.
- Inspection of personal appearance and uniforms.

SUMMARY

The host position can function in many different ways according to the type and size of restaurant along with the restaurant's organizational structure. The host must be able to take pressures such as handling a mealtime rush, accommodating various party sizes, effectively taking care of guests in a hurry, and assisting families with unruly children; he or she must never allow those pressures to affect his or her performance with the guests.

The host should be competent in tactfully handling table delays by offering to seat guests in the lounge, when possible, where they can order drinks and appetizers until their table is ready. It is important to keep communication going by giving realistic waiting times and keeping guests informed of the situation. The selection of tables that will provide maximum comfort for guests to fully enjoy their meal is also important. The host/hostess has the responsibility to control the seating flow in order to maintain a smooth tempo for the entire restaurant, as guests are alternately seated in servers' stations allowing for a smooth flow of service.

Among the many professional courtesies that the host should perform are helping guests with their coats, pulling out chairs for guests to be seated, and opening and presenting a menu in front of each guest. Also, he or she should be flexible during the busy times and assist with bussing tables, pouring coffee, filling waters, and helping with orders. The host, when also acting as the cashier, should be attentive in handling any guest complaints, and be sincere when inquiring about the guest's dining experience.

When taking telephone reservations and/or "to go" orders, a specific procedure should be followed to ensure accuracy at all times. The host/hostess should also be familiar with the community in order to provide guests with directions and points of interest within the community.

The host will often have additional duties and therefore must be able to control the front-of-the-restaurant operations, including proper planning and assignments.

DISCUSSION QUESTIONS AND EXERCISES

1. What will determine the duties and responsibilities of a host?
2. When a guest's name is known, why should it always be used?
3. What should the host tell guests when they will have to wait 15 minutes or more for a table?
4. How should guests be seated?
5. Explain a table management system.
6. When should guests be seated in the center of the dining room and why?
7. How should guests' coats be handled?
8. How should menus be presented to guests?
9. When the restaurant is extremely busy, what other duties is the host often expected to perform?
10. Why would the host-cashier process the payment of a guest check before seating arriving guests?
11. How should the host, when acting as cashier, handle any guest complaints?
12. What procedure should the host follow when taking a guest's reservations?
13. What procedure should the host follow when taking a "to go" order?
14. Describe five duties that a host may have to perform.
15. List five items that could be discussed at a menu meeting.

10

Banquet, Catering, and Buffet Service

learning objectives

After reading this chapter and completing the discussion questions and exercises, you should be able to:

1. Understand the difference between a banquet, catered event, and a buffet.
2. Recognize the value of using an Event Plan Details work sheet.
3. Understand that a time schedule is a critical factor in allowing an event to flow smoothly.
4. Understand the difference between *approximate, guaranteed,* and *confirmed* number of guests and know the relevance of each to the foodservice operator.
5. Know the importance of clearly defining the menu, including portion sizes and degree of cooking doneness.
6. Explain the differences between an open bar, cash bar, and open–cash combination bar.
7. Understand the guidelines and options in preparing a buffet.
8. Recognize the various options in selecting dinnerware.
9. Know how to calculate a room's capacity for comfortable seating.
10. Recognize the most typically used table sizes.
11. Know the guidelines for table and seating arrangements.

Banquet, catering, and buffet service can accommodate any size group ranging from a dozen to an unlimited larger number of guests. The capacity of the room will dictate the number of people that can be served. A banquet, catering, or buffet menu can be limited and served quickly, or it may consist of several courses, elaborately presented and served. It may be a traditional breakfast, lunch, or dinner menu.

A *banquet* is a dining event that typically honors a special guest(s), such as a business awards lunch, or in celebration of a special occasion, such as a school graduation banquet. Many foodservice operators have fixed banquet menus that are limited to the choices offered on the menu. This is a very important feature of banquet-style service because it helps the establishment accommodate a diverse clientele. Another important feature which sets banquet style service apart from restaurant service is that all elements of the event are predetermined: the date, number of guests, the type of tables used, start and end time, and style of service used. This helps the establishment order the correct amount and type of food in addition to accurately scheduling employees.

A *catered event* is where the menu is created for the specific occasion. The nature of the catered event typically influences that menu, such as a wedding reception, birthday party, anniversary party, Christmas or New Year's Eve party, bar or bah mitzvah, or any other special occasion. The menu is always predetermined. Occasionally a second choice may be offered to guests or to guests who may have dietary restrictions. A catered event could be on or off premise. An on-premise catered event takes place at a restaurant or hotel. An off-premise catering event can take place away from a restaurant or hotel in a natural environment such as a botanical garden, near a scenic waterway, or at a historical landmark.

A *buffet* allows guests to select the food and serve themselves. The buffet may be formal or informal and is appropriate with either a simple or an elaborate menu. The advantages of a buffet are, a restaurant establishment can service a large group of guests in a short amount of time and they can provide a wide variety of food to accommodate many likes and dislikes. Guests like buffets because they can choose what suits their personal portion size and taste.

Banquet, catering, and buffet service are generally used to accommodate larger groups of guests. Foodservice establishments use these types of service because they have components that allow for ease of service and limited number of employees to serve large number of guests for all kinds of special occasions. Table 10–1 compares banquet, catering, and buffet service by location, advantages, and disadvantages for each.

TABLE 10–1
BANQUET, CATERING, AND BUFFET SERVICE COMPARED

Type of Service	Location of the Event	Advantages	Disadvantages
Banquet—food is plated and served to a large number of guests by a limited number of servers for a specific occasion.	Typically in a room which is on the property. The room can have special dividers to allow the establishment to increase or decrease the number of guests that can be accommodated.	All elements of the event are predetermined	Food choices are limited
		Can serve a large group of guests	There can be lag time between the first and last tables being served and food can get cold.
		Can be customized to fit the specific needs of the guests	
Catering—foodservice where the food may or may not be plated but large numbers of guests are served in a limited amount of time by a limited number of servers for a specific occasion.	*On-premise catering*	Same as above	Same as above
	Event takes place under the same circumstances as banquets		
	Off-premise catering	Same as above	Can be difficult to move food, equipment, and staff to the desired location.
	Event can take place anywhere away from the property and can be customized to meet the guests needs		
Buffets—food is placed on tables and on chaffing dishes. Guests help themselves to food items from the buffet line. Servers will serve beverages to guests and clear plates.	In a restaurant setting special room, or on location.	Same as above	Need to purchase special equipment such as chaffing dishes and service utensils.
			Buffet can get messy
			Certain types of food do not hold well on buffets so menus are limited

12. Know how to set up a head table, lectern, and podium.
13. Know how to place table numbers.
14. Be aware of room temperature in achieving guests' comfort.
15. Be aware of choices in tablecloths, napkins, table skirting, and chair covers and bows.
16. Understand the various options available for floral décor and table and room decorations.
17. Understand beverage and chocolate fountains.
18. Be aware of ice carvings and ice molds.
19. Understand the procedure for coatroom checking using double theater tickets.
20. Know how to arrange a portable stage.
21. Know the correct placement when arranging the U.S. flag with one or more other flags on display.
22. Recognize the importance of lighting in creating the desired atmosphere and enhancing a food presentation.
23. Be aware of what may be needed for sound systems, background music, and the use of a piano.
24. Know how to coordinate valet parking.
25. Explain the conditions that affect pricing.

THE EVENT PLAN

A banquet, catered event, or buffet always begins with a checklist of details followed by a level of professional service that enhances every detail of the event. The checklist should be thorough and complete in identifying everything that the foodservice operator is capable of providing. Furthermore the customer may not be aware of all the options that can add to the success of the event. Therefore the checklist serves to provide additional choices for the customer to consider.

The typical checklist would include, but would not be limited to, the following, as presented in Figure 10–1.

Customer Information

Customer information includes the name, address, telephone number, mobile number, fax number, and e-mail address of the person responsible for scheduling and paying for the event. It is essential for the foodservice operator to be able to conveniently contact the customer as the time for the event approaches. The type of function is also identified, such as, a women's club lunch and meeting or a wedding reception.

Date and Time Schedule

The date, day, and arrival and departure times of the event must be identified and scheduled with enough advance notice to adequately prepare for and deliver first-rate service. Accommodating the customer's time schedule is a top priority for the foodservice operator. Therefore it is important to know the exact time that the customer would like the service to begin. When the menu is served on time, prepared and cooked to the highest quality, and perfectly presented, the customer's guests will be satisfied. The experienced foodservice operator knows the amount of time required for preparation, cooking, and serving.

When the food serving time is preceded by other activities occurring, beginning and ending time frames for those activities should be established; such as a set time for cocktails, hors d'oeuvres, bar service, speaker(s), entertainment, dancing, or photography. There are occasions when a specific time frame cannot be established so an approximate time frame should be determined. The foodservice operator must always be prepared with a contingency plan for time delays. And when the unexpected happens, a logical alternative choice should be presented to the customer. For example, if half the guests attending an event are delayed for an hour due to a traffic backup, an alternative could be to hold the meal and offer appetizers to the guests who have arrived.

The amount of time needed to complete all of the necessary work, from start to finish, for a successful banquet, catered event, or buffet should be determined. Therefore the customer must be able to inform the foodservice operator of the actual or approximate guest departure time from the event.

Number of Guests

An *approximate number of guests* attending the event must initially be determined in order to plan the details and identify the costs. Several days before the scheduled event, the customer will authorize a *guaranteed number of guests* attending, which is the minimum number that the customer is committed to pay for. If it is a large event that involves special ordered items, such as a wedding cake, then a week or more advance notice would be required. The *confirmed number of guests* served may be more or less than the guaranteed number, but the customer is responsible for paying for whichever is greater, the guaranteed or the confirmed number of guests.

The foodservice operator prepares an additional amount over the guaranteed number to be served. That amount will depend upon the size of the guaranteed number. For example, when the guaranteed number is 30, then it would be appropriate to prepare for 36, 20 percent over the guaranteed number; if the guaranteed number is 100, then

Customer Name ______________________________ Telephone # ____________
Address ______________________________ Mobile # ____________
______________________________ Fax # ____________
Type of Event ______________________________ E-mail ____________

Date ____________ Cocktails served ____________ Speaker(s) (start time) ________ (end time) ________
Day ____________ Hors d'oeuvres ____________ Entertainment (start time) ________ (end time) ________
Arrival Time ________ Bar service ____________ Dancing (start time) ________ (end time) ________
Departure Time ____ Food served ____________ Photography (start time) ________ (end time) ________

Number of Guests: Approximate Number ________ Guaranteed Number ________ Confirmed Number ________

MENU ____Banquet ____Catered ____Buffet ____Cake Order
Menu Items______________________________ ______________________________
______________________________ ______________________________
______________________________ ______________________________
______________________________ ______________________________
Beverages ______________________________ BAR SERVICE ____Open ____Cash ____Combination
______________________________ Drink Choices ______________________________
______________________________ Brands ______________________________

Room Location ______________________________ Table Set-up: _____ Banquet _____ Round _____ Conference
Table Arrangement ______________________________ Number of Chairs at Each Table _____
Table Numbers / Names ______________________________ Head Table: _____ Banquet _____ Round
______________________________ Number of Chairs at Head Table _____
______________________________ Room Floor Plan *(see attached diagram)*

ACCESSORIES
Tablecloths (color) ____________ Napkins (color) ____________ Type of Napkin Fold ____________
Chair Covers (color) ____________ Bows (color) ____________ Table Skirting (pleat/pattern style) ____________
Candles (type) ____________ Candelabras ____________
Floral Arrangements (name specific flowers & details for each arrangement – real or artificial)
Centerpieces ____________ Baskets ____________Sprays ____________
Canopy ____________ Plants ____________ Trees ____________
Room Decorations ____________ Balloons (colors) ____________ (size) ____________(wording) ________
Fountains: Beverage (type & mix) ____________ Chocolate (list items for dipping) ____________
Ice Carving(s) (name of design & size requested) ______________________________
Coat Rack / Coat Checking (instructions) ____________ Lectern ____________ Speaker Podium ____________
Portable Stage (height) ____________ (size) ____________(skirting type & color) ____________
Flags (placement location)____________ (name of flags and order of arrangement) ____________
Tripod(s) (sizes) ________ (placement location) ________ Easel(s) (sizes) ________ (placement location) ________
Lighting Effects (list all area requiring special lighting) ______________________________
Sound System / Microphones: ___ Cordless ___ Lavaliere ___ Standing ___ Lectern ___ Table
Background Music (start & end time) ____________ (type of music / requested music) ____________
Piano (date checked for tuning) ________ (placement location for the piano) ____________
Registration Table(s) (size & number of tables) ________ (number of chairs) ________ (electrical requirements) ________
Miscellaneous Items: (big screen television with DVD, costume rental, menu printing, large notepad & marker for meetings, etc.)
____
Valet Parking (guests' arrival time) ________ (departure time) ________
Special Requests ______________________________

ESTIMATED CHARGES
Guaranteed guest number of ______ at $ ________ per guest for a total of...................... $ ____________
(The final charge will be for the guaranteed guest number or confirmed guest number, whichever is greater)
Beverage Service (wine(s), espresso) $__________ Bar Service $____________.................... ____________
Accessory Items ______________________________
______________________________ ____________
Gratuities: Servers $ ________ Bartenders $ ________ ____________
Estimated Total (not including tax)................... $ ____________
Deposit Amount................................ $ ____________

Figure 10–1
Event Plan Details.

Figure 10–2
Event Menu. Courtesy of Lake Isle Country Club Caterers.

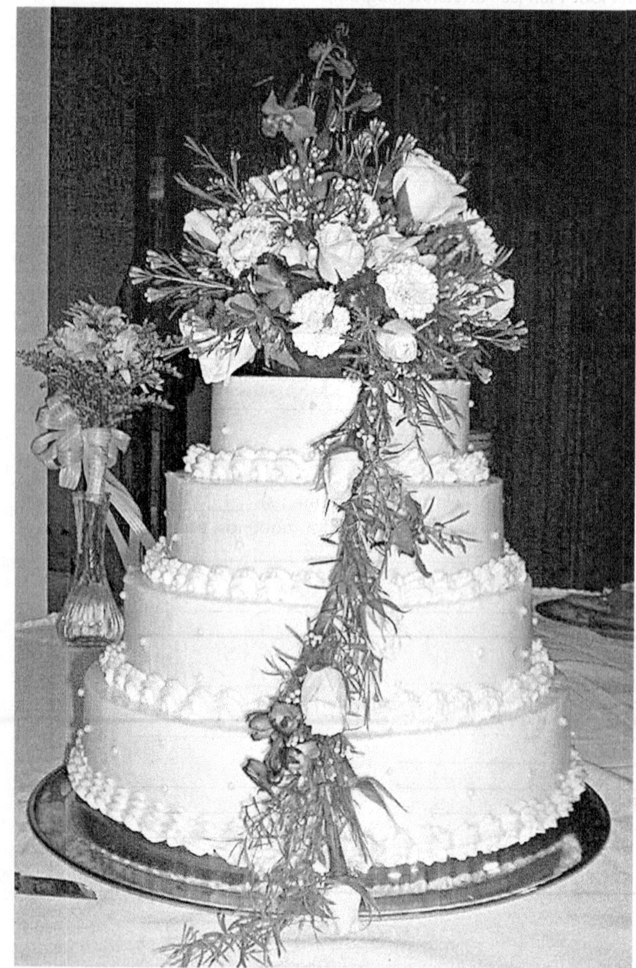

Figure 10–3
Wedding Cake.

it would be appropriate to prepare for 110, 10 percent over the guaranteed number. The amount that is to be prepared over the guaranteed number should be discussed with the customer to find out if any unusual circumstances may exist that could influence a greater number of guests attending—for example, an important topic being presented at a business lunch meeting or a prominent speaker that may attract more guests than anticipated. The actual number of guests served is verified by the number of dinner plates used.

When the foodservice operator prepares a cost estimate for the customer, the percentage number over the guaranteed number is calculated into the cost of the guaranteed number. This protects the foodservice operator if the actual number is greater, the same, or less than the guaranteed number of guests.

MENU

The menu will be identified according to the type of event and service required: banquet, catered, or buffet. The nature of the event and time of the year can affect the menu choices that the customer may consider. For example, a summer wedding reception might include a selection of fresh fruit appetizers or carved watermelons for a buffet table. The menu chosen and item portion sizes should be clearly identified—for example, prime rib 6 ounce cut cooked medium or grilled salmon 8 ounce. This reduces the possibility of the customer being dissatisfied with a portion size or degree of cooking doneness. Also if children are attending the event it would be helpful to know the approximate ages and number attending to determine if a second menu selection should be considered. Furthermore if a guest has a dietary restriction a special individual meal could be prepared; or if a guest was being honored perhaps a special dessert may be requested.

There are occasions when the customer may want to have copies of the event menu printed so that guests attending the event will know the food and beverage items that will be served. When this occurs the menu is typically printed with the name of the host, the title of the menu, such as "Wedding Menu," and the food and beverage items printed in the order that those items will be served, as shown in Figure 10–2.

Cake Order

When a cake is requested for a wedding, anniversary, birthday, or special event dinner, it must be prepared and presented exactly to the customer's request. The foodservice operator should have a choice of two or three specialty bakeries that could fulfill the order; and know the capabilities and pricing for each bakery. The size and complexity of the cake will determine the amount of advance order time required. Figure 10–3 is an example of a decorative wedding cake.

Beverage

The foodservice operator should always be able to recommend alcohol and nonalcohol beverages that complement the food being served. An understanding of wines, as discussed in Chapter 6, is an important part of the foodservice operator's function in helping the customer to make a selection that is paired with the menu when wine is to be served.

Nonalcohol beverage choices may include sparkling cider in lieu of champagne, plain or flavored mineral waters, iced teas, and specialty coffees or espresso that may be paired with a dessert.

BAR SERVICE

There are occasions that may include bar service, such as prior to a dinner. The time allotted for the bar service is often a time frame for guests arriving to socialize prior to a dinner being served; for example, from 7:00 p.m. to 8:00 p.m. cocktail reception with dinner being served at 8:00 p.m.

A number of drink choices (liquor, beer, wine) would be presented to the customer along with specific brands that the customer's guests may request. When the customer determines the number of drink choices and identifies the specific brands to be served, the foodservice operator can calculate the charge for the bar service.

The bar service can function as follows:

Open bar—paid for by the customer, whereby the guests do not pay for the drinks.

Cash bar—also referred to as a no-host bar where the guests pay for their drinks.

Open bar–cash bar combination—this occurs when the customer may agree to pay for the first one or two drinks with drink tickets that are given to each guest prior to or upon arrival. If the guest desires additional drinks after the tickets have been used then he or she would be required to pay for those drinks.

The foodservice operator typically has a portable full functional bar that can be conveniently set up and in place to serve guests as shown in Figure 10–4.

Figure 10–4
Portable Bar for Cocktail Reception (10 on the Park, Time Warner Building, NYC). Courtesy of Restaurant Associates.

SERVICE PRESENTATION

If hors d'oeuvres or beverages are to be served on handheld trays during a social time prior to a banquet or catered event, *butler service* would be provided. This type of service is discussed in Chapter 3.

A sit-down individual plate service, commonly known as *American service,* is the typical method of service for most banquet or catered events. The food is plated in the kitchen and individually served to guests. The service is fast, efficient, and equal portion sizes are maintained with each serving. This type of service is also discussed in Chapter 3.

Buffet service allows guests to choose among the food items being presented and serve themselves. The typical buffet is set up in the following order:

1. serving plates
2. salad selections

(a)

(b)
Professor Louise Hoffman and Associate Professor Jean F. Claude

(c)

Figure 10–5
(a) Hors d'ouvre/appetizer Buffet Table. Courtesy of Johnson & Wales University.
(b) Buffet Tables. Courtesy of Hospitality Management Program, New York City College of Technology and
(c) Dessert Buffet Table. Courtesy of Johnson & Wales University.

3. vegetables
4. potatoes/pasta/rice
5. rolls and butter
6. entrée(s)
7. dessert plates
8. desserts

The arrangement presents the food items in their natural order and allows the guests to fill their plates first with the items costing less, leaving enough space for an adequate portion of the entrée.

The average single-line buffet can comfortably accommodate 40–50 guests within 15 minutes, with an average of three guests per minute going through the line. The speed at which the line moves will be determined by the variety of foods and the extent of the food presentation; the greater the variety the more time needed for guests to make selections. A double-line buffet, allowing guests to serve themselves from both sides of the table, will accommodate twice the number of guests within the same period of time. Several buffet tables could be set up to accommodate a large group with an elaborate presentation. An example would be a buffet table for Hors d'oeuvres/appetizers as shown in Figure 10–5a, which also may include salads, salad dressings, fresh fruit, cheeses, breads, and crackers; a second buffet table for the entrée(s), sauces, vegetables, and potatoes/pasta/rice as shown in Figure 10–5b—carving station could also be placed at this table; and a third table for desserts as shown in Figure 10–5c.

When planning the menu for a buffet service it is important to include food items that hold up well on a serving line along with being easy for guests to serve themselves. The visual presentation is enhanced by placing risers, trays, and chafing dishes at various angles to the table. Trays can be slightly elevated in order to slant toward guests and placed at different heights to add interest. When serving unusual food items or items not easily recognized, the name of the item printed on a small card should be conveniently placed next to the item. Also when the food items become depleted with about one-quarter to one-third remaining in bowls or on trays replace or remove then put in smaller bowls or trays to retain a fresh and full appearance.

The food items should at all times be kept at their recommended safe food temperatures: 140°F or above for hot foods and 41°F or below for cold foods. Chafing dishes are typically used for hot foods and large pans filled with crushed or small cubed ice can hold platters, trays and bowls for cold foods. And for certain events the use of a hot or cold well buffet table (to insert trays and pans) provides additional safety and flexibility.

Dinnerware

The choice of dinnerware should be banquet weight, which is lighter than the traditional dinnerware and thus more comfortable to handle. White-color dinnerware fits all decors and is traditionally used, although the right dinnerware can increase the perceived value of the meal. Therefore the foodservice operator may have several choices from inventory or from rental sources that complement a menu, theme, and décor as well as the customer's preference. For additional information on dinnerware, banquetware, drinkware, flatware, and holloware visit www.oneidafoodservice.com

ROOM LOCATION

A restaurant, hotel, resort, or club may have several rooms that can accommodate small to large groups. The rooms may adjoin and be configured to fit the needs of a particular function—for example, a room to serve cocktails and hors d'oeuvres as guests arrive next to the room where guests will be served dinner. The choices should be presented to the customer so that the room(s) location can be reserved in advance.

ROOM FLOOR PLAN

The size of the room determines the seating capacity for banquet, round, and conference size tables. If banquet table seating (long tables lined up in a row) is planned then the total square footage of the room is divided by 12. For example, if a room is 60 by 80, the total square footage is 4,800 (60 × 80 = 4,800) divided by 12 (4,800 ÷ 12 = 400), seating for 400. If traditional seating (individual or round tables) is planned then the total square footage of the room is divided by 15 (4,800 ÷ 15 = 320), seating for 320. Figure 10–6 shows a room setup for banquet table seating. Figure 10–7 shows a room setup for round table seating.

If the room has an unusual layout, such as long and narrow or has floor to ceiling columns, then allowance should be made for adequate spacing. The seating arrangements should allow for the comfort of the guests and provide easy traffic flow for safe and efficient service. Also additional space will have to be allowed for if a portable bar, hors d'oeuvre buffet table, or piano are to be set in the room. For example, if a portable bar and hors d'oeuvre table is set up for a cocktail hour prior to a full-service menu being served with traditional seating, then the following calculations would be appropriate: 4,800 square feet room, 1,200 square feet allowed for the bar, hors d'oeuvre table and stand-up socializing prior to the dinner being served, and 3,600 square feet allowed for tables (3,600 ÷ 15 = 240), seating for 240.

Figure 10–6
Banquet Table Seating. Courtesy of Lake Isle Country Club Caterers.

Figure 10–7
Round Table Seating ("Gala" Liberty Science Center, Jersey City, NJ). Courtesy of Restaurant Associates.

When setting up the tables it is critical to remember to set up for the number that is on and above the guaranteed number of guests. For example, if the customer has guaranteed the guest count number to be 220, and had requested the foodservice operator to be prepared to accommodate 12 more over the guarantee, then seating for 232 would be adequate. If 5-feet round tables with seating for 8 at each table were being used then 232 divided by 8 ($232 \div 8 = 29$) would equal 29—therefore, 29 tables to be arranged and set up for service.

A room floor plan diagram either hand-drawn or computer generated should accompany the contract agreement with the customer's approval. Figure 10–8 is a diagram that shows 3 buffet tables and 16 banquet tables set according to the customer's preference. This is of the utmost importance for certain events that require a head table or conference table seating for meetings or seminars, a stage, podium placement, buffet tables, room decorations, etc.

Table Setup

The tables should be set up well in advance of the event, allowing enough time to be thorough and complete. Tablecloths should be draped approximately 1 inch above each chair. The tables should be set with the appropriate plates, beverage glasses, coffee cups, saucers, and flatware to accommodate the menu being served. Each table setting should be approximately 24 inches wide and 15 inches deep. This will allow a comfortable space for guest seating and dining, as well as adequate serving room. Tables and chairs should be arranged so that guests can be conveniently seated and served. Chairs, when in use, will normally extend 18–20 inches from the table edge and 18 inches in width. Allow 24–30 inches from back to back (when in occupied position) for comfortable service between tables. When a head table is being used, the other tables should be arranged so that the majority of the guests will be able to view the head table. The server is typically assigned 12–18 guests to serve, depending upon the menu and the method of service.

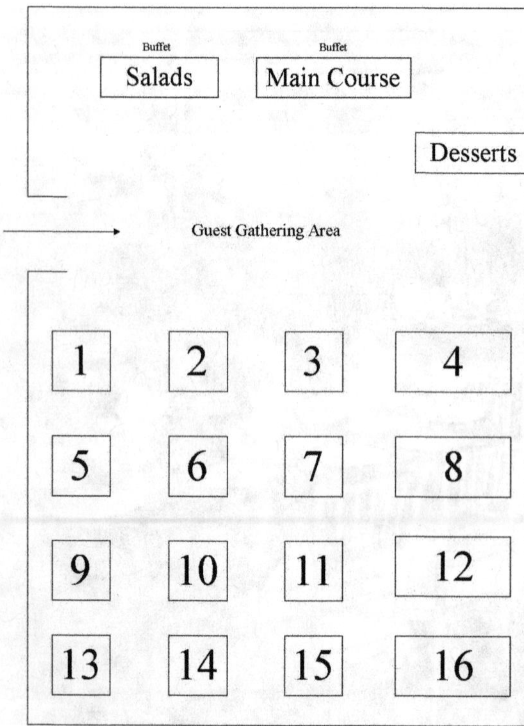

Figure 10–8
Floor Plan Diagram.

TABLE SIZES

The typical table sizes with seating capacity are as follows:

Length	Width	Seating
Banquet Table Sizes		
4 feet	30 inches	4 (5 or 6 if chairs are added to the opposite ends of the table)
6 feet	30 inches	6 (7 or 8 if chairs are added to the opposite ends of the table)
8 feet	30 inches	8 (9 or 10 if chairs are added to the opposite ends of the table)
Round Table Sizes		
4 feet	round	6 or 7
5 feet	round	8 or 9
6 feet	round	10 or 11

Conference Table Sizes

6 feet	18 inches
8 feet	18 inches

Conference tables are used for groups holding meetings, but can also be used for buffet or display tables. If needed for meal service, the tables can be placed together side by side forming a 36-inch-wide dining table with opposite seating.

TABLE ARRANGEMENT

Banquet tables can be arranged in several different configurations for dining, buffets, and elaborate food presentations. Some examples are as follows:

- U-Shape—where several banquet tables are set to form the shape of the letter "U," with chairs around the outside. The inside of the "U" is covered with *table skirting* or *draped tablecloth* reaching approximately 2 inches above the floor. This layout is often used for business meetings or discussions that immediately follow the meal service.
  Table Skirting is easy to install and is secured and held in place with clips, tape, or T-pins. The skirting is available in a variety of pleat styles and patterns. Valances that would attach along the top of the skirting can also be added for a bolder appearance, and are available in a number of styles.
  Draped tablecloth is held in place with masking tape. Head tables and buffet tables can easily be draped with tablecloths. For a head table, one tablecloth is draped over the front of the table reaching approximate 2 inches above the floor and secured with masking tape. A second tablecloth is draped in the usual manner. For a buffet table the front and back of the table would each be covered and secured with masking tape, and topped with a third tablecloth draped in the usual manner.
- Hollow Shape—where banquet tables are set to form a square or rectangle, leaving the center open. Both sides of the tables are covered with table skirting or draped tablecloth reaching approximately 2 inches above the floor. This layout is ideal for a formal buffet setting. The hollow center could accommodate a large ice carving. The carving would set in a pan on top of a skirted square table. A drain hose connected to the pan and attached to a 5-gallon bucket placed under the table to control the flow of water as the ice slowly melts. The base of the pan would be covered with parsley or other greens.

Head Table

A head table is usually reserved for honored guests, speakers, or the bride and groom, parents (relatives), and the wedding party. When the room is set with a head table, it should be set apart from, and face, the other tables. The front of the head table should always be covered with table skirting or draped tablecloth reaching approximately 2 inches above the floor.

If requested, a head table can be placed on a portable stage that is raised from 6 to 36 inches above the floor, depending upon the nature and circumstances of the event.

There are occasions where the head table may be set apart from the other tables by an above-average-size centerpiece such as a tall floral arrangement, signifying the distinction of the table. This is often the case when a speaker podium is to be used. The table is set close to and off to one side of the podium allowing for speakers to easily come forward to the podium with the least amount of distraction.

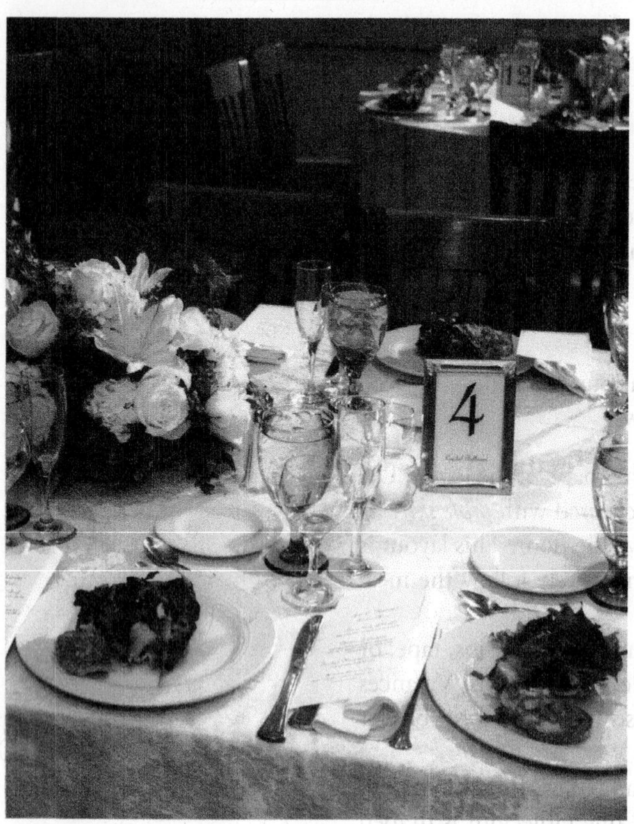

Figure 10–9
Table Numbers. Courtesy of Lake Isle Country Club Caterers.

Table Numbers/Names

Table numbers or names are used when the customer requests assigned seating for guests. This is often the case for functions that may have distinguished guests who would need to be seated near a head table or speaker podium and also for events that sell tickets, whereby a group of individuals or a business may purchase tickets for a complete table. The table numbers as shown in Figure 10–9 or names are printed on cards and placed in the center of the table or clipped to a centerpiece. The numbers or names are removed by the service staff when all of the guests are seated.

Room Temperature

The room temperature will rise when the room becomes fully occupied. Therefore, the room temperature should be five to ten degrees cooler prior to guests' arrival. The foodservice manager should be familiar with the cooling and heating conditions of each room. It is important to be able to establish temperature settings that will accommodate the guests' comfort during any season of the year. If a room temperature is either too hot or too cold, the guests will be uncomfortable, which can result in not enjoying the event.

ACCESSORIES

There are a number of additional items and services that the foodservice operator may be able to offer customers. These are items and services that can enhance the event and be an added source of revenue for the foodservice operation. Each item is individually priced and added to the total cost of the event. The items and services may include the following:

Choice of Linen Colors

Tablecloths, napkins, and chair covers and bows are available in different fabrics and a variety of colors. Table skirting comes in various pleat and pattern styles. All of these items are available from local rental stores and from national linen rental companies. The national companies are able to fulfill size and quantity requirements within short notice and ship to any location. The websites of those companies include: www.linennstuff.com, www.fabulousevents.com, www.bbjlinen.com, www.dovelinen.com, and www.tabletoppersinc.com.

There are many different types of napkin folds that add a distinctive look to the table. Napkin presentations are explained and illustrated in Chapter 3. The specific napkin fold selected for the event should be noted, such as "Bird of Paradise" or "Rose." For a quick reference to napkin folding, visit www.napkinfoldingguide.com or www.napkinfolding.net

Chair Covers

Chair covers are often used for distinguished guests, the bride and groom, or for a specific table. Chair covers with bows add a special touch of elegance and are available in a variety of colors.

Candles

Candles offer an added accent to each table and should be placed in the center of the table or evenly placed on banquet tables at a height that is not distracting to guests, as shown in Figure 10–10. If a formal event requires the use of candelabras, then it is important to remember to use dripless candles.

Figure 10–10
Candelabras placed on banquet tables.

Floral Arrangements

The foodservice operator, at the request of the customer, often coordinates with a floral designer and local florist in providing the floral arrangements for an event. This may be the case for wedding receptions or special dinners where fresh flowers are the preferred choice, as shown in Figure 10–11.

There are occasions when customers request artificial silk flowers for table centerpieces. The artificial silks allow for flexibility in choosing colorful and/or exotic flowers. The additional advantage is the absence of any floral scents that could activate allergy conditions for some guests. The cost of artificial silks is relatively stable versus the cost of fresh flowers that will fluctuate according to seasons and general availability. The artificial silks can often be rented or, if purchased, can be offered by the host as gifts to guests to take upon leaving the event.

Baskets of fresh flowers or colorful sprays often add decorative accents to a room when appropriately placed by an entrance or near a head table. Plants and trees, real or artificial, are excellent choices to accent parts of a room or to create an aisle that will serve to guide guests' movement. A floral canopy can add an elegant touch to the entrance of a wedding reception or festive event.

Figure 10–11
Floral Table Centerpieces (Corporate Dinner, Diker Pavilion, Natural Museum of The American Indian, NYC). Courtesy of Restaurant Associates.

Room Decorations

An atmosphere can easily be created with a few appropriately selected room decorations. Good judgment is the key factor in selecting items such as photographs, art, floral decorations, balloons, mobiles, and special effects lighting. The foodservice operator can work closely with a party-supply rental store in providing ideas and items that can meet the customer's expectations. The facility itself and the nature of the event may often dictate the appropriate decorations.

Balloons are a popular choice and come in numerous colors and sizes that can be decoratively placed on tables, chairs, arches, and throughout the room. Greetings and messages can also be printed on balloons that further add a personal touch. The balloons should not be prepared and put in place too far in advance of the event. Under normal temperature conditions, latex and Mylar balloons will retain helium for several hours.

Beverage and Chocolate Fountains

Fountains have an excellent display effect in attracting the attention of guests. A beverage fountain allows guests to easily approach the fountain to fill or refill their cups or glasses. While in use, a service person would be assigned to maintain the necessary beverage quantity for the fountain to adequately function. Beverages should always be chilled before pouring into the fountain. If champagne or cider is to be used it is important to not allow the beverage to remain in the fountain too long or it will become flat.

Chocolate fountains can fill a room with a delightful aroma as melted chocolate is pumped up the inside of the fountain and flows over the tiers. Items for dipping such as fresh strawberries, marshmallows, cookies or biscuits are placed on nearby trays within easy reach for guests. While in use, an attendant should be readily available to promptly wipe up any messy drips from guests' use.

Fountains are typically positioned to the side of a room near an electrical outlet and the cord taped to the floor to avoid any possibility of a guest tripping. Depending upon the amount of use, many foodservice operators prefer to rent fountains from full-service rental stores versus owning the units.

Ice Carvings

Ice carvings are a work of art and can add an elegant touch to any event. Many unique designs in various sizes are carved by professionals skilled in the art of ice carving, as shown in Figure 10–12. The ice carving professionals will have photos of their work for prospective customers to review as can be viewed in the following website: www.icesculpturedesigns.com. Many of these talented people are also accomplished chefs working in prominent restaurants, hotels, resorts, and clubs within local communities. Once the design is decided upon, the amount of time needed to do the ice carving can be determined and scheduled.

Ice molds may be ideal when a smaller display would be appropriate. A sculpture mold is filled with water, placed in a freezer, and removed when ready to use. The mold is cut along a marked bead, peeled away, and discarded. The result is a decorative ice sculpture that is placed in an appropriate size pan. As it slowly melts, the water can be absorbed with dry bar towels that are covered with parsley or other greens.

Coat Rack/Coat Checking

As weather conditions prevail, a conveniently located coat rack for guests' coats, hats, raincoats, or umbrellas should be provided. But for events that take place during cold weather where most guests would be wearing coats, the foodservice operator may be asked to have one or more attendants assigned to coatroom checking. This is efficiently accomplished with the use of double theater tickets: One ticket is hung on the hanger with the coat, and the other is given to the guest. The coats are hung on the rack in the order of the ticket numbers. When the event is over, the coatroom attendant(s) will be able to quickly return guests' coats.

(a)

(b)

Figure 10–12
(a) Ice Carving for Business Event and (b) Replica of building carved in ice.
Courtesy of Ice Sculpture Designs.

Lectern or Speaker Podium

There are events that require the use of a lectern or speaker podium and the foodservice operator will need to be prepared to accommodate those requests. If a lectern is to be used it is normally placed on top and at the center of a banquet table that has been prepared as a head table. Lecterns can be small and simple, with folding sides and top for easy portability, or large and equipped with a microphone, reading light, and perhaps the name and logo of the restaurant or hotel prominently displayed on the front. One or more glasses with a pitcher of ice water can be placed near the lectern or podium as per the customer's request.

If a speaker podium is to be used, it may need to be set up with a microphone, computer connection for PowerPoint, space in front for a floral display, or anything else relevant to a speaker's presentation. It is important to double-check that all technology is functioning properly prior to the event taking place.

Portable Stage

Stages are typically used to support a head table, speaker's stand, and band or orchestra. The height of the stage is determined by the size of the room: The larger the room the higher the stage. Portable stages range in height from 6, 12, 24, and 36 inch heights with 4 by 4 or 4 by 8-foot adjoining sections. The front part of the stage that faces the guests should be covered with appropriate skirting from the edge of the stage to the floor.

Flags

There are certain event gatherings that request to have flags displayed, and when that occurs the foodservice operator should be able to accommodate those requests. The rule in displaying flags is as follows: When the U.S. flag is displayed with the flags of other countries, states, schools, colleges, universities, clubs, and various organizations on a stage or as part of a room display, the U.S. flag should be placed to the right of any other flag and slightly higher than the flag of another country. When a speaker is addressing an audience, however, and flags are beside or behind the podium; the U.S. flag should be placed to the speaker's right as he or she faces the audience. Other flags should be to the speaker's left.

Tripods and Easels

The customer may request the foodservice operator to set up a display area using skirted tables, tripods, and easels. There may be the need to display business products, company awards, family memorabilia, an individual's accomplishments, art objects, etc. Special lighting may also be necessary for the display. If the display request requires more than what the foodservice operator can accommodate, the foodservice operator should be able to suggest the names of companies that specialize in creating exhibit displays.

Lighting Effects

The foodservice operation should be able to accommodate the basic lighting needs of most events. For example, hors d'oeuvre or buffet table can be enhanced with the right degree of lighting; softening the lights to create a relaxed mood as food and beverages are served, a stage or speaker podium may need spot lighting. Whatever the lighting requirements may be, all the lights must be tested and adjusted to the desired levels prior to the guests' arrival.

Sound System

The event may require the use of microphones for speakers and/or entertainers. The microphones could be either cordless, lavaliere (neck), standing, attached to a lectern or podium, or placed on a table. The foodservice operator should be experienced and familiar with the types of sound systems that will provide the best-quality sound and functions for each specific use. The sound system should be tested, adjusted, and ready for use prior to the guests' arrival. The foodservice operator should also be able to suggest the names of reputable companies that specialize in sound systems as well as Disc Jockey service.

Background Music

A customer may request to have soft background music playing during a cocktail and hors d'oeuvres time and/or during dinner to add to the atmosphere. The specific times for the music to be played should be noted and followed. If the event is a Christmas party or has an Italian menu theme then the music selected could appropriately fit the event. Also to be included would be the music that the customer has specifically requested.

Piano

A piano is often available in many fine restaurants, hotels, resorts, and clubs for guests' entertainment. When a piano is to be used for an event, the foodservice operator should make certain well in advance that it will be in tune, and again check several days prior to the event. The piano should be placed in the most appropriate location in accordance with the customer's preference.

Registration Table

A registration table is used at certain events that require guests to turn in or fill out a registration form, pick up a name tag, possibly pay a fee, or simply to turn in their invitation to the event. The foodservice operator may be asked to set up one or more registration tables as per the request of the customer. Typically, banquet tables with table skirting along the front and sides of the tables are used, with chairs placed behind the tables. Electrical outlets and extension cords are conveniently placed for the customer to use his or her computer(s) and printer(s).

Miscellaneous Items

The foodservice operator may be asked to provide a big-screen television with a DVD player for the customer wanting to have a video presentation as part of the event. A customer may request to have someone in costume stationed at the entrance of the room to greet guests, the costume being associated with the theme of the event, such as a ship's captain for a New England seafood menu. There are rental stores that can accommodate most reasonable requests. Menu printing may be requested for a multiple-course formal dinner. A large stand-up notepad with marker may be needed for a business session that follows a lunch or dinner meeting.

Valet Parking

When valet parking for guests is provided, the time schedule for guests to arrive is an important factor in determining the number of attendants to schedule for the event. For example, if guests will be arriving within a short period of time, say between 7:30 and 8:00 p.m., more attendants would be needed. The same is true for departure time. The experienced foodservice operator will know exactly

Figure 10–13
Ice Carved Serving Bowls and Vases. Courtesy of Ice Sculpture Designs.

Figure 10–14
Artisanal Cheese Station. Courtesy of Restaurant Associates.

what it takes to keep traffic flowing smoothly in and out of the facility's parking areas. If there is the need for limousine service the foodservice operator should be able to suggest the names of reputable companies that can professionally deliver the chauffeured service.

Special Requests

The customer may request to have a cocktail-hour buffet table serving seafood appetizers from ice-carved bowls and vases, as shown in Figure 10–13, an artisanal cheese buffet station, as shown in Figure 10–14, or a custom-created dessert for an event or for an honored guest, as shown in Figure 10–15; or perhaps have several servers join to sing Happy Birthday to a certain guest. Most special requests can be accommodated when properly planned and scheduled.

The foodservice operator should also be prepared with names of bands, solo instrumentalists, singers, and professional photographers to answer a customer's request for possible choices. The customer would be responsible for determining the best choice for the occasion and event.

Estimated Charges

The pricing for a banquet, catered event, or buffet is based upon several factors which include the following:

- The type of foodservice operation (restaurant, hotel, resort, or club): *Upper Priced*—which is the finest food and beverage selections with superb service and elegant accessory details in a highly rated property. *Mid Priced*—represents most banquet, catered events, and buffets, where the food, beverage, service, and accessory details are carefully chosen and professionally presented. *Budget Priced*—where the food, beverage, and service choices are limited to the dollar amount that the customer can afford to spend.
- The reputation of the restaurant, hotel, resort, or club. When a high level of quality and service is performed that consistently meets customers expectations, then the property's reputation commands a higher price.

Figure 10–15
Custom Dessert. Courtesy of Restaurant Associates.

Gratuities

A gratuity for the service staff of 18–25 percent of the total food and beverage charge is typically added to the final bill. The percentage assigned is often determined by the going rate within the local foodservice industry.

Deposit Amount

A deposit amount can vary from 10 to 50 percent of the total estimated dollar amount of the event and is normally due at the time a contract agreement is signed. Experienced foodservice operators have policies in place that set forth the terms and conditions for deposit amounts, gratuities, and cancellations.

Cancellations

A cancellation policy that clearly defines the terms, conditions, and charges if a customer cancels should be reviewed with the customer before the contract agreement is signed. If something occurs that forces a customer to cancel the contract all or part of the deposit may have to be forfeited. The determining factors would be to what extent food and beverage products had been ordered and prepared. Once the costs are identified, along with adding a service charge for the foodservice operator's professional services time, the balance of the deposit may be returned to the customer.

SUMMARY

The functions and many details that can be involved in a banquet, catered event, and buffet are presented and explained. Through the use of an event plan details work sheet the foodservice operator can review important details with a customer. The event plan insures that both the guest and establishment agree and understand the expectations of the event. It is a valuable tool which is the foundation of a successful event. There are accessory details that the customer may not be familiar with but will often appreciate being made aware of in order to choose additional services that can further enhance his or her event.

Three types of bar service—open, cash, and combination open–cash bars—are explained. The guidelines for setting up and presenting different types of buffet lines are reviewed. Topics ranging from selecting the right dinnerware, being able to calculate a room's seating capacity, chocolate fountains, and ice carvings to the various conditions that affect pricing are presented and discussed.

DISCUSSION QUESTIONS AND EXERCISES

1. Contrast the differences between a banquet, catered event, and a buffet.
2. Why is it important to have a complete list of event plan details available to review with a customer?
3. Explain why the time schedule is a critical factor in allowing for an event to function smoothly.
4. Define approximate guest count, guaranteed guest count, and confirmed guest count.
5. Name two or more menu details that are important to discuss with the customer.
6. Contrast the difference between an open bar, cash bar, and combination open–cash bar.
7. List five key factors for a successful buffet including food safety.
8. What should be considered when selecting dinnerware?
9. Calculate the banquet seating for a room that is 50 feet by 30 feet.
10. What are the most popular table sizes used for banquet and catered events?
11. Explain the guidelines for seating arrangements.
12. Explain how a head table is set up.
13. When would table numbers be used and where would the numbers be positioned?

14. Approximately how many degrees cooler than normal should a room be set for prior to an event?
15. What are the different choices available when choosing tablecloths, napkins, table skirting, and chair covers and bows?
16. Explain the benefits of silk floral arrangements.
17. List several food items that could be placed on trays next to a chocolate fountain.
18. What should be considered when deciding on an ice carving?
19. Describe the procedure for coatroom checking with the use of double theater tickets.
20. What are the typical sizes and heights of a portable stage?
21. Explain how to position the U.S. flag when displayed with another flag, and explain the one exception to that rule.
22. When a piano is requested by a customer, what should be checked well in advance?
23. How does the event's time schedule for valet parking affect the number of attendants working?
24. What is the average gratuity range and how is it determined?
25. When pricing a banquet, catered event, or buffet, what are the factors considered?

appendix A
Common Menu Terms

À la (ah-la) After the style or fashion.

À la broche (ah-lah-brosh) Cooked on a skewer.

À la carte (ah-lah-cart) A separate price for each item on the menu.

À la king (ah-lah-king) Served in a cream sauce with mushrooms, green peppers, and pimentos.

À la mode (ah-lah-mode) Usually a dessert (pie) served with ice cream.

Al dente (ahl-den-ta) Cooked firm to the bite—pasta.

Aioli (all-i-oli) A sauce made of garlic and olive oil.

Amandine (ah-mahn-deen) Almonds added.

Ambrosia (am-broh-zha) Fruit mixture of oranges, grapefruit, bananas, cherries, and shredded coconut.

Antipasto (ahn-tee-pahs-toh) An appetizer that can have a variety of Italian meats, cheeses, olives, and vegetables.

Aspic (ass-pik) A clear jelly made from meat, fish, poultry, or vegetables.

Au gratin (oh-grah-tin) Foods with bread crumbs, cheese, or sauce topping usually made by browning top.

Au jus (oh-ju) Meat served in natural juices.

Basted Cooking juices (drippings) spooned over meat while cooking.

Battered Covered with flour or other starch mixture.

Béarnaise (bear-naz) A sauce usually containing butter, egg yolks, tarragon, shallots, and white wine or vinegar.

Béchamel (bay-shah-mehl) A white sauce usually containing butter, flour, milk, and seasonings.

Bill of fare List of foods on the menu.

Bisque (bisk) Cream soup usually made with seafood (shellfish).

Blanquette (blang-ket) White stew usually made with veal or poultry.

Bombe glacé (bongh-glaz-ay) Frozen dessert usually made with cake, ice cream, or a combination of several dessert items, and molded in a round ball.

Bon appetit (bone-ah-pet-tee) "A good appetite to you," "May you enjoy your meal".

Bordelaise (bohr-dih-layz) A brown sauce usually made with meat stock, beef marrow, butter, carrots, onions, red wine, bay leaf, and a variety of seasonings.

Borscht (borsht) A beet soup, may also include cabbage.

Bouillabaisse (boo-yah-bays) A fish stew usually made with several types of fish and vegetables.

Breaded Rolled in bread crumbs (plain or seasoned), cracker crumbs, cornmeal, or other dry meal, generally used prior to pan- or deep-frying.

Brioche (bre-ohsh) A sweetened soft bread with eggs and butter.

Brochette (bro-shet) Meat chunks broiled, grilled, or baked on a skewer, often with onion, green or red pepper, and tomato.

Cacciatore (kah-che-ah-toh-reh) An Italian sauce usually made with tomatoes, garlic, onions, peppers, sausage, and spices.

Calamari (kah-lah-mah-re) Squid.

Canapé (kah-nah-pay) Small bread, toast, or cracker spread (topped) with tasty food mixtures and served as an appetizer.

Cannelloni (kan-a-lo-ne) A pasta stuffed with cheese and/or spicy meat and served with Italian tomato or meat sauce.

Capers Small flower buds from the caper plant that have been pickled.

Carbonara (car-boh-nah-rah) A sauce usually made with cream, butter, onion, peas, bacon, Parmesan cheese, and various seasonings.

Carte du jour (kahrt-du-joor) Menu of the day.

Chanterelle (shahn-the-rehl) A funnel-shaped mushroom mild in taste.

Chantilly cream (shahn-tee-lee) Vanilla whipped cream.

Chantilly sauce (shahn-tee-yee) A mixture of thick sauce supreme and whipped cream.

Chateâubriand (shah-toh-bree-ahn) A roasted tenderloin of beef, center cut.

Chiffonade (sher-fon-ad) Shredded vegetables used as a topping for salads or soups, or as a garnish or bedding.

Chive (ch-eye-vuh) Slender, green, dried onion tops.

Chorizo (choh-re-soh) A mild or spicy Mexican pork sausage.

Chowchow A spicy hot relish usually made with pickles and pickled vegetables.

Chutney (chuht-ne) A sweet-and-sour condiment that is usually made of fruits or vegetables.

Cobbler A deep-dish fruit dessert.

Compote (kahm-pote) A stewed fruit mixture.

Consomme (kon-so-may) A clear broth.

Couscous (koos-koos) Crushed wheat grain often cooked by steaming and served as an alternative to potatoes or rice.

Crème brûlée (krehm broo-lay) Cream custard with a caramelized sugar glaze top.

Creole (kree-ol) Style of cooking common in Louisiana, prepared with tomatoes, peppers, onion, and unique seasoning blends.

Crêpe (krehp) A thin pancake.

Crêpes suzette (krehp-soo-zeht) Crêpes cooked in a sweet orange sauce consisting of sugar, lemon juice, butter, and oil from the skins of Mandarin oranges.

Croquettes (crow-kets) A mixture of chopped cooked foods, shaped into small balls, rolled in egg and bread crumbs, and deep-fried.

Croutons (crew-tahns) Bread cubes sautéed and seasoned.

Currants Small red or black dried fruit from a shrub related to gooseberries.

Drawn butter Melted butter.

Duchesses potatoes Mashed potatoes usually made with egg yolks, butter, milk, salt, ground white pepper, and nutmeg.

Duxelles (ducks-elz) Finely chopped mushrooms, shallots, and garlic sautéed in butter and then simmered in a stock and made into a coarse paste.

En casserole (ahn-kahs-eroll) Baked or served in an individual dish.

Endive (ahn-dev) A leafy salad vegetable with a bitter taste.

Escargot (es-kar-go) Snails served as an appetizer.

Escarole (ehs-kah-rohl) A curly leaf salad vegetable similar in taste to endive.

Feta (feh-tah) A Greek white cheese that has been pickled.

Filet (fih-lay) A boneless loin of meat or a boneless strip of fish.

Filet mignon (fih-lay-meen-yoon) Tenderloin of beef.

Flambé (flahm-bay) Flamed.

Flan (flahn) A caramel custard.

Florentine (floor-ahn-teen) Prepared and/or served with spinach.

Foie Gras (fwah-grah) Goose or duck liver, of a pâté.

Fondue (fon-du) Melted or blended for dipping bread, meat, etc.; most common is cheese fondue; dessert fondues often feature chocolate or caramel for dipping fruit.

Frappé (frap-pay) A frozen drink served over crushed ice.

Fricassée (frick-ah-see) Stewed meat or chicken served with thickened white sauce.

Gazpacho (gahs-pah-choh) A cold tomato and vegetable soup.

Glacé (glaz-ay) A glazed coating made by reducing fish, meat, or poultry stock.

Gnocchi (nyoh-ke) A small Italian dumpling usually made from potato.

Gouda (goo-dah) A smooth mild Dutch cheese.

Granita (grah-ne-tah) A flavored frozen beverage.

Gratinée (grah-tan-ay) A food that is sprinkled with bread crumbs and/or cheese and baked until browned.

Gruyère (grue-yair) A sharp dry cheese with a nutlike flavor.

Guava (gwah-vah) A tropical fruit with a sweet flavor.

Gumbo A soup usually made with seafood or chicken, tomatoes, peppers, and various ingredients and spices.

Hollandaise (haw-lawn-dez) A sauce made with egg yolk, butter, and lemon juice.

Hors d'oeuvres (ohr-durv) Savory foods served before meal as appetizers, to stimulate the appetite.

Hush puppies A popular southern dish of deep-fried cornmeal.

Indian pudding A baked pudding made with cornmeal, milk, eggs, brown sugar, and raisins.

Jardinière (jar-duhn-air) A mixture of vegetables.

Jarlsberg (yahrls-berg) A Norwegian cheese with large holes, like Swiss cheese, and a smooth nutlike flavor.

Julienne (julie-en) Thin strips of food about 2 or 3 inches long.

Kabob (keh-bahb) Cubes of meat and other foods, such as peppers, onion, and tomato, grilled or broiled on a skewer.

Kimchi (kihm-che) A Korean relish usually made from spicy, pickled vegetables.

Kipper (kih-per) A cold, smoked herring.

Kiwi (ke-we) A fruit with brown skin, green flesh, and tart taste.

Knockwurst A large smoked German sausage.

Kosher A method of cooking that strictly follows Jewish dietary laws.

Kumquat (kuhm-kwaht) A mildly bittersweet citrus fruit.

Langostino (lang-goh-ste-noh) A large prawn that has the appearance and taste of a small lobster tail.

Leek A very sweet type of onion.

Lox Smoked salmon.

Mango A fruit with a juicy light orange flesh and a pineapple and peach taste.

Marengo A chicken or veal sautéed in olive oil with tomatoes, mushrooms, and olives.

Marinara (mah-re-nah-rah) An Italian tomato sauce with various spices.

Medallions Small round cuts of food, often round cuts of meat.

Meringue (mar-rang) Baked dessert of beaten egg whites and sugar.

Meunière (moon-yair) A lightly floured piece of fish, sautéed in butter, seasonings, parsley, and lemon juice.

Milanaise (me-lan-ayz) A food item that is breaded, sautéed, and topped with Parmesan cheese.

Mornay (mor-nay) A white cheese sauce.

Mortadella (mohr-tah-dehl-lah) A spicy Italian pork and beef sausage.

Mousse (moos) A chilled, light, whipped dessert made with cream, egg white, gelatin, and flavoring; or a cold molded purée of meat, fish, or poultry.

Mozzarella (moth-sah-rehl-lah) A soft white mild Italian cheese.

Münster (moon-ster) A semi-soft German cheese with a light pungent flavor and aroma.

Napoleon A layered pastry with custard or cream filling.

Neapolitan (ne-oh-pah-le-than) A layered ice cream and cake dessert, layered in different colors of ice cream and cake.

Newberg A creamed seafood dish made with egg yolks, sherry, and various spices.

Panettone (pa-neh-toh-neh) A bread with candied fruit.

Parboiled Boiled until partially cooked.

Parfait (par-fay) A chilled dessert of layered ice cream, fruit, whipped cream, and/or other confections served in a parfait glass.

Parisienne potatoes Small round potatoes that can be cooked by boiling, steaming, or baking.

Parmesan (pahr-meh-jzahn) A hard sharp Italian cheese that is served grated and used as toppings for salads and soups.

Pastrami (pa-stra-mi) Beef that has been slowly cured with spices.

Pâté (pah-tay) A meat or fish mixture often baked in a small pastry shell.

Pâté de foie gras (pah-tay-de-fwah-grah) A goose or duck-liver pâté.

Pesto (pehs-toh) An Italian sauce made of olive oil, garlic, basil, and cheese.

Petite marmite (puh-teet-mahr-meet) A consommé made with beef, chicken or turkey, and vegetables, such as carrots, peas, and celery.

Petits fours (puh-tee-foor) Small layered and frosted cakes or cookies, or small fruits glazed with sugar.

Pilaf (pee-lof) Rice that has been cooked slowly with onions and stock.

Piquant (pee-kahnt) Heavily seasoned.

Polenta Boiled cornmeal.

Prâline Almonds or pecans caramelized in boiling sugar.

Primavera (pre-mah-veh-rah) Fresh spring vegetables served as part of a main dish.

Prosciutto (proh-she-oo-toh) Dry-cured smoked ham.

Provençale (pro-vahn-sahl) An item usually cooked with tomatoes, garlic, and spices.

Provolone (proh-voh-loh-neh) A hard, sweet-tasting Italian white cheese.

Purée (pu-ray) Fruits or vegetables that have been sieved or blended into a thick liquid, also a thick soup.

Quiche A mixture of cream, eggs, Swiss cheese, and various other ingredients baked in a pie shell.

Radicchio (rah-de-ke-oh) A small red leaf lettuce.

Ragoût (rah-goo) A stew of highly seasoned meat and vegetables.

Ramekin (ram-kin) A small oven-proof baking dish used for individual food portions.

Ricotta (re-kah-tah) A soft bland Italian cheese.

Risotto (re-soh-toh) Sautéed grains or rice that is boiled in stock and seasoned with cheese.

Rissole (ree-soh-lay) Browned.

Romano (roh-mah-noh) A hard Italian cheese with a strong flavor and aroma.

Roquefort (roke-furt) A French white cheese made only in Roquefort, France.

Roulade (rue-lad) Thin meat that can be braised or sautéed and rolled around stuffing.

Scalappine (skah-loh-pe-na) Small pieces of veal.

Scampi Shrimp in butter sauce.

Shallot An onion variety.

Shiitake (she-e-tah-keh) A Japanese mushroom.

Sorbet (sore-bay) (or sherbet) A frozen mixture made with fruit juice or fruit purée.

Soufflé (soo-flay) A baked, fluffy, light egg mixture combined with ingredients such as cheese, spinach, or chocolate.

Spumoni (spoo-moh-ne) An Italian ice cream made with chocolate, vanilla, and cherry flavors along with candied fruit.

Stir-fry To cook vegetables alone or with meat or poultry in oil over high heat in a wok, frequently stirring to retain the crispness of the vegetables.

Sweetbreads The thymus glands of young animals such as calves and lambs.

Tortoni (tore-toh-ne) An Italian vanilla ice cream topped with crushed almonds or macaroons.

Tournedos (toor-nuh-doe) Small-size tenderloin steaks.

Trifle A decorative dessert made with several layers of sponge cake and fresh fruit, soaked with brandy or rum, and topped with custard or whipped cream.

Truffles A fungi-like tuber similar to a mushroom but with a strong aroma; or can be ganache-filled rich chocolate candies.

Velouté (vel-oot-eh) A thick cream sauce made from fish, veal, or chicken stock.

Vichyssoise (vee-shee-swaz) Potato and leek soup served cold.

Vinaigrette (vee-neh-gret) A dressing made with oil, vinegar, salt, and pepper.

Watercress Green type of small crisp salad leaves used on sandwiches, in salads, and as garnishes.

Wiener schnitzel (vee-ner-schnit-zl) Breaded veal sautéed and served with lemon wedge.

Wonton Noodle stuffed with ground pork or chicken served in Oriental soup.

appendix B

Wine Terminology—General, Sight, Smell, and Taste

GENERAL

Acetic Vinegar smell and taste. Spoiled wine.

Aeration Letting a wine "breathe" before drinking it, preferably in the glass, in order to soften the tannins and improve the overall quality. Red wines benefit most from aeration.

Alcoholic Used to describe a wine that has too much alcohol for its body and weight, making it unbalanced. A wine with too much alcohol will taste uncharacteristically heavy or hot as a result. This quality is noticeable in aroma and aftertaste.

Awkward Poor structure, clumsy, or out of balance.

Backbone Full bodied, well structured, and balanced by a desirable level of acidity.

Backward Used to describe a young wine that is less developed than others of its type and class from the same vintage.

Balance A wine has balance when its elements are harmonious and no single element dominates.

Character Describes distinct attributes of a wine.

Clean Wine without disagreeable aromas or taste.

Closed Wines that are concentrated and have character yet are shy in aroma or flavor.

Complexity Displays subtle, layered aromas, flavors, and texture.

Cooked Wine that has been exposed to excessively high temperature; spoiled.

Delicate Light, soft, fresh—usually describes a white wine.

Dense Describes a wine that has concentrated aromas on the nose and palate. A good sign in young wines.

Dumb Describes a phase young wine undergoes when the flavors and aromas are undeveloped. The same as "closed."

Earthy Used to describe both positive and negative attributes in wine. At its best, a pleasant, clean quality that adds complexity to aroma and flavors. The flip side is a funky, barnyard character that borders on or crosses into dirtiness.

Elegance Well balanced and full wine with a pleasant distinct character.

Fading Describes a wine that is losing color, fruit, or flavor, usually as a result of age.

Flawed Wine that is poorly made and shows faults.

Flinty Extremely dry white wines such as Sauvignon Blanc. More often an aroma than flavor. Smell of flint struck against steel; a mineral tone.

Floral Tasting and smelling of flowers. Mostly associated with white wines.

Fresh Having a lively, clean, and fruity character. An essential for young wines.

Fruity Having obvious aroma and taste of fruit(s).

Graceful Describes a wine that is harmonious and pleasing in a subtle way.

Grapey Characterized by simple flavors and aromas associated with fresh table grapes; distinct from the more complex fruit flavors (currant, black cherry, fig, or apricot) found in fine wines.

Grassy Aromas and flavors of fresh-cut grass or herbs. A signature descriptor for Sauvignon Blanc.

Harmonious Well balanced, with no component obtrusive or lacking.

Hearty Used to describe the full, warm, sometimes-rustic qualities found in red wines with high alcohol.

Heady High in alcohol.

Herbaceous Herbal or vegetal in flavor and aroma.

Length The time the sensations of taste and aroma persist after swallowing. The longer the better.

Light Soft, delicate wine; pleasant but light in aroma, flavor, and texture.

Madeirized The brownish color and slightly sweet, somewhat caramelized and often nutty character found in mature dessert wines.

Mature Ready to drink.

Meaty Describes red wines that show plenty of concentration and a chewy quality; they may even have an aroma of cooked meat.

Medium-Bodied Good weight and texture but softer than "full-bodied."

Nouveau A light fruity red wine bottled and sold as soon as possible. Applies mostly to Beaujolais.

Oaky Describes the aroma or taste quality imparted to a wine by the oak barrels or casks in which it was aged. Can be either positive or negative. The terms *toasty, vanilla, dill, cedary,* and *smoky* indicate the desirable qualities of oak. *Charred, burnt, green cedar, lumber,* and *plywood* describe its unpleasant side.

Peak The time when a wine tastes its best—very subjective.

Potent Intense and powerful.

Raw Young and undeveloped. A good descriptor of barrel samples of red wine. Raw wines are often tannic and high in alcohol or acidity.

Robust Means full-bodied, intense, and vigorous, perhaps a little too much so.

Rustic Describes wines made by old-fashioned methods or tasting like wines made in an earlier era. Can be a positive quality in distinctive wines that require aging. Can also be a negative quality when used to describe a young, earthy wine that should be fresh and fruity.

Simple Light wine with limited aromas, flavors, and texture, similar to thin.

Stale Wines that have lost their fresh, youthful qualities are called stale. Opposite of fresh.

Stalky Smells and tastes of grape stems or has leaf- or hay-like aromas.

Stemmy Wines fermented too long with the grape stems may develop an unpleasant and often dominant stemmy aroma and green astringency.

Vegetal When wines taste or smell like plants or vegetables.

Vinous Literally means "wine-like" and is usually applied to dull wines lacking in distinct varietal character.

Yeasty Fresh dough, biscuit-like aroma and or flavor.

SIGHT

Appearance Refers to a wine's clarity, not color.

Brilliant Absolutely clear appearance of a wine.

Browning Describes a wine's color, and is a sign that a wine is mature and may be faded. A bad sign in young red (or white) wines, but less significant in older wines. Wines 20–30 years old may have a brownish edge yet still be enjoyable.

Cloudiness Lack of clarity to the eye. Fine for old wines with sediment, but it can be a warning signal of protein instability, yeast spoilage, or re-fermentation in the bottle in younger wines.

Hazy Used to describe a wine that has small amounts of visible matter. A good quality if a wine is unrefined and unfiltered.

Legs The drops of wine that slide down the sides of the glass when it is swirled.

Murky More than deeply colored, lacking brightness, turbid, and sometimes a bit swampy, mainly a fault of red wines.

SMELL

Acetic Vinegar smell. Spoiled wine.

Acrid Describes a harsh or pungent smell that is due to excess sulfur.

Aroma Traditionally defined as the smell that wine acquires from the grapes and from fermentation. Now it more commonly means the wine's total smell, including changes that resulted from oak aging or that occurred in the bottle—good or bad. "Bouquet" has a similar meaning.

Bouquet Wine's aroma from aging.

Cigar Box Another descriptor for a cedary aroma.

Cedary Denotes the smell of cedar wood associated with mature Cabernet Sauvignon and Cabernet blends aged in French or American oak.

Dirty Covers any and all foul, rank, off-putting smells that can occur in a wine, including those caused by bad barrels or corks. A sign of poor winemaking.

Esters The aromatic compounds of wine.

Mercaptains An unpleasant sulfur smell found in some very old white wines.

Musty Having a moldy or mildew smell. The result of a wine being made from moldy grapes, stored in improperly cleaned tanks and barrels, or contaminated by a poor cork.

Nose The smell, aroma, or bouquet of wine.

Nutty Aroma found in sherry, Madeira, port, and "cooked" wine.

Perfumed Describes the strong, usually sweet, and floral aromas of some white wines.

Pungent Having a powerful, assertive smell linked to a high level of volatile acidity.

Smoky Aromas caused by low acid, tannin, or both. Imparted from the oak barrel.

Toasty Wine aroma derived from the fire bending of the oak barrels staves.

TASTE

Acidic Used to describe wines whose total acid is so high that they taste tart or sour and have a sharp edge on the palate.

Acrid Describes a harsh or bitter taste that is due to excess sulfur.

Aeration Letting a wine "breathe" before drinking it, preferably in the glass, in order to soften the tannins and improve the overall quality. Red wines benefit most from aeration.

Aftertaste The taste or flavors that linger in the mouth after the wine is tasted, spit, or swallowed. The aftertaste or "finish" is the most important factor in judging a wine's character and quality. Great wines have rich, long, complex aftertastes.

Aggressive Unpleasantly harsh in taste or texture, usually due to a high level of tannin or acid.

Astringent Extremely dry acidity, bitter; gives a dehydrated sensation in the mouth.

Austere Used to describe relatively hard, high-acid wines that lack depth and roundness. Usually said of young wines that need time to soften, or wines that lack richness and body.

Bite A noticeable level of tannin or acidity. Desirable in rich, full-bodied wines.

Bitter Along with salty, sweet, and sour, this is one of the four basic tastes. Not a desirable trait in wine, it often signifies too much tannin.

Blunt Strong in flavor and high in alcohol.

Body Tactile impression of weight or fullness on the palate. Commonly expressed as full-bodied, medium-bodied, or medium-weight, or light-bodied.

Brawny Used to describe wines that are hard, intense, and tannic and that have raw, woody flavors. The opposite of elegant.

Briary Describes young wines with an earthy or stemmy wild-berry character.

Bright Used for fresh, ripe, zesty, lively young wines with vivid, focused flavors.

Brut A general term used to designate a relatively dry-finished Champagne or sparkling wine, often the driest wine made by the producer.

Burnt Describes wines that have an overdone, smoky, toasty, or singed edge. Also used to describe overripe grapes.

Buttery Rich, creamy aroma and flavor associated with barrel fermentation, often referring to Chardonnay.

Chewy Deep, heavy, tannic wines that are full-bodied with mouth filling texture.

Cloying Describes ultra-sweet or sugary wines that lack the balance provided by acid, alcohol, bitterness, or intense flavor.

Coarse Usually refers to excessive tannin or oak. Also used to describe harsh bubbles in sparkling wines. The opposite of smooth.

Corked A wine that has been tainted with moldy smell from a bad cork.

Depth Describes the complexity and concentration of flavors in a wine. The opposite of shallow.

Dry No sugar or sweetness remaining. A fruity wine can be dry.

Empty Similar to hollow or devoid of flavor and interest.

Extra-Dry A common Champagne term not to be taken literally. Most Champagne so labeled is sweet.

Extract Richness and depth of concentration of fruit in a wine. Usually a positive quality, although high-extract wine can also be highly tannic.

Fat Full-bodied, high-alcohol wines low in acidity give a "fat" impression on the palate.

Finesse Delicate and refined texture and structure.

Finish The lasting impression, or aftertaste, of a wine on the palate. Can be long or short.

Firm High in acidity or tannins, usually describes young reds.

Flabby Soft, feeble, lacking acidity and mouth feel.

Flat Having low acidity; the next stage after flabby. Can also refer to a sparkling wine that has lost its bubbles.

Fleshy Soft and smooth in texture with deep flavor.

Full-Bodied Rich, mouth-filling texture and weight on the palate; opposite of thin.

Green Tasting of unripe fruit, tart, and sometimes-harsh flavors and texture.

Grip A welcome firmness of texture, usually from tannin, which helps give definition to wines such as Cabernet and Port.

Hard High in acidity or tannins that do not allow flavor perception.

Harsh Astringent or burns the palate. Wines that are tannic or high in alcohol.

Hollow Lacking in flavor.

Hot High-alcohol content that tends to burn. Acceptable in Port wines.

Jammy Sweet concentrated fruit character.

Leafy Describes the slightly herbaceous, vegetal quality reminiscent of leaves. Can be a positive or a negative, depending on whether it adds to or detracts from a wine's flavor.

Lean Lacking in fruit.

Lingering Used to describe the flavor and persistence of flavor in a wine after tasting. When the aftertaste remains on the palate for several seconds, it is said to be lingering.

Lively Young wines that are fresh and fruity with bright vivacious flavors.

Lush Wines that are high in residual sugar.

Malic The green apple-like flavor found in young grapes that diminish as they mature.

Off Dry A slightly sweet wine.

Pruny Having the flavor of overripe, dried-out grapes. Can add complexity in the right dose.

Puckery Describes highly tannic and very dry wines.

Raisiny Having the taste of raisins from ultra-ripe or overripe grapes. Can be pleasant in small doses in some wines.

Rich Intense, generous, full flavors, and texture.

Round Smooth flavors and texture; well balanced, not coarse or tannic.

Soft Describes wines low in acid or tannin (sometimes both), making for easy drinking. Opposite of hard.

Spicy Spice flavors such as anise, cinnamon, cloves, mint, nutmeg, or pepper.

Structure A wine's texture and mouth feel—a result of a particular combination of acid, tannin, alcohol, and body.

Subtle Describes delicate wines with finesse, or flavors that are understated rather than full-blown and overt, a positive characteristic.

Supple Describes a smooth soft texture, mostly with reds.

Tanky Describes dull, dank qualities that show up in wines aged too long in tanks.

Tannin The mouth-puckering substance, mostly in red wines, that is derived primarily from grape skins, seeds, and stems, but also from oak barrels. Tannin acts as a natural preservative that helps wine age and develop.

Tart Sharp tasting because of acidity. Occasionally used as a synonym for acidic.

Thin Lacking body and depth, unpleasantly watery.

Tight Describes a wine's structure, concentration, and body, as in a "tightly wound" wine. *Closed* or *compact* are similar terms.

Tinny Metallic tasting.

Tired Limp, feeble, or lackluster.

Velvety Having rich flavor and smooth texture.

Volatile (or Volatile Acidity) Describes an excessive and undesirable amount of acidity, which gives a wine a slightly sour, vinegary edge. At very low levels (0.1 percent), it is largely undetectable; at higher levels it is considered a major defect.

appendix C

Spirit Brands and Related Cocktails

AMERICAN BOURBON WHISKEY

STRAIGHT BOURBON

Ancient Age
Beams Choice
Ezra Brooks 90
Evan Williams
Gentleman Jack
Jack Daniels
Jim Beam
Jim Beam Black
Knob Creek
Mattingly & More (M&M)
Old Crow
Old Forrester
Old Grand Dad
Makers Mark
Bookers
Wild Turkey
Wild Turkey 101

BLENDED BOURBON

Beams Blend 8 Star
Kessler
McCormick
Seagrams 7 Crown
Brokers Reserve
Monarch

STRAIGHT RYE WHISKEY

Old Overholt
Wild Turkey Rye

CANADIAN WHISKEY

BOTTLED IN CANADA

Black Velvet Sipping
Canadian Club
Canadian Mist 1885
Canadian R&R
Crown Royal Sp. Resv.
MacNaughton
Northern Light
Seagrams Crown Royal
Seagrams V.O.
V.O. Bold

BOTTLED IN THE UNITED STATES

Black Velvet
Canadian Mist
Lord Calvert
MacNaughton Lt. Wt.
Monarch Canadian
Potters Crown Canadian

COMMON BOURBON WHISKEY COCKTAILS

CC—7
Manhattan
Mint Julep
Old Fashioned
7&7
Whiskey Sour

IRISH WHISKEY

Black Bush Irish
Bushmills Irish
Bushmills Single Malt
Jameson
Jameson 1780
Tyrconnel
Tullamore Dew

SCOTCH WHISKEY

BLENDED SCOTCH

Ballantine
Black& White Grant's
Chivas Regal
Clan MacGregor
Cutty Sark
Dewars (White Horse)
Grants
J&B
Johnnie Walker Blue
Johnnie Walker Red
Old Smuggler
Passport
Pinch
Scoresby
Sheep Dip
Teachers

BLENDED SCOTCH – 12 YEAR

Buchanan's Deluxe
Chivas Regal
Johnnie Walker Black

BLENDED SCOTCH —15 YEAR

Haig & Haig Pinch
Glenfiddich Solera

SINGLE MALT SCOTCH

Balvenie
Cardhu Highland Malt
Cragganmore
Dalmore
Dalwhinnie
Glenfarclas 12 Year
Glenfiddich Ancient
Glenkinchie
Glenlivet
Glenmorangie 10 Year
Glenmorangie 18 Year
Glenmorey 12 Year
Glenmoray Tin
Glendronach
Highland Park
Knockando
Lagavulin
Laphroaig
Macallan 12 Year
Macallan 18 Year
Oban
Talisker
Tambowie
Tamnavulin

COMMON SCOTCH COCKTAILS

Rob Roy
Rusty Nail
Scotch Mist

COGNAC AND BRANDY

TERMS

V.S.—Very Superior
V.S.O.P.—Very Superior Old Pale
X.O. Extra Reserve—Usually denotes the oldest cognac from a particular producer.

Brandy

AMERICAN BRANDY

Christian Brothers
Clear Creek
Domain Charbay
E&J
Korbel
Lejon
Martel
Monarch
Paul Masson
Potters

IMPORTED BRANDY

Asbach Uralt
Boulard Calvados
Don Pedro
Funador
Maraska Sliovitz
Metaxa
Presidente
St. Remy VSOP
Viejo Vergel

Cognac

Courvoisier VS
Courvoisier VSOP
Hennessey VS
Hennessey VSOP
Hennessey XO
Martel VS
Remy Martin Louis XIII
Remy Martin VSOP
Remy Martin XO

GRAPPA

Acqua Di Amore
Clear Creek
Peak

LIQUEURS

(Liqueurs listed with identifiable flavors)

LIQUEURS—FLAVORS

Amaretto Di Saronno—almond
Bailey's Irish Cream—chocolate
Benedictine—herb spice
B & B—cognac
Carolans Irish Cream—chocolate
Chambord—cognac/raspberry
Cointreau—orange
Crème de Bananas—bananas
Crème de Cocoa—chocolate/vanilla
Crème de Cassis—currants
Crème de Menthe—mint
Crème de Noyaux—almond
Curacao—orange
Drambuie—scotch/honey
Frangelico—hazelnut
Godiva—chocolate
Galliano—anise-vanilla/licorice
Goldschlager—cinnamon (100 proof)
Grand Marnier—cognac/orange
Irish Mist—honey
Kahlua—coffee
Kamora—coffee
Midori—honeydew
Ouzo—licorice
Peppermint Schnapps—mint
Sambuca—licorice
Sloe Gin—plum
Southern Comfort—bourbon/peach
Tia Maria—Jamaican coffee
Triple Sec—orange
Tuaca—cocoa
Yukon Jack—Lt whiskey

GIN

AMERICAN GIN

Gilbey's
Boords
Gordon's
McCormick
Monarch
Potters
Seagrams Extra Dry
Seagrams Lime Twisted

IMPORTED GIN

Beefeater
Boodles
Bombay
Tanqueray

COMMON GIN COCKTAILS

Gibson
Gin Tonic
Gimlet
Martini
Tom Collins

RUM

JAMAICAN

Bacardi Anejo
Bacardi Solera

PUERTO RICO

Bacardi 8
Bacardi Dark
Bacardi Light
Bacardi Limon
Bacardi 151 (proof)
Captain Morgan
Captain Morgan Spiced
Castillo
Lemon Hart
Malibu
Mt. Gay
Ronrico

VIRGIN ISLANDS

Cruzan Clipper
Monarch
Montego
Potters
Redrum

COMMON RUM COCKTAILS

Cuba Libra
Piña Colada
Mai Tai
Daiquiri

TEQUILA

Aguila Blue Agave
Arandas Oro
Baja
Cuervo 1800
Cuervo Anejo
Don Julio
Giro
Herradura
Hussongs
Jose Cuervo Gold
Jose Cuervo White
Monarch
Monte Alban
Montezuma
Pancho Villa
Patron Anejo
Patron Reposado
Patron Silver
Pepe Lopez
Potters
Puerto Vallarta 100% Agave
Sauza Commerativo
Sauza Hornitos
Tarantula Azul
Torada
Tres Generationes
Two Fingers
Rio Grande
Sauza
Matador

COMMON TEQUILA COCKTAILS

Bloody Maria
Margarita
Tequila Shot
Tequila Sunrise

VODKA

Absolut—Sweden
Absolut Citron—Sweden
Belvedere—Poland
Finlandia—Finland
Gibley's—U.S.
Gordon's—United States
Kamchatka—U.S.
Lukweska—Poland
Popov—U.S.
Skyy—U.S.
Smirnoff—U.S.
Stolichnaya—Russia
Tanqueray Sterling—U.K.

COMMON VODKA COCKTAILS

Bloody Mary
Chi Chi
Cosmopolitan
Gibson
Gimlet
Greyhound
Kamikazi
Lemon Drop
Martini
Salty Dog
Sea Breeze
Screwdriver
Vodka Collins
Vodka Martini
Vodka Rocks
Vodka Tonic

COMMON MIXED DRINKS

B-52
Black Russian
Champagne Cocktail
Collins
Colorado Bull Dog
Creamsicle
Dr. Pepper
Eggnog
Fuzzy Navel
Godfather
Boiler Maker
Brave Bull
Godmother
Golden Cadillac
Grasshopper
Harvey Wallbanger
Long Island Iced Tea
Melon Ball
Midori Sour
Mimosa
Café Royal
Cape Codder
Mud Slide
Pink Lady
Pink Squirrel
Presbyterian
Whiskey Sour
White Russian

ALCOHOL COFFEE/TEA DRINKS

B-52
BFK
Blueberry Tea
Café Diablo
Café Jitz
Café Pucci
Café Royal
Hot Apple Toddy
Hot Toddy
Irish Coffee
Jamaican Coffee
Kioke Coffee
Mexican Coffee
Nudge
Royal Street Coffee
Spanish Coffee

appendix D

Ales, Lagers, and Nonalcohol Beers

TYPES OF ALES

Altbier "Alt" in German means "old." This style of top-fermenting light ale is cold conditioned, making them more in taste like lagers than ales.

Barleywines A high-alcohol ale (7.5–14 percent) with a dark brown hue, usually bittersweet, it is matured for a long time in casks.

Bitters Style of English ale that is dry and usually served draft. Should not be served too cold.

Brown Ale A strong, dark-colored ale that is somewhat sweet, from the stewing of barley. Brown ale is stronger than pale ale and lightly carbonated.

Cream Ale Mild and sweet ale made in the United States.

Golden Ale Light to medium body with some hop aroma and clean finish.

India Pale Ale Fruity, super-premium ale that has a strong flavor of hops. India Pale Ale sometimes has a touch of oak.

Lambic A spontaneously fermented style of wheat beer unique to Belgium. Usually full bodied with an acidic, yeasty palate.

Pale Ale Dry, delicate flavored, English-style ale.

Porter Deep brown ale, lighter in body than a stout, originating in London in 1722.

Scotch Ale Strong, malt style ale, which is often served as a nightcap. Can be served in winter with hearty food.

Stout Descended from Porter, stout is a thick, sweet, and relatively low-alcohol content.

Trappist There are six breweries operated by monks of the Trappist order, typically producing strong, fruity, sedimented ale, bottle conditioned, undergoird fermentations in the bottle.

Weisse German word meaning "wheat." Top fermented, most are light and tart in taste with bread or yeast aroma.

COMMON ALE BRANDS

Alaska Amber—U.S.
Bridgeport Blue Heron—U.S.
Full Sail—U.S.
McTarnahan's—U.S.
Napa Ale Works – U.S.
Rolling Rock—U.S.
Thomas Kemper—U.S.
Widmere Hefeweizen—U.S.
Widmere Hop Jack—U.S.
Widmere Wildberry—U.S.

COMMON STOUT BRANDS

Anderson Valley—U.S.
Guinness—Ireland
McAuslan—Canada
Murphy's Irish Stout—Ireland
Napa Ale Works—U.S.
Red Hook—U.S.
Youngs & Co.—U.K.

TYPES OF LAGERS

American Lager Largest selling beer in the USA with broad categories. Derived from European Pilsners, clean and crisp with more carbonation and less hop character.

Bock A strong lager that is served very cold, usually bottom fermented. It is full bodied, sweet, and sometimes syrupy.

Dortmunder From the German city with the same name. Their export style of beer is pale and medium dry, with more body and alcohol content than pale lagers from Munich to Pilsen.

Dry Styled in Germany with thorough fermentation creating high-alcohol content. Popularized by Japanese brewers. The American version has no "beery" aftertaste with conventional alcohol content.

Ice Developed by Labatt of Canada.

Marzen Originally brewed in the month of March for consumption in the summer months. Eventually became a malty, medium-strong version of the Vienna-style beer.

Munchener Dark brown lager with a sweet malt and slight hop flavor that is more creamy and aromatic than light lagers. The dark color and malty flavor come from roasted barley.

Pilsner A very dry, pale lager. Lots of hop aroma. A true Pilsner can only come from the town of Pilsen, Czechoslovakia. Most light lagers are styled after Pilsner beer but have less body and character.

Vienna Amber-red kilned malt producing style beer. Originally produced in Vienna.

COMMON LAGER BRANDS

Amstel Light—Holland
Asahi—Japan
Budweiser—U.S.
Bud Light—U.S.
Coors—U.S.
Corona—Mexico
Dos Equis XX—Mexico
Fosters—Australia
Grolsch—Holland
Harps—Ireland
Heineken—Holland
Henry Weinhard—U.S.
Henry Weinhard Dark—U.S.
Lowenbrau—Germany
Michelob—U.S.
Miller Genuine Draft—U.S.
Miller Lite—U.S.
Moosehead—Canada
Samuel Adams—U.S.
Sapporo—Japan
Saxer Lemon—U.S.
St. Pauli Girl—Germany
Steinlager—New Zealand
Thomas Kemper—U.S.
Tsing Tao—China

COMMON NONALCOHOL BEERS

Bavaria Malt Bier—Germany
Bitburger Drive—Germany
Buckler—Holland
Dortmunder Union—Germany
Gerstel Brau—Germany
Grolsch—Special Malt, Holland
Haake Beck—Germany
Kaliber—England
O'Douls—U.S.
Sharps—U.S.

website reference

CHAPTER 1 THE PROFESSIONAL SERVER

www.restaurant.org	National Restaurant Association
www.edfound.org	The Education Foundation
www.dol.gov/whd/state/tipped.htm	Federal and State Minimum Wage Laws

CHAPTER 3 TABLE SETTINGS, NAPKIN PRESENTATIONS, AND TABLE SERVICE

www.napkinfoldingguide.com www.napkinfolding.net	Napkin folds with step-by-step instructions

CHAPTER 6 WINE AND BEVERAGE SERVICE

www.nraef.org	Serv Safe Alcohol® Responsible Alcohol Training
www.foodandwinepairing.org	Food and Wine Pairing Guide
www.riedel.com (wine glass guide)	Styles of wine glasses
www.bjcp.org/2008styles/catdex.php	Beer styles
www.hopsaficionado.com	Craft beer

CHAPTER 10 BANQUETS, CATERING, AND BUFFET SERVICE

www.oneidafoodservice.com	Dinnerware, banquetware, drinkware, flatware, and holloware
www.linennstuff.com www.fabulousevents.com www.bbjlinen.com www.dovelinen.com www.tabletoppersinc.com	Linen Rental Companies for tablecloths, napkins, chair covers and bows, and table skirting
www.icesculpturedesigns.com	Ice Carvings

index

Note: The locators followed by 'f' and 't' refer to figures and tables sited in the text

W

Y

Z